Best wishes

Barry

How to
PROFIT
from the
ART PRINT
MARKET

Practical Advice For Visual Artists

2ND Edition

Barney Davey

Legal Notices

Table of Contents

How to Profit from the Art Print Market
Second Edition

Introduction

From the moment I picked your book up until I laid it down, I was convulsed with laughter. Someday I intend reading it.—Groucho Marx

I promise that if you will be unlike Groucho and grace me by reading this book, you will come away with a clearer understanding of the art print market and be better equipped to make good decisions and prosper from it. From personal observations, I know that artists who succeed in the art print market will enjoy greater financial rewards and recognition by doing so. This book is written to help guide you to success as a print artist.

I have added 30% more content and four chapters to this edition. The remaining balance of copy has been updated and rewritten to make it current with current market conditions. This second edition is (much like the print industry and the world at large) very different from 2005. Looking back, the sweeping changes that have occurred in the art print market and the world are simply astounding.

Since 2005, we have witnessed a massive global change in how goods, products and services are produced, created and delivered. We find ourselves growing more connected via social media, and this – together with our rising reliance on the Internet for entertainment and news – has fractured and nearly broken traditional media.

A combination of disruptive forces has shaped the changes in the art print market since this book's first edition. These include the housing-market crunch that caused the near collapse of the U.S. economy; the globalization of manufacturing; the penetration and acceptance of ecommerce, along with the increase in use and reliance on the Internet by marketers of all sorts; the rise in big-box retailing; the decline of independent art print retailers; the demise of most art-print and picture-framing tradeshows; the shrinking size and influence of trade media; and the influx of cheap oils from Chinese oil-painting-factory villages.

Gaining an understanding of the nature of the print business is critical for visual artists seeking success with it. While there are numerous excellent books on the business of being an artist and on art marketing, including many published since 2005, next to none provide more than a couple of pages or paragraphs regarding the ins and outs of the print market – if they offer anything at all.

There are a couple of notable constant values that appear in both the first and second editions of this book. One is that getting into print remains the best way for visual artists to generate a secondary source of income from their creative efforts. The other is that knowing how the whole industry works is essential for those who want to learn how to profit from the art print market. While the means for making a success in the market are as different and as varied as the new world around us, you will find the advice in this book is as solid as ever in helping you make the best and most-informed career choices regarding the print market.

Since 2005, I have kept a finger on the pulse of the market by maintaining and growing my connections in the art world. The hundreds of posts I have published on my Art Print Issues blog, [www.artprintissues.com], are a testament to my commitment to keep my readers and followers up-to-date on the news, events, techniques, products and people that impact the business of visual artists. I continue to do art marketing workshops. The results of these efforts and the knowledge gained from them are at the heart of this book.

My 15-year tenure with DECOR magazine and its sister tradeshow, Decor Expo, gave me access to many of the industry's most successful print publishers (both self-published and established catalog publishers) and allowed me to observe their traits and techniques. With the first of edition of this book, I distilled those experiences to share them with visual artists.

Returning readers of the second edition will find the comments from those distilled experiences remains steady. All readers will find that the new factors influencing how artists can best succeed in the print market today are given in-depth coverage, which accounts for both the additional and substantially revised content.

I initially developed my expertise with DECOR because I found that artists seeking to break into the print market needed practical advice on entering the business. Since repeat customers for advertising and tradeshow space fueled my sales, it was crucial to offer insights and information to increase their chances for success. Upon leaving, I started presenting workshops to spread my knowledge, and I quickly realized that more artists could be reached and helped with a book such as the one you hold in your hands.

If my readers gain not only a better grasp of the art print market but also the ability to judge the best course of action for themselves (based on their individual capabilities and resources), then my aspirations for this book will have been met. Best wishes to all the intrepid souls who embark upon an art print market career. Send me a postcard from the top!

I owe a grateful nod to my wife, Mary, for her love, her patience and her support during long late-night hours spent bringing this edition to life. It was my mother, Mary, a talented painter with a deep passion for fine art, who gave me a love of art and a respect for those who make it. Without her influence, this book may have never happened. I owe a special thanks to the countless visual artists, photographers and graphic designers who have inspired me with their work and encouraged me with their kind comments about my book, book and workshops.

Many thanks are offered to Marissa, and the rest of the team at FirstEditing. com, for a fine job polishing the copy. A debt of untold gratitude goes to the talented and imaginative Megan McLaughlin of 9 Speed Creative [www.9speedcreative.com], who is responsible for the enhanced layout and graphic redesign of the second edition. Together, these collaborators and supporters contributed to making this book better for you.

Barney Davey

To see far is one thing, going there is another. —Constantin Brancusi

Chapter One
Goals and Vision

Every artist was first an amateur.
—Ralph Waldo Emerson

The primary goal of this book is to help you gain an understanding of how to become a successful published artist whose original works are selling as reproductions in the art-print marketplace. As publishing is not for every artist, it can also serve as a sounding board to help you decide – or at least get closer to making an informed decision – whether or not publishing your art as a self-publisher or in concert with an established art-print publisher is the path for you to take.

Defining the Term "Print"

Before we go further, let's allow that the art world is one where confusing terms and contradictions exist. Since the word "print" is used in the title of this book, and it is a prime example of a term with confusing yet synonymous meanings in the art world, it is imperative to provide a clear definition of "print" as it pertains to this book.

The terms "print" or "prints" in this book are meant to discuss those works of art on paper or canvas that are primarily reproductions of originals and which are always sold in multiples. Typically, these prints are reproductions of original art works created using oils, pastels, acrylics and watercolors. It also includes fine art photographs and high-concept graphic designs. Exceptions are prints that are not reproductions, but which were originally created as prints; for example, computer-generated digital images, etchings, monotypes and those serigraphs which are designed as original prints as opposed to reproductions or original paintings..

While I acknowledge there are many other methods of creating art on paper, canvas and other substrates, I must emphasize that this book concerns itself with posters, open edition prints, canvas transfers, limited edition offset prints, giclées and serigraphs, primarily those marketed to the mainstream populace.

Another use of the term "print" comes from the body of artists, educators, gallerists, museums and collectors whose interest and work revolves around what I call the printmaking community. Printmaking is an ancient art. It is still taught at universities, where students can major in printmaking. It is epitomized by the art sold by members of the International Fine Print Dealers Association [www.ifpda.org].

Many in the printmaking community who specialize in media such as linotypes, woodcuts, monotypes, serigraphs, etchings, collographs, aquatints, mezzotints and so forth, take a more elite connotation of the word "print." They often eschew prints made for the mainstream market, and many find the use of the term "'print" to describe reproductions offensive. Nevertheless, the term, like giclée, has made it into the parlance, and no amount of angst will change it. In this book, the term "elite prints" conveys works of art that come from the printmaking community.

It becomes obvious then that one can hear the word "print" used to describe a piece of art and yet, without further clarification, be clueless as to what the word means or how the print was made. Are we describing an open edition lithographic offset reproduction, fresh from the offset press, or an original graphic etching made from a plate created by Rembrandt 300 years ago? It is not wrong to use the term "print" to identify artworks on paper that are of different origins, but it is confusing without further explanation.

What Is a Dealer, and How Are They Different from Retailers or Gallerists?

You will also see the word "dealer" used throughout this book. For our purposes – and within the industry in general – dealers are those who buy art at wholesale and sell at retail. The term encompasses not just gallerists, the brick-and-mortar art retailers, but also art consultants, high-end interior designers, and those who may not have a retail location but who own, trade, buy and consign art, and includes those who have the capability to exert great influence over the buying decisions of major collectors, museums and corporate art buyers.

The contemporary art market can be broken down (fairly or not) from a price point of view into three tiers. Here, the term "contemporary" is not used to describe a particular style of art, but rather to denote those pieces of art that are currently available through dealers, gallerists and other channels in a high-to-low price continuum. The three tiers are as follows:

1. High-end fine art galleries, museums, and auction houses, as well as important dealers and interior designers, typically found in major metropolitan areas, resorts and at the high-end consumer art shows (including Biennale Venice, Art Basel, Art Basel Miami and Art Palm Beach). Expect to see them selling fine art originals, elite prints and sculpture.

2. Middle market galleries, art consultants and dealers, and some interior designers, selling higher-priced limited edition giclées, serigraphs, sculptures, offset limited edition prints and moderately priced originals. This group also includes some online art retailers.

3. Poster and frame shops, lower-end galleries, mass-market retailers, furniture stores and contract design firms selling posters, open edition prints and some lower-priced, offset limited edition prints, giclées. This group includes most online art retailers.

This book aims to help those who wish to see their works sold in the middle and lower tiers of the market, which – if viewed as a pyramid – would form the base and bulk of the art market in terms of numbers of buyers. There are potentially tremendous rewards and recognition to be gained from serving these areas of demand for art. And, contrary to what many think, there are plenty of examples of artists who have had it all, meaning they have enjoyed representation at chic Manhattan galleries and also benefited from having their work reproduced and sold to the mass market.

Calvin Goodman, in Art Marketing Handbook – the 531-page tome that was the bible for art marketers for decades, and which is still available from the publisher – long maintained that the print market, as it is considered in this book, was not a great opportunity for economic gain for artists.

Later, Goodman went on to say he was wrong on this point. He acknowledged that an esteemed artist who he watched for two decades, Arthur Secunda, while not becoming wealthy, managed to do well with poster publisher Haddad's Fine Arts (www.haddadsfinearts.com).

According to Goodman, Secunda found that being in posters helped him maintain his studios in France and California, and he believed the exposure did not hurt his original print and collage market. In fact, Goodman reports, Secunda credits his posters with not only spawning imitators, but also helping to popularize his name and imagery.

There are no guarantees that by reading this book you will achieve the status of Arthur Secunda or secure a lofty position in the top tier and the lower tier of the market simultaneously as he did. You will, however, be assured of gaining a greater understanding and appreciation of how the art-print market operates in the middle and lower tiers. You will learn about the similarities in traits and attributes that artists already successful in this market share, and you will come away with a clearer idea on how you can best benefit from the potential the market offers.

As you will come to see, the decision to publish is the first of many you must make along the way to earning reward and recognition from having your work sold in the print market. The decisions you make will put you on one of the many paths to print-market success for artists.

I wish it were possible to provide you with all the ways artists have made gratifying careers in the print market. This would not then be a book, but an encyclopedia requiring far too much shelf space and time to read. Instead, I will give you examples of artists I have known or whose careers I have had the opportunity to study.

To start, we explore the following questions and sentiments in this chapter:

- What do you want to achieve with your art?
- Do you have a mission statement?
- Is commercial success included in your vision for personal achievement?
- Ambition is not a dirty word
- Can you visualize a career with high integrity, sales and bank account?
- Is it worth pursuing a career with potentially high repute and low bank balance?

For those of you who desire to put yourself on the road to publishing, this guidebook will help you decide which forks, among the many you will encounter, are best taken to lead to a successful art print career. At this point, the temptation is too great to resist quoting the venerated philosopher who said these things:

When you come to a fork in the road, take it.

You got to be careful if you don't know where you're going, because you might not get there. (Yogi Berra)

My goal here is to be more accommodating than Yogi's advice in that I intend to help you make good decisions when you reach the many forks you'll encounter upon entering the art-print market – good decisions that will help you to get somewhere with your art-print career.

It would be hard to imagine you took the time and spent the money to find and read this book if you do not already have the idea of making some money – if not a full-fledged business – from your art. I encourage you to make pursuing your goals the journey, and not the destination, when you face a choice at a fork in the road.

What do You Want to Achieve with Your Art?

The choices begin with you defining what sort of artist you are or want to be regarding your success on a commercial level. If you plan to sell your work, you can make three choices regarding your art career from a marketing and sales perspective:

1.   Be a professional full-time artist whose art pays the bills;
2.   Be a professional part-time artist who earns extra money from an unrelated capacity to pay the bills;
3.   Be an accomplished amateur artist who makes occasional sales.

We will examine each of these choices with the admonishment there is no wrong choice. They are all right choices, depending on your desires, abilities and circumstances. Don't waste time or breath with anyone who wants to argue the validity of making one of these choices over another. It is not their life or career.

As it should be, the choice will always come down to what is right for you. It can take some serious soul searching on your part to come up with the choice that best suits your situation, but few other choices you will ever make will have more impact on your career as an artist. It is worth putting in the time to clarify for yourself which choice best suits you.

According to www.dictionary.com, an artist by definition is:

One, such as a painter, sculptor or writer, who is able by virtue of imagination and talent or skill to create works of aesthetic value, especially in the fine arts.

Inarguably, the term is much broader than that, but for our purposes it suffices to define the artists drawn to read this book.

On Being a Full-Time Artist

Being a full-time artist is a brave career choice. It can be humbling to learn it is a pursuit where the odds are stacked against enjoying great success as a professional. It is an area where salaried or hourly jobs are virtually non-existent, and this is true whether one seeks to make it on Broadway, in feature films, or as a writer or recording artist. For most, it is a daunting task to make one's art pay the bills without other means of support.

Visual artists compete in a crowded and competitive field. As in other areas of the arts, success is achieved not by talent alone, but also ambition, luck, selfishness and unforeseen circumstances.

One unique advantage visual artists have over others who strive to make a career in the arts is that they have more latitude to make their own decisions and drive their own careers – if they have the talent, desire and wherewithal to do so.

This book will most help those who possess the right stuff and decide developing a print-market career is worthy goal. Perhaps it will help some readers decide they are missing some elements in the success capability quotient, and as such they will choose not to pursue a career as a print artist, or at least not as a self-published artist.

The good news is that if you have the right stuff, you can exercise much more control over your career than artists in other fields can. Recording artists, writers and actors are far more reliant on a whole host of people, luck and circumstances to make their careers successful than are visual artists (although, today, print-on-demand technology in book publishing and music publishing allows writers and musicians more opportunities than ever). This is not to minimize that outside influences have a great deal to do with the success of visual artists. They do; visual artists are also reliant on powers beyond their control to make their success. It is just that as a visual artist, you have more ability to create your own situation and make your own luck.

In this book, you will find stories about successful self-published artists, each with different looks and styles, who share common traits and attributes that helped shape their careers and brought them unqualified success. These artists took control of their future and fortune in their own ways.

A word about success: invariably, outsiders measure it in terms of fame and fortune, which can be a good measure for many artists as well. Nevertheless, success, as it pertains to artists or anyone for that matter, is truly and wholly a personal definition.

Success is getting what you want from your art. The reality is that the notions and opinions of others with regard to how successful you are, or will be, are not important. Of course, the opinion of collectors, dealers and gallery owners – and of some critics – can be important to your fame and fortune. However, none of them can tell you what success means to you.

Being a full-time professional artist means committing yourself to making a business of your art. As a professional, you have to take actions and make decisions that will influence how you create your art. It is common that some artists, upon realizing what it takes, decide not to pursue a full-time art career. Some correctly decide they would rather work part-time so they can avoid making compromises on what to create and have less need to pay attention to all the business requirements of getting art marketed and sold.

What is the Difference between Marketing and Sales?

Many people tend to confuse these terms, considering them synonymous when in reality they are two different activities. The most basic way of explaining it is to say that activities that generate interest and bring someone to the gallery are marketing activities (for example, postcards, advertising, brochures, blogs and websites); a sale, on the other hand, is the activity of engaging someone and asking them to buy. Marketing leads the prospect to the product. Selling convinces the prospect to purchase the product.

On Being a Part-Time Artist

It is a given that being a successful full-time artist is difficult to achieve. For the purposes of this book, I define "full-time" to mean a career in which the artist pays all the bills and earns a living from the fruit of the labor of creating and selling art. If you have a part-time job to make ends meet, even if it is working in a gallery, a frame shop or a museum, you do not meet the full-time artist criteria.

Being part-time can be pleasurable and satisfying for many artists. If you are one of those people who are multi-talented and enjoy, for example, programming computers by day and creating art by night, you might be lucky enough to have the best of both worlds. Who knows, if your art is the sort that finds a ready audience, you may be compelled some day to make computer programming your hobby. You would not be the first artist who crossed over from some other field, even if creating an art business was not the original intent.

The leap to fame and fortune is, in many cases, more of a long walk to the destination of full-time artist. Robert Bateman, a Canadian national treasure and one of the all-time most successful artists in the print market, is an example. Far from an overnight success, he did not sell his first work until he was in his thirties. Moreover, he kept his day job as a teacher until he was forty-six years old.

For many artists, their ideal would be to work at creating magnificent pieces of art that magically sold at worthy and regularly escalating prices – with little or no involvement from them in the actual marketing and sale of their art. As it often goes in life, the ideal and the real do not synchronize.

It is not likely you can find any successful artist who has had no hand in the marketing and sales of his or her art. If one is successful and is not involved, it is a safe bet they were involved earlier, before they achieved the success that allowed them to concentrate fully on creating new work.

On Being a Serious Hobbyist

Is commercial success truly included in your vision for personal achievement? Creating art is a deeply passionate and pleasurable pursuit for many artists. As such, the idea of turning their passion into a business is abominable to them. I am an accomplished fine woodworker and former president of the St. Louis Woodworkers Guild. I used to daydream about turning my hobby into a business and making fine furniture for others as a way to make a living. The daydream was no different from that of many talented would-be professional visual artists – including some readers of this book. In my fantasy, I would quit my job and create a new occupation by doing woodworking full time. Two separate instances helped to disabuse me of trying to fulfill my flight of the imagination.

The first was a letter to the editor of one of the many woodworking journals I faithfully subscribed to for years. It was a letter to tell all the hobbyists wannabes they should think hard before they quit their day job. In it, the writer told the story of a woman who came into a professional woodworker's shop and fell in love with a chair he had made to sell.

She was delighted to find out the price was only $100 and inquired about the price of having three more made to complete a table she already owned. The price for the remaining three chairs was set at $200 each. Naturally, she was surprised and asked why they were double the price of the first one. The simple reply was, "The first was fun to make."

To complete his thought, the woodworker's letter went on to describe a neighbor – an accomplished hobbyist with all the necessary talent and tools to be a professional – who was building a fine cherry chest of drawers. He told how the neighbor had spent months building it, hand cutting dovetail drawer joints, carved legs and so on; and then had spent even more months completing the piece with painstaking care, sanding and hand rubbing applications of stain and finish. It was a masterpiece when done. To the lament of the woodworker, the neighbor's finished piece was something the likes of which he, the professional, would never build or sell, because he could never charge enough to pay for his time.

The second incident involved my brother-in-law. He is an artist in sheet metal and a master mechanic. I have seen the incredibly beautiful result after he cut apart a 1955 two-door and a 1956 four-door Chevy Bel Air automobile and created a fabulous convertible out of the pieces. He and his talented brothers have built numerous hot rods and drag cars, which they race at tracks throughout the Midwest.

After seeing his ability and passion for building hot rods, I suggested he quit his seemingly dull job at the sign-making plant and open up a speed shop or a custom car shop to build hot rods for other people as a source of income. He looked at me incredulously for a while and said, "Why would I want to do that? It would ruin my hobby. I work at my job so I can enjoy the time I spend in the garage."

When I heard that, not long after reading the woodworker's letter to the editor, it sealed the fate of my woodworking career too. I realized the reason I do woodworking is to have a pleasant pursuit with a creative outlet that allows me to design and build objects at the speed I choose – not on someone else's time and budget.

The moral here is, no matter how talented you are as an artist, it is possible that for personal reasons you will decide it best not to make it a career. As I will state later in this chapter, there is no shame in enjoying a successful career; likewise, there is no shame in choosing to remain a hobbyist. The choice is not a reflection on your talent and creativity as an artist; it is a personal choice only you can make.

For many creative people, one of the most difficult things they have to do is reconcile the fact that, despite their talent, they are not going to become a famous artist, musician or what have you. Often it is because of situations or circumstances out of their control, while other times it is owing to their actions; but whatever the cause, it still blocks them from fulfilling their fantasies of stardom in their chosen field.

If it seems that the opportunity to be on stage in front of an audience, or to be the star of a glittering art opening, has passed you by; you may need to work on how to resolve and overcome the feelings such awareness brings. Perhaps because you are an artist, you are more sensitive to finding yourself in this place with the realization that things did not go your way.

Coming to grips with these feelings – whether it is through therapy, faith, spirituality or by spending your energy on worthy goals within your grasp – can make the difference between being happy or not. Becoming a big star artist with your own publishing company may not be attainable; but if you have the talent, nothing can stop you from using your skill to create art that will live beyond you and, in all likelihood, generate you a decent living too.

While you cannot always choose the outcome of your circumstances, you can always choose how you react to them. To understand this and acknowledge your complete control over your ability to choose your reaction will provide you with tremendous personal power. Realizing your ability to choose your reaction to adverse conditions and remaining positive is how you elevate yourself in even the most difficult situations. Keep that in mind the next time life gets you down.

If the idea of choosing your reaction appeals to you and you want a role model to consider, look to Viktor E. Frankl and his powerful book, Man's Search for Meaning. If Frankl could find ways to choose to be positive during his five years incarcerated at Auschwitz and at other Holocaust internment camps, then by comparison, even profound personal and professional disappointments can be dealt with in ways that, instead of destroying us, make us better people. Frankl has inspired many, including Stephen Covey, who wrote glowingly about Frankl's story in one of the bestselling personal-growth books ever, The Seven Habits of Highly Effective People.

Art is a gift to the future, and in the future your art will be valued for what it is and not by how much money you made from it in your lifetime. As such, the choice to be a serious amateur artist will always be a viable one, even if the path to making decisions about how to apply it for your personal situation has its painful moments.

What was any art but a mould in which to imprison for a moment the shining, elusive element, which is life itself? — Willa Cather

Do You Have a Mission Statement?

Having a mission statement is a way to create a touchstone to help you make good decisions and guide you in your career, as well as in your personal life. A well-executed mission statement is dynamic. It changes as you pass through stages of your life and career. Regardless, its essence will remain constant, just as those things that define you as a person have remained a constant as you have evolved in your life.

If you want some help with creating a mission statement, the free mission builder at the Franklin Covey website is helpful: www.franklincovey.com/missionbuilder. It was developed in part by the aforementioned Stephen Covey, author of The Seven Habits of Highly Effective People.

If you have not read Covey's perennial classic and bestseller on self-improvement, a book that remained on the charts for more than a decade, then I suggest you put it on your must-read list. It is not an easy, simplistic "Chicken Soup" kind of book to read, but it is positively worth the effort if personal self-improvement and personal leadership are things you want to develop in your life.

What Do I Want to Achieve with My Art?

The answer to this question is as personal as what you want to create. It ties directly in with having a mission statement. It is as important to know what you want to achieve as it is to know what you want to create. You need a road map to get where you are going, or you will not go anywhere.

Imagine you have been dropped into a big city in another state and you want to get home. Would having a map, and planning to use the map, not help you get there quicker? Spend all the time you need to think about the question of what you want to achieve, and come up with an answer that is believable and achievable. It will pay dividends beyond your imagination.

A mission statement helps you develop a sense of what is important. An action plan helps you prioritize what steps you need to take to achieve the goals you set for yourself

Do you envision yourself as a multi-millionaire artist whose editions sell out quickly, or would making enough money to pay the rent and keep the Volkswagen van running make you happy? Would you like to put your kids through college based on your art sales, or does picking up pocket change to pay for a few paint supplies float your boat?

Only you can come up with the answer to what you want to achieve with your art. When you are comfortable with your goal, then you can start to tackle the rest of the puzzle insofar as how you are going to turn your goals and dreams into your reality. Many artists are living their dreams. You can be one. First, find your true North Star, and then proceed to break it down into manageable increments to keep on track with your goals.

Is Being Commercially Viable Part of My Definition of Success as an Artist, and Will I Have to Make Creative Sacrifices to Achieve Success?

In order for the world around you to know and enjoy your art, you will need commercial success. You do not have to sell your soul and should not have to make unbearable creative sacrifices to enjoy success as you define it. However, being able to incorporate suggestions from coaches, agents, mentors, publishers and occasionally even collectors can improve your odds of having greater success.

As with life itself, there are many choices. You choose what to create and what to do with your creation. You choose to pursue art as a career, enjoy it as a serious hobby, or find some middle ground between the two. Earlier, I mentioned how the artist Arthur Secunda neatly managed to straddle the poster market without hurting his high-end print and collage market. If anything, he felt it gave him and his art greater visibility.

Enjoying a career similar to artists you admire, both for the imagery they create and the business model they use, can be yours. However, you must work equally as hard at making good informed choices about your career as you do about creating the best art you can.

Ambition is Not a Bad Thing

Ambition coupled with talent is often the key driver in determining how far someone's career goes. This applies whether you are a salesperson, an artist or a bookkeeper. It can make the difference in how a career develops, and it can make a huge difference at the top, especially in modern art.

Often it is the artist who is the best connected to the right dealers, publicists, journalists and centers of influence who gets the most acclaim. Those things do not just happen. In these cases, the artist is fully complicit in socializing with these people in just the right way. If you study the highly successful fine artists of the twentieth century, whether it is Picasso, Jasper Johns, Robert Rauschenberg and Jackson Pollock, Thomas Kinkade, Bev Doolittle, Robert Bateman, Terry Redlin, or other popular print artists, you will not find any lacking ambition.

There is No Shame in Being Successful

Suffering from the high repute, low bank balance or starving-artist syndrome is just that: suffering. Despite how fiction and fantasies see this as somehow romantic, it is not a prescription for producing an environment conducive to creating your best art.

Isn't it more shameful not to be successful if you truly believe in your art and crave for it to be known? If few people ever see or appreciate your art, then wouldn't it be a shame to have your creativity go unnoticed when your desire was to share it? Instead, wouldn't it be better to have a goal of being successful, and using the success for the good of your family, your community and the world at large? How much good can anyone who is starving do for themselves, much less others?

The art world is full of examples of artists who have achieved the model of high recognition, high integrity and high sales, resulting in a high bank balance. There is nothing to stop you from working to accomplish the same in your career. What you need to do is be able to accurately assess your resources and then base your goals and expectations upon that. Use this book to help you begin to take control of your career.

If the artist is true to self and not vying for commercial trade, art is the creative concept taken from the heart of each individual who practices art. It's the formula for being an artist of high repute, and low bank balance. Reality tells us that there has to be some commercial use for the art we produce otherwise it's going to remain unsold and unviewed. OK, most commercially successful artists are producing what those who are not so successful call rubbish. But I find that the best driving force is eating, so maybe commercialism makes better artists.
— Batty's Bulletin (found on the Internet)

Chapter Two
Understanding Art-Print Media

Instead of trying to render what I see before me, I use color in a completely arbitrary way to express myself powerfully.
— Vincent Van Gogh

It is important for clarity's sake to identify the various media in which original works are reproduced as prints – at least, those that comprise the bulk of the market of the middle and lower tiers.

The reason to discuss print media here is because the other decisions you will make with regard to self-publishing or seeking a publisher are driven to some extent by what kind of art print best suits your work. For instance, if you create novel pieces that incorporate teddy bears, you are best suited for the poster market with those images. On the other hand, if you create large abstracts, it is probable that serigraphs or giclées will be your medium of choice, although oversized posters using this genre is a growing market segment.

There are economics around producing and marketing different types of media. You will find it typical that publishers who sell posters do not sell more expensive limited edition and higher end works. That means you have different decisions to make regarding which medium you believe best represents your art or best represents your chances for success in publishing, and what companies to prospect for and approach if you are inclined to collaborate with an established publisher.

The following list is neither encyclopedic nor a detailed technical explanation of print types, but rather a brief description of the types of prints that buyers at fine art tradeshows, such as ArtExpo New York, or lower end print tradeshow, such as Decor Expo Atlanta, will most often encounter.

Serigraph or Silkscreens

Usually, serigraphs are reproductions from an original, but they also can be an original graphic. In reproductions, either the artist or a person known as a Chromist identifies in minute detail by shape on a separate screen each individual color in a piece of art. With an original graphic, you find the piece designed and created as a serigraph.

Although modern materials have replaced them, silkscreens were originally made from stretched silk, ergo the name. With each individual color separated, and with an opening on its screen to allow ink to be squeegeed onto the art paper in a special press, the printing process begins. Some intricate silkscreens have 100 or more colors meaning that each print must pass through the press 100 times. A run of 350 prints in a limited edition can cost upwards of $50,000 or more to produce, depending on the number of screens in the job.

Serigraphic work today has been largely automated, and as a result it is a medium that crosses over between the top- and middle-tier shows. Hand-pulled serigraphs, often pulled by the artist, are still widely used by the printmaking community. Middle-tier publishers and artists also incorporate automated serigraphy with digital printing to create mixed media art.

Just as the art community used serigraphs to counter the negative connotation of silkscreen printing, which is an inexpensive method used by commercial printers, giclée was brought into the art lexicon to overcome negativity toward using the common term of digital print.

Giclée

"Giclée" (pronounced "zhee-clay") from the French language is a neologism or invented name. It is used to describe the process of making fine art prints from a digital source using ink-jet printing. The word can be found in the French language as "le gicleur," which translates to "nozzle." Specifically the French term "gicler" is used to mean "to squirt, spurt or spray."

This digital print format is the most broadly used form of limited edition prints sold today. And, it is now, due to increased print speeds and lowered printing costs, making serious inroads into the open edition print and poster market. It took years for the giclée print to gain full acceptance in the industry because of the controversy surrounding the colorfastness reliability in its early stages, and because it was computer-generated. New and continuously evolving equipment and archival inks, dyes, solvents, printing processes, substrates and finishes have all but eliminated the criticism. An inevitable initial resistance to technological advances contributed to the hesitancy for many in the art community to embrace the giclée as a legitimate medium.

The format warrants further discussion. Print-on-demand technology (POD) has become one of the most transforming developments for artists in our lifetime. Giclée printing is just one form of POD. You see POD footprints in music and literature, and its far-reaching effects have changed those fields as well. It is a freeing technology in that it puts the ability to create fine reproductions in the hands of artists, without their having to resort to traditional methods of producing and distributing their work.

Giclée is a broad term that covers five different methods of creating reproductions on a variety of substrates. They are:

1. Digital art created using computer-generated images (some use the term "original giclée prints," which I find confusing for the collector);
2. Digital photographs output on a digital printer;
3. Scans of original works created as reproduction giclée prints;
4. Digitally enhanced scanned images or photographs, reworked or altered with software programs such as Corel Painter or Adobe Photoshop before being printed;
5. Giclées, photographs, or any digital image that is embellished or otherwise reworked after being printed.

Due to the widespread use of the giclée medium throughout the industry, rather than go into an in-depth look at giclées here, you will find that Chapter Sixteen of this book is devoted to them.

Limited Edition Reproduction

This term is primarily used to describe art on paper via the traditional four-color offset printing process, although you will find some six-color press runs used today. While still used by some art publishers to sell offset limited edition prints, this has faded as a viable option in the onslaught of giclée prints.

Incidentally, the record for largest limited edition print, "Sacred Ground" by Bev Doolittle, was an offset print. It has more than 69,000 prints in the edition. (An interesting side note is that Doolittle returned to the limited edition market for the first time in eight years in 2007. Her publisher, Greenwich Workshop [www.greenwichworkshop.com] issued the new piece in (you guessed it) giclée format. The story goes that Doolittle was working in stone lithography to create this new image, but there were problems with producing in that format. The next step was to move to the giclée format as a replacement.

There were two sizes of prints made as separate editions of the "Beyond Negotiations" acrylic original. The total number of pieces in both editions was about 4,000, and they sold out at the publisher level rather quickly, proving Doolittle's drawing power was still effective, although not to the massive degree it was the late '80s and early '90s.

Offset printing is not as dominant as it once was because the only cost effective way to afford an offset print edition is print it all at once. The cost per piece for open editions is usually not reasonable for less than 1,000 copies. This means you, or your publisher, are betting there will be enough sales to break even on the printing and marketing costs, other overheads notwithstanding. Time-limited pieces, as Doolittle's "Sacred Ground," abated this problem, but they are a rare anomaly to the normal process and are not an effective marketing tool these days.

The giclée printing process has eroded the limited edition on paper market segment for obvious reasons. All the same, on a cost per piece basis, offset limited edition pieces cost less to produce than giclées and still have appeal to some publishers and collectors. Spend time at any art tradeshow now and you'll be hard pressed to find artists or publishers offering limited edition offset lithographs.

Open Edition Reproductions

In their heyday, you would find the editors of art trade magazines using "open edition reproduction" to describe offset lithographic prints as those images printed without any graphic or type on the surface, and sans the fly spec bold print acknowledging the publisher. Today, the public and those within the industry use the term "poster" to synomonously mean open edition print. However, reading the next description reveals why using the term in this way is technically incorrect.

Posters

Here the classic definition of a poster is an offset lithographic image with type or other graphic elements included as part of the print. A classic example is the vintage poster. Henri Toulouse-Lautrec and other French graphic artists of his day popularized this format. They designed prints specifically to "post" advertisements. It is from this use that the term poster came about. Thus, despite the lack of uniformity, there is a true distinction between posters and open edition prints in art lexicon. As you know, the term poster is widely used to describe art on paper in open edition, regardless of the distinctions noted here.

The "poster" moniker has stuck to the offset litho-medium with artists, publishers and consumers. In this book, as per general usage within the industry, you will find the word "poster" used to describe both posters and open edition prints.

Canvas Transfers

Now here is an interesting product. It has been around for decades. Thomas Kinkade is the most famous and prolific artist to have used canvas transfers. This format initially made up almost all of his limited edition prints, although he too succumbed to the lure of giclée printing. Canvas transfers can be produced for less than giclées and still create results that make it hard to believe they are reproductions. Kinkade used offset prints to diversify his pricing, offering them as a way to differentiate product sold through galleries not in his gallery program.

Canvas transfers start out as normal offset prints. The first step is to apply a special clear acrylic coating that binds to the ink. After hardening, the prints are bathed in a chemical-and-water solution until they soften so the paper can be removed from the bound acrylic and ink top layer. A thin adhesive paper goes between the hardened layer and a canvas substrate. The final step is to mount the layers to the canvas using a heated vacuum press. There are other methods, such as binding the paper directly to the canvas, but the chemical bath process produces the best results.

The cost to create a canvas transfer and have it stretched on a frame runs from $0.50 to $2.00 per united inch. You calculate united inches by adding the outside dimensions of the length and the width of the stretched imaged area. Thus, a 16" x 20" canvas image has 36 united inches with a cost of $18.00 to $72.00. Even at the high price, it is less than the cost of a giclée printed on canvas and mouted on stretcher bars.

The effect is something that looks like an original, especially when additional coatings are added to the canvas transfer after it is stretched. Sometimes clear gels are applied to give the effect of brushstrokes on the pieces. Other times, paint highlights are added. Kinkade has had van tours to galleries with his highlighters featured … go figure. An obvious advantage is canvas transfers, unlike prints on paper, require no glass or plastic to protect them. This way, they show great in galleries and on the walls of collectors.

Now that you are well informed with some basics on the different kinds of prints that are most often seen in the marketplace, you may have a clearer idea of which of these methods best suits your own art and needs. By coming to grips with the question of what medium best suits you and your art, you can progress to other decisions regarding whether you should self-publish or seek a publisher. Should you decide on the latter, you will be better prepared to target publishers who use the medium you have chosen as ideal for your art.

Photography

That photography is a fine art medium is a well-established fact. Practically from its first days, visual artists have used photography as a means to express themselves. American photographers Alfred Steiglitz and Edward Steichen were pioneers in making photography fine art, and efforts by the Metropolitan Museum of Modern Art have been instrumental in maintaining this as a fine art medium.

Today, with the tremendous array of digital equipment, photographers are better equipped than ever to make unique artistic visions from their work. It is a long established fact that photography is a much more difficult medium to break into the print market with than painting. When asked why this was so, I used to say that most people didn't appreciate the art in photography and incorrectly believed that had they been standing in the same spot with a high-priced Hasselblad or Nikon camera, then they too could have taken the same photo.

In an interesting twist, with the availability of powerful and affordable digital cameras, I think more people now understand it takes the eye of an artist to create a fine art photograph. That is, they now have the equipment within financial grasp and realize it is not about the box that shoots the picture; rather, it is the creative person's talent behind the camera that creates a fine art image. That is, in part, why I believe photography as a fine art medium is growing in status.

Digital Art

I met Bonny Lhotka [www.lhotka.com] when she was exhibiting at ArtExpo. Years have faded my memory, but my best recollection says it was in Los Angeles in the early 1990s. As a founding member of the Digital Atelier [www.digitalatelier.com], she is a pioneer digital artist. She was far ahead of her time then. I am sure the show was both an experiment and a disappointment as she was well ahead of her time in presenting such work.

Along with the other founding members of the Digital Atelier, Dorothy Simpson Krause and Karin Schminke, Bonny combines traditional studio and media techniques to produce original fine art and variant editions using the latest computer equipment and imaging hardware and software. I have blogged about the Donnie Awards, which are awarded to winners of the Digital Art Contest sponsored by MOCA (the Museum of Computer Art. [http://moca.virtual.museum/]).

The point is that digital art as an art form has arrived. I predict that as younger generations – who have been exposed to virtually everything digitally – grow older, digital art will become increasingly important in the world of art.

Digital Painting

According to Wikipedia, digital painting is an emerging art form in which traditional physical-medium painting techniques – such as watercolor, oils, impasto, etc. – are applied using digital tools: a computer, a digitizing tablet and stylus, and special software. Digital painting differs from other forms of digital art, particularly computer-generated art, in that it does not involve the computer rendering from a model. The artist uses painting techniques to create the digital painting directly on the computer.

Many photographers have crossed over to digital painting. Notable among them is Marilyn Sholin. She is the autor of The Art of Digital Photo Painting. Marilyn founded the Digital Painting Forum [www.digitalpaintingforum. com] in 2005 as a way to help photographers and other visual artists learn how to harness the increasingly powerful tools at their disposal to make art.

Convergence Media

I first used the term "convergent media" in a guest blogger post for www. AbsoluteArts.com, which is one of the most heavily trafficked consumer art sites. Here is part of the post:

The process of creating art using digital means is involved and multi-stepped. There is image capture, whether through digital photography or image creation using a Wacom Tablet or other hardware/software combinations. There is a manipulation of the imagery through any number of software programs, such as Painter, Photoshop, Illustrator and so on. Then comes the output onto a myriad of substrates, including paper, canvas, vinyl, metal, wood and more. To produce a final desired result, the artist must print or collaborate with a printer on calibrating the equipment to get the output desired. Often pieces are further enhanced post printing to make them unique, one-of-a-kind and original.

To my mind, the term convergent media makes more sense. It reflects the usage of mixed media, which is an ages-old and widely accepted art term. Mixed media describes a multi-stage process of using different techniques and media to render an original piece of art. Convergent media does the same thing but implies the use of technology not available to previous generations of artists.

I do not know whether convergent media will catch on as a useful descriptor for art made through a digital process involving cameras, scanners, tablets, software and printers, but I like to think it will. The artists using these tools are every bit as creative as those who draw and paint, and they visually express themselves in ways traditional painters cannot.

It was only through the extensive use of digital tools that a box office hit such as Avatar (earning $1 billion worldwide in a week) could be made. Likewise, there is stunning digital art – convergent media, if you will – that can only be made using digital tools. If you are a traditional painter, I do not advocate abandoning your tools or craft in favor of a computer; but if you are so inclined, there are new vistas to be conquered with them.

There is much more to say about each of these and other art print processes. The intent here is not to burden you with more than you need or want to know, but to give you some guidelines and basic understanding of the overall commercial art market from a print-medium perspective.

There is a similarity to the previously discussed decisions regarding being a full-time or part-time artist in that there is no wrong choice here. Your decision about which medium to use often will come down to considering economics, subject matter, personal preferences and competition.

Naturally, if you have inputs from a publisher, it will help influence your decision.

Later on, I'll provide some ways for you to spot trends in current art themes. Keep in mind that while you sleuth for trends, you should also look for which media various publishers use. Doing this will help you make more sense of the business on multiple levels.

Chapter Three
First Things First

It's not what you see that is art. Art is the gap.
— Marcel Duchamp

It may seem odd to have chapter three labeled as "First Things First." However, the prior chapters laid the groundwork so that now we can start asking the most important questions about your quest to break into the print market. This chapter will challenge you to start organizing actions based on what is important, as well as what is most urgent, in launching your print-market career.

Homage must be paid here once again to the brilliant Stephen Covey, because the title for this chapter is borrowed from "Habit Three: First Things First," from his enormously influential The Seven Habits of Highly Effective People. That Covey feels strongly about this habit is obvious; he has since devoted an entire book to the subject, aptly titled, First Things First. He uses this phrase to talk broadly about personal leadership and how, if you do not tackle that which is the main thing first, you are dooming yourself to wasting time, if not to outright failure.

For our purposes, we will narrow the concept down to deciding where your art fits into the market and what actions you should take to support that decision. Getting into the print market requires the three D's: Desire, Discipline and attention to Details.

Having your own effective plan will help you implement the three D's. The plan will also help you avoid making mistakes or wasting time and money, and it will give you the best chance for success on the path to profiting from the art-print market.

Answering these questions will help you get first things first:

- How can I tell if my art is appropriate for publishing?
- Are there reasons to avoid the print market?
- Which media best suits my art?
- Should I be thematic or show a range of work?

- Should I self-publish or seek a publisher?
- Can I do both?
- Is there another alternative?

How Can I Tell whether My Art is Appropriate for Publishing?

You may instinctively know that your art is appropriate for being published; it is likely the reason you are now reading this book. Nonetheless, you can use the following to help make this determination. You will know your art is right for the art print market if:

- your originals are getting prices that take too many collectors out of your buying pool;
- your art is in such demand that you could have sold your originals many times over;
- you cannot produce on a schedule to meet the demand for your originals;
- you desire or need a secondary source of income from your art;
- you are creating art specifically for the print market.

If you answered with affirmative responses to these questions, you are a great candidate to jump on the art-print bandwagon.

Are There Reasons to Avoid the Art Print Market?

Yes, and the reasons to avoid this market include the following:

- Your subject matter is too esoteric or inappropriate to be workable in the mainstream print market.
- If your original work is not moving, you may compound your situation by investing in the print market. If this is your case, most publishers will grasp this whether you tell them or not, because it is their job to have a finger on the pulse of the market. This is not to say you would never get a bite from a publisher, but it is far less likely if your originals are not already selling well.
- Alternatively, upon investigation, it could be that you decide not to pursue publishing.

If reading this book helps you make the decision not to pursue publishing, it is just as good a reason for me to have written it as convincing another artist to take the print plunge. The idea is to help stimulate your thinking and deepen your knowledge so you come up with the right conclusions and act on them appropriately. You do not want to have regrets later on.

Which Media Best Suits My Art?

Deciding which media best suits your art can be tricky. I mentioned teddy bears earlier. If you are painting them, or similar content, then open edition prints or posters are where your art will find greatest acceptance. Red Skelton was a famous and well-liked comedian who was also an artist with a successful career painting clowns that were sold as limited edition prints. His celebrity allowed him to move beyond posters with this genre. Without it, I think the art would have had far less appeal to collectors.

When I wrote the first edition of this book in 2005, I said that it takes some thinking and investigating on your part to decide where you think your art fits in the mix of art-print alternatives, and that there were price points across the board. Artists could be in inexpensive limited-edition prints, medium-priced giclées or sky-high-priced serigraphs – or the inverse of any of those scenarios – and would still have made a right decision. While these things remain true, the poster and the limited-edition-on-paper market are not as feasible now as they were five years ago. The opportunities for artists to capitalize on them have dwindled with their decline.

Then, as now, you have to decide what feels right for you and listen to what the market is telling you. You may get feedback from collectors and publishers that differs with your own perceptions of where your art fits in the marketplace. Should you get such advice, pay attention to it.

In the past, attending tradeshows and consumer shows along with studying trade magazines were the best, quickest and easiest ways to learn what was going on in the industry. You could pick up on shifts in prices, subject matter, sizes, media and many other tidbits that together would inform you of the overall trends. With the dominance of the giclée medium, being aware of these shifts in the industry is not as necessary for helping you pick the right medium for your work.

Should My Work be Thematic or Show a Range?

Many artists are talented in that they can paint a variety of subjects and themes equally well. They enjoy stretching themselves to try new things. However, displaying a command of unrelated themes and media does not make success in the print market easier. The way to success for artists in the market is to become recognizable for something in particular. If I say "cottages," then unless you have been living in the proverbial cave, you are going to reply, "Thomas Kinkade." LeRoi Neiman is as well known for his colorful sports images as P. Buckley Moss is for her quaint Amish scenes, and so on.

When it comes to collectors and keeping your galleries happy, being thematic is a huge plus. Your dealers and galleries need to know you are willing to work hard at creating more images for their buyers. This is not to say you cannot paint what you want to paint, but if you are making a business of it, you need to establish a look and style that is uniquely yours. Once established with a look or style, you need to stay with it. Being recognizable for a style will take you far in the art print market.

Alternatively, you can look for a publisher who will feed you ideas on what is needed to meet developing trends, but it becomes much more of a hit-and-miss proposition for all involved, and the probability of finding a publisher who would take you on in that kind of capacity is small. So pick something and stay focused on it. If, after a while, it becomes obvious the fish are not biting, you can change to something with better marketing prospects.

Keep in mind some poster publishers are perfectly fine with the idea of you painting under an assumed name – a Nom de Brusse, if you will. Most are not looking for you to make personal appearances for them anywhere. As such, there is the possibility you can create a look for a poster line that is different from the images marketed to collectors of your originals. Think of it as moonlighting, or guilty pleasures. Remember, Arthur Secunda managed to be a hit poster artist without damaging his original sales in tony New York galleries. Without knowing for certain, I feel confident Secunda's work was not sold in the licensing market.

Should I Self-Publish or Seek a Publisher?

This question started me on counseling artists during my 15 years with DECOR magazine: Should I self-publish? My short answer then was, "Yes, if you can, but seek a publisher if not." Just a few years ago, self-publishing was an expensive and daunting task for most visual artists. The lack of financing or qualified help to get to market forced them to seek a publisher.

Today, things are much different. Working with an art publisher is more difficult and less promising than in the past. Given the current market conditions, in most cases I would not advise an artist to seek a publisher until they have fully explored their options for self-publishing their work.

First Things First

I say "yes" to self-publishing because when you successfully self-publish, the rewards are greater and the control of your artistic life remains in your hands. Also, if you should decide, for whatever reason, that self-publishing is not the best thing for you, then having done it will give you a greater appreciation for what a publisher does when you decide to throw in with one.

Formerly, in my first edition, I gave odds that most readers would seek to find an established publisher. I said this based on my experience and by judging the number of successful self-published artists versus those working with publishers. As with so many other decisions, this is not about being wrong or about one choice being better than another. It is really about making the right choice for your situation.

Before it seems like I have completely thrown in the towel on the idea of seeking a publisher, I want to state that there are still opportunities with publishers. I know artists who have made recent arrangements with publishers and who are now working towards making a rewarding income, despite the serious downturn in the national economy and in the art market in recent years, which are both are still working to overcome the near disastrous effects on them.

If you have a full-time job to pay the bills, and do not have unpaid staff whose assistance would provide you more time and energy, self-publishing is going to be trickier for you than for those who do and can more fully focus on making art. However, if you have help and are already making substantial income from your art, you are a good candidate to move forward with a self-publishing business plan. Do not let lack of staff be a reason to not pursue the print market. Instead, adjust your goals according to your available resources. You can still get there, it just may take longer.

In subsequent chapters, we will look at examples of successful self-published artists and of successful artists who work through professional art publishers. We also will explore ideas on developing a marketing plan for each scenario. I am talking about these things now as a way to get you thinking about them, and to continue to do so as you move through this book and progress towards making career decisions regarding how you will get your art published.

Can I Do Both?

Some of you will want to try having a publisher and also do some self-publishing as well. This is perfectly fine, as long as your publisher does not mind. Some are open to such ideas; others will be restrictive with you on where else you can market your work. It is something you will need to investigate and keep in mind as you begin contacting publishers.

Some artists license their images to publishers as posters, while marketing other images in different formats on their own. This is a typical situation for many artists whose publisher cannot handle their volume of creative output. You have to work out what is best for you and your publisher.

Remember to ask many questions when you negotiate with a publisher (Chapter 7 is devoted to how to work with a publisher). Do not be intimidated, and do stick up for yourself. You have a right to make a living. If a publisher only wants to cherry-pick your images, then you cannot allow yourself to be tied to such exclusivity, unless you really want to be a starving artist.

Is There an Alternative?

Artists often ask if there is an alternative to the choice of self- publishing versus working with a publisher. My simple answer is, no. If you want to gain sales and fame from the print market, you either have to do it for yourself or have a publisher do it for you.

Back in the days when it took a substantial investment of tens of thousands or more to break into the print market, I would cringe when contacted by naïve artists who believed buying a single ad or a single booth in a tradeshow would launch their careers, or just give a positive return on investment. A typical scenario was an artist who had borrowed money from her parents to make a couple of limited edition prints, and who was then asking about using her credit card to buy some ads and booth space to promote the pieces.

In this instance, we are looking at someone committing thousands of dollars to try to start a career with two prints, a couple of full-page ads in DECOR, and barely enough money to get into a tradeshow. In my professional opinion, this is a prescription for failure.

My advice to that artist was take the money and go on the vacation of a lifetime – and make it so exotic and extraordinary that she would talk about it the rest her life. This is because if you choose to go into self-publishing unprepared and under-funded, you are – as they say at the poker table – dead money. I am not trying to scare you; I just want you to be realistic about what you are trying to do. Besides, I already know there is no amount of advice that will stop those fully committed to what they are doing.

Okay, we have described the top-level opportunities in publishing and briefly discussed the merits and pitfalls of each. Although you still need more information about self-publishing and using a publisher to be able to make a decision about which is best for you, you are much closer than you were on page one.

By reading this far, you have begun to determine what is most important in the self-publishing versus seeking-a-publisher decision process. And, you are beginning to gain some insight on other decisions you'll need to make to get your print career on track. In other words, you have your attention focused on first things first.

Chapter Four
Traits and Attributes of Self-Published Artists

Those who do not want to imitate anything, produce nothing.
— Salvador Dali

In every endeavor where one wishes to succeed and indeed exceed the masters who have come before them, studying the tools and techniques of those masters is the basic prescribed method of improvement. Learn everything you can about how they did it, and then do it better.

It is human nature to push for faster, stronger, more beautiful and more consequential. We have intelligence, and we use it to strive to better our surroundings and ourselves. Studying successful self-published artists to discover what they have done to gain their triumphs is natural and logical.

When we study the careers of successful self-published artists, certain traits and common attributes become obvious. The list that follows is arguably not exclusive. Nevertheless, there is no argument in saying that each item is critical in successfully launching and sustaining a self-published art career:

- Talent
- Art that resonates with a large group of collectors
- Financing
- Personnel, usually a spouse, devoted family member or close friend
- Willingness to prodigiously continue to create art within the same thematic range in order to continue to supply the dealer and collector base
- Ambition

Using the above points, evaluate whether you possess the qualities and capabilities outlined. If you match up in all categories, you are a prime candidate for a top-notch self-published art career. Conversely, if your frank evaluation finds you lacking in one or more of these critical areas, your climb to career success in the art-print market will potentially be more difficult. However, having an unusual abundance of one of the above attributes can be a great help in overcoming deficiencies in another.

Although the art business enjoys a certain glamorous quality, it is still a business. Your success is dependent on how well you run yours. While your business is one that depends on you tapping your creative well to make work worthy of the market, it also requires your involvement to treat it seriously and run it professionally. There may be rare cases in the early going where an artist remains isolated from the business aspects and is still successful, but huge odds are stacked against any who initially avoid participating in the business.

Talent

If you are following the advice from this book, you are performing self-assessment in many ways, not the least of which is talent. Unfortunately, many talented artists do not enjoy the commercial success of their less talented contemporaries. This phenomenon extends beyond the visual arts. Why else would pretty faces sporting reed thin voices top pop charts? Why do some visual artists make fortunes despite critics dismissing them as hacks? The answer is that hitting the big time in any field takes more than talent. This is especially true in the arts, where tastes are subjective and the level of sophistication of the mass consumer is low. This is not to short change talent, because if you lack that, your road will be rocky.

For some people, talent within themselves is hard to gauge. In the visual arts, talent is subjective, thus providing the opportunity for some artists with a lesser talent to delude themselves into thinking their work is being received better than it is in reality. Often this delusion comes from the best intentions of family and friends, who – lacking the critical facility or experience to give honest advice on artistic talent – spur the artist into believing their talent is greater than it truly is.

For some whose aspirations are larger than their talent, it can be painful to come to the realization that they fall short in this category. All the same, if they draw an accurate bead on their ability, they are likely to avoid even further pain in the form of financial setbacks and career disappointments. The bottom line is to get critical opinions from qualified, but otherwise uninterested, parties.

In my career, I have seen artists with too little talent optimistically come into the gallery where I worked or into the booth of a publisher at a trade show. Each was hoping to find acceptance. Instead, what they typically found was polite rejection. If you find yourself in such situations and if you have the courage, you can ask for a quick appraisal with the caveat that you would deeply appreciate an unvarnished estimation. Asking for honesty does not always work; some will dismiss you without critique, simply to be done with it. Regardless, it is always worth asking.

In certain areas, sports for instance, it is harder to hide a lack of talent. If you cannot hit a curve ball, you will not make it to the big leagues, no matter how good an athlete you are otherwise. Look at Michael Jordan, perhaps the best basketball player ever, who strived for two years hoping to ignite a second career in baseball after conquering basketball. Jordan learned that despite his natural athletic gifts, hitting a major league curve ball is not easy – so much so that he gave up and went back to glory and more NBA titles.

What does that mean to you as an artist? That talent matters, but that you can make up for a lack of it if in some areas if you can excel in other areas. This is not to say you can be really bad and also be successful, but there is plenty of evidence that some artists with less than stellar ability – whose work is far below museum quality – still make a great living.

Consider an artist in a niche; pet portraits, for example. While there may be those who have a greater talent at rendering their subjects in a most artistic way, the lesser artist who has a deeper affinity for the animals he or she paints, and who may have a tireless outgoing networking capacity, may completely swamp the more talented artist in prints sold. This example proves there is more to success than just painting the picture. No one will argue that Andy Warhol was the most talented artist to pick up a paintbrush; instead, his genius was in his clever artistic concepts and in how skillfully he managed the social aspects of the art business, and this is what made him larger than life.

The bottom line is, if you have talent, you can learn technique and make a go of it. If you lack talent, your ambition and business sense will need to be off the charts to get there. Taking an honest, brutal assessment of your own talent is often hard to do. Nevertheless, it can help you adjust to what you need to do on the side of imagery, content and style. Do not take on more than you can handle; it will only add to your frustration. The sports cliché is, "Staying within yourself."

Art that Resonates with a Large Group of Collectors

If you can see the fish, and they are not biting, then you need to switch bait. Simply, buyers must like your art. It may seem obvious, and I hope that it was for you before reading it here. Possessing the knowledge that you are painting for the approval of others is proof to yourself that you are conceptually on board with what it takes to make an art print career. Yes, of course you are painting for yourself too. What needs to happen is an alignment of your artistic vision and your collectors' desires.

The point of your art business is not making art. Your business is really about supplying collectors, dealers and gallery owners with art that they want. Not surprisingly, dealers enjoy developing collectors who will come back and buy more art similar to what they first bought. If you are doing well in landscapes and then switch to painting trains, good luck. Your collector and dealer bases have now moved back to square one.

Thomas Kinkade [www.thomaskinkade.com] built a $100 million dollar business around painting cottages, nostalgic scenes of homes and beautiful romantic vignettes. I imagine some days when he sits to paint cottage number ... (pick one), that it requires great discipline to do the work and is more a chore than a labor of love at times. This is a personal impression, because although I sold his company advertising and booth space for years, I do not know him.

Regardless of whether you admire the man for his success or vilify him for it, he is the most successful limited edition artist of all time. Whatever his talent or motivation, he personifies the three D's (Desire, Discipline, Details.) He continues to stay at the easel and crank out the product today. Kinkade succeeds by having first found a subject matter and style with enormous compelling appeal to a large group of collectors and then relentlessly continuing to – in a manner of speaking – feed the beast.

Kinkade rarely receives credit for creating a huge number of art collectors, including many among them who had never set foot in a gallery before finding him. Inarguably, some of his collectors grew in sophistication and ultimately sought more sophisticated art – maybe yours.

Compare the art of P. Buckley Moss [www.pbuckleymoss.com] and her nostalgic scenes, with Wyland [www.wyland.com] and his ocean art, and you will note that each built their business selling to different kinds of collectors by finding a theme and style that resonated with them. They then continued to layer on more of the same, year after year.

These are but three of innumerable self-published artists who have created success by developing a subject matter with a look and style that collectors enjoy. The artists follow up by continuing to supply their collectors with more of the same. You will need to consider how you can emulate developing a look and style of painting for your own business. It is a key component of the whole picture.

Repetition is the mother of all skill.
— Tony Robbins

Financing

The adage "it takes money to make money" is as true in the art print business as it is anywhere else. This is where having the intangible of luck can play a crucial part in the development of your business. That is, if you already have money, you can self-finance. If you have access to someone who believes in you and who has money, you are also in luck. If, like most people, having excess funds available to throw at a somewhat risky business venture such as art print publishing is not a reality for you, you need to be creative in a whole new way – and that would be in raising money.

The number one reason why small business startups fail is lack of adequate funding to keep them afloat while they find footing and develop a client base. It is the same, maybe even more so, for self-published artists. Brilliance is not required, because among all the attributes and traits that cause would-be self-published artists to fail (or to not even try), lack of financing is the number-one reason. It is the all-time killer of small business startups.

In the first edition of this book, I remarked that almost all readers would be better candidates for seeking a publisher than for self-publishing, with inadequate financing as the reason. I went on to say, "I am not in the business of dashing hopes, but I would rather be known for that and save some of you from problems you never imagined possible – and for laying out the brutal honest truth of what you might be considering – than for cheerleading you into financial ruin. Having a garage full of unsold paper, crushing debt and broken optimism is a much harsher reality than admitting you don't have sufficient funds to get started self-publishing."

Now, some five years later (in what seems like eons in some ways) things have changed beyond the imagination of all involved, then or now – not only in the art print business, but in the world of business and communication in general. Things we considered reliable, bedrock marketing vehicles and things we took for granted, such as tradeshows and trade magazines, have disappeared or been marginalized to mere shells of their former selves. Now you are faced with new challenges, but also new opportunities.

Given the current market conditions, I have revised my thinking and advice. That is, rather than start searching for a publisher, I believe most artists can do as well – or even better – financially if they work on selling their art direct. Despite the difficult economic conditions that exist in 2010, there are many opportunities for artists to manage their careers. With the advent and acceptance of the giclée format and e-commerce, artists can find ways to get to market as never before. When you sell for yourself, you need to move much less product to generate the same income than you would with a publisher.

Regarding financing, there are no tricks to tell you. Artists who are already successful hardly ever discuss their early financing adventures, so anecdotes about how they did it are rare and not readily available. Some may have had luck with wealthy family members, but reality says more found luck in the residue of hard work. That is to say, in the early stages they built their businesses little by little, and then continued to invest earnings back into the business.

A lucky few might have hit it right with a look that defined a trend or created one and caught fire from inception; but hoping for, or trying to plan for, similar results to build your career would be as wise a buying lottery tickets to fund your retirement. It is much better to heed Aesop's Fable about the hare and the tortoise when it comes to strategizing for your career.

There is an abundance of successful, self-published artists who are not well known outside their dealer and collector base. They are not media stars or publicity hounds, yet they have fabulous careers and enjoy nice incomes from their art. You do not find them advertised in trade journals or mentioned in consumer magazines. Nevertheless, they have managed to build successful ongoing careers in the print market. Most are mining some niche where they have built a following and where they do not have to rely on establishing a huge dealer network to sell their art.

Sometimes I think they have the better of it, just as I think of those fine actors who work the stage – not on Broadway, but at the better Repertory Theatres found in large cities across the country. They are well paid, and they get to practice their craft to the best of their ability and travel to new cities where they reside for a time and enjoy obscurity rather than fame. Fame these days comes with a steeper price than ever, as the plethora of entertainment news attests.

In my opinion, there is nothing wrong with an art career out of the limelight. The same is true for symphony musicians and others in the arts. It is good work if you can get it and sustain it. Think of a competent, well-paid major league ball player: one who is both respected by his teammates and who avoids the hot lights of publicity. He takes pleasure playing the game, but he still enjoys a degree of anonymity better-known players gave up long ago.

Anecdotally, many unheralded yet successful self-published artists started slowly and then steadily grew their business. They started out at local shows, hustling like everyone else, getting attention any way they could to make sales. Then they moved on to regional shows and juried affairs, all the while improving their art and marketing skills and studying the moves of those they admired, especially those already enjoying self-published success. At some point, they amassed enough money to leverage marketing and publicity to their advantage.

There are examples self-published artists who started out working for an established publisher, but who, for reasons too different and numerous to mention, used their success and reputation to go on and start their own operations. The results are as varied as the reasons they left the relative security of working for publishers. Those with many of the traits and attributes outlined at the beginning of this chapter have done well. Those who bolted without good business skills and a plan, or without financing or proper support (and so forth), have struggled – and some have outright failed, only to end up back with a publisher.

To make it in self-publishing, you need to have money already (lucky you), be able to borrow it, or you need to be able to grow into a position of having a cash flow to pay for your publishing business. I do not know of other ways to do it. Some combination or permutation of these three methods is possible, but you have to have access to cash to get your self-publishing business off the ground.

Personnel, Usually a Spouse, Devoted Family Member or Close Friend

Here again, we are talking luck of the draw. If your spouse has a career he or she enjoys, lacks management and marketing skills, or is up to his or her ears running a household with three kids or similar, and if your sister, brother, best friend and other candidates are likewise involved, I'm sorry: you drew a bad lot on this attribute. Your hill to the top of the successful self-published artist heap is going to be steeper to climb.

There are numerous examples of successful self-published artists who had the good fortune to have someone who believed in them 100% on their side. Equally important was that these supporters were often capable of helping them in the critical areas of marketing and management. Lacking this asset is as lethal to a self-published art career as any other attribute except a lack of financing. Moreover, in studying successful self-published art careers, I have found that having these two attributes is always in the mix.

Hard as you might try, it is near impossible to pull off doing all the work yourself. How are you alone going to create the images, raise the money, market the work and manage the business? This is not to say it is impossible, but it is rare.

Any artist who has succeeded solely on their own has vast left- and right-brain capabilities and is highly organized and keenly competitive, along with being an ambitious and talented painter with an eye for what collectors want. He or she would be equally adept at handling marketing, sales, promotion and management duties while still finding time for a life, much less sleep. This is a tall order indeed.

"Monomaniac on a mission" is the apropos quote I borrow from Tom Peters, from his bestselling business book, co-authored with Bob Waterman, In Search of Excellence: Lessons from America's Best Run Companies. It best describes many of those whose support helped drive the success of the art industry's most well-known self-published artists.

A prime example is the spouse of P. Buckley Moss. Moss has derived much of her success from the driven marketing leadership of her husband. The duo worked as hard as any self-published artist team ever has at building their business through their dealer network. The success they have enjoyed as a result is tremendous. The notable 20th-century impressionist Richard Thompson had his son and daughter-in-law as his business partners. His is another example of the built-in marketing management attribute.

The late Marty Bell and her husband, Steve, built a fabulous business around her art. It included a devoted collector society, something she shares in common with P. Buckley Moss. When Thomas Kinkade looked for an idea to express his artistic talent and build an art print career, he emulated Marty Bell's romantic cottage theme that she had successfully created years earlier. He, like Bell, Moss and others, used his images to build a loyal fan base – or "collector society," as many publishers call them.

You cannot find a better example of a superb result from collaboration than that of P. Buckley Moss and her devoted spouse. The result of their collaboration was that she was featured on the cover of Parade, the Sunday supplement delivered to tens of millions of households each weekend. The story had her with numerous other people listed on the cover with picture, occupation and annual income. It is a feature Parade has done from time to time called, "What People Earn."

In the article, readers found a thumbnail headshot of P. Buckley Moss among dozens of pictures of millionaire basketball players and everyday folks, such as police officers, librarians, truck drivers and schoolteachers. Each had their annual salary listed below their names, and under Pat's was the amount of $600,000. Considering this story ran in the mid-1990s, the income was notable – and still is today – especially for a painter known for nostalgia work, Amish children, country life and geese.

We will never know if this was her personal income or if it included that of her husband. My guess is that it was not inclusive of his salary, which would flow to her in other ways – and nor does it matter. Either way, 20 years later, it is a greater figure than many reading this book can imagine as a personal income. To earn a half million-plus annually is to truly be in clover.

The point is that there are artists making lots of money out there, and the majority of them have trusted partners, often family members, who are instrumental in growing and supporting their businesses. It is difficult to recruit a willing person with the right qualifications if you do not already know one, especially because of the likelihood they will need to work on the promises of things to come, with little or no income at the outset.

It is a harsh reality to realize that launching a full-fledged art-publishing business is near impossible to do alone. So if you have that marketing maven, that "Monomaniac on a mission" targeted or recruited, then you are blessed. You have filled a crucial component of the successful self-publishing-needs matrix.

Willingness to Continue Thematically Creating Art in Order to Supply Collector Interest and Your Dealer Base

We discussed this attribute earlier when I mentioned Thomas Kinkade's discipline in sticking to what makes him successful. Still, even with his success, it is easy to see that he yearns for acceptance in other ways. For example, he has a line of plein-air images that are, in my estimation, a refreshing departure from (and better than) his cottages and nostalgic work. Nonetheless, his collectors are not wild for the stuff. Although it gives him a creative outlet besides his cottages, I believe that if he were trying to become a multi-millionaire based on his plein-air style, he would be up the proverbial creek without a paintbrush or paddle.

The reality, which can be a cruel taskmaster for some artists – even multi-millionaire artists – is that if they are going to continue to feed the beast, they must continue to paint in a style and thematic range that is comfortable to their collector base.

The same is true of other artists. Imagine the sublime blues-recording artist Eric Clapton attempting to switch gears and create a collector base with a rap album. The more success you enjoy, the more people in your supply chain you have depending on you to continue to paint those cottages or what have you. You've got employees, dealers, printers and even magazine and tradeshow reps (as was formerly the position of yours truly), hoping and pulling for you, encouraging you to continue with zest to create and market art that sells at ever increasing speed and prices.

For some artists, this is not a burden, but a joy. There are those who simply enjoy creating images in the same vein, who are not bored with yet another marine wildlife painting or Impressionistic landscape and so on. To those, I salute you for your ability; you should be relieved not to carry the weight of feeling penned in by circumstances and success. To those of you who feel the weight and succeed despite it, may the blessings of your success help lift you and otherwise make your life so sweet that you carry your weight without grudge or gripe.

Ambition

If you lack this, skip to the chapters on seeking a publisher. No joke; it is that simple. Either you possess it, just as you may possess artistic talent, or you don't. Ambition is not a technique you can study to improve upon. It's either there or it's not — simple as that. It's an innate trait, built into your DNA. Yes, we all have it to some extent, but you know what I am talking about: the burning desire to enjoy success and be somebody, come hell or high water. Ambition and competitiveness are close allies in success. I mentioned earlier that selfishness is an attribute that contributes to success; I also believe it is a component of ambition.

The previously mentioned Michael Jordan is a case in point. Like all pro ball players, he spent decades traveling around the country, for six months at a time, to play ball – and then he spent more time to tend to public appearances and promotional activities, all because he is driven. Mark Twain spent enormous amounts of time away from his family in his writing studio or traveling, either to speak or for other reasons. How many top visual artists obsess on their work? Too many to count or list.

I will say most average people lack they capacity to fully understand how driven the many elite performers, artists or athletes are in order to succeed. Likewise, it may be difficult for the achievers to realize the depth of their desire, or understand how it makes them different. There are numerous examples of artists and other high achievers who had to sacrifice something to make their goals. Consider the career of P. Buckley Moss. She made about 100 one-person gallery shows, annually, for 15 years. There are tremendous sacrifices in adhering to such a demanding schedule. Not surprisingly, she learned to paint on airplanes to best use her time.

Ambition, like talent, comes from different depths in each of us. If you are fortunate enough to understand your own, you can use that knowledge to help harness your success, or at least accurately gauge how far you can or want to go with it. If you did use the Mission Builder program mentioned in Chapter One, perhaps it helped you gain some insight into your own makeup and drive.

Let's look back once more at Michael Jordan, because his achievements are legendary. He is a fierce competitor who would never accept defeat without giving it his all, whether playing a "friendly" game of ping-pong or a card game in the locker room. His desire to win and to be the best inspired his teammates to be better than they would have been on their own. Those attributes combine into leadership, both personal and organizationally. As the driving force in your business, your competitiveness, ambition and leadership abilities will make a huge difference in your success.

When deciding whether to self-publish or seek a publisher, or to be a full-time, part-time or amateur painter, there is no shame in making an honest evaluation and concluding you do not have the fire in the belly to go through the gyrations to gain all the sales and success that you might. Remember the woodworker's story; it applies here as well. Fortunately, you get to define what success is for you.

When I sold advertising in the heyday of thick robust issues published by DECOR magazine, I had one artist who advertised infrequently. When he did, he invariably pulled the best reader response of any ad in the issue. After noting this occur for sometime, I visited him and encouraged him, much like I had for my brother-in-law, the hot rod builder, (are you getting the impression here that I am a slow learner or a dogged optimist?) to embrace his success and advertise monthly and really push his sales envelope.

He explained to me that having the ability was not a good enough reason for him to do it. He already knew he could have substantially greater sales by being more visible, but he didn't want the headaches that went with it. That is, more staff, more shipping, more printing, more this and that. Go figure, because I had others advertising with me at that time who would have done anything to get his results. It they had the chance, they would have eagerly pursued every possible sales opportunity open to them. Sadly, many were just getting by and could not afford the advertising I envisioned for this artist. Life's twists are strange, cruel and hard to comprehend at times.

If you are not as driven, passionate and ambitious about success with your art career as you are about creating your art (if not more so), then reaching the top as a self-published artist is likely not your cup of tea. It requires drive and much personal leadership to succeed as an art entrepreneur, and ambition is a key ingredient in that success.

Do yourself an enormous favor, because it is vitally important for your choice of career path. Be honest with yourself regarding your depth of ambition as you contemplate your career as a self-published artist. If your actions and deep desires do not match your wishes, your self-publishing dreams are in jeopardy.

Fortune favors the bold.
— Basil King

Chapter Five
Economics of Self-Publishing

The holy passion of friendship is so sweet and steady and loyal and enduring in nature that it will last through a whole lifetime, if not asked to lend money.
— Mark Twain

This chapter will not cover all aspects of finance as it relates to a successful art career. There is enough in that subject for a complete book. The objective here is to inform readers of some of the typical and specific costs involved in self-publishing art, and to provide some basic formulas for calculating your launch prospects.

In this chapter, you will discover some of the financial variables involved with starting and operating a self-publishing enterprise for artists. The intent with these basics is not to be inclusive of every financial aspect of your career, because the complexities involved in launching and maintaining a self-published art career, or any small business for that matter, are not feasible for this type of book.

Trying to understand the variables necessary to make blanket statements about what it would cost to get an art-publishing career off the ground is a daunting task. One of the most frequent questions artists ask is how much it will cost them to launch a successful art print career. When pushed for an answer in the days before I wrote the first edition of this book, I would apply the S.W.A.G. Factor (either "Scientific" or "Stupid" Wild-Ass Guess, depending on how well you like the answer) and toss out $100,000.

In 2005, $100,000 was a shocking, if not nearly unbelievable, figure to hear. Nevertheless, in the context of going from relative obscurity to attaining a degree of national prominence, it was accurate. Now, more than five years later and under today's difficult economic conditions, the number is more shocking and overwhelming. However, if you examine all the other changes that have taken place in the market place, they are just as outrageous.

For now, we will examine the economics involved in the start up costs a successful art print career, then and now.

Because history is an important teacher to each of us, I felt it imperative to leave the following in: a breakdown of how, in 2005, an artist could easily spend $100,000 to break out as a nationally or internationally known artist. While one today could still spend the same amount of money on the same marketing vehicles, such as tradeshows and trade magazines, the return on investment is not as assured as then. Regardless of timeframes, knowing these figures informs the budgeting process.

The following is the broad-brush budget plan I suggested in 2005. The dollar figure is for a bold rollout campaign over the course of 12 to 18 months. In that time, one could easily spend upwards of $100,000 to launch a publishing career. While that understandably is a hard-to-swallow figure, it does not include all the attendant costs in making a successful operation run.

Keep in mind you are spreading these expenditures over a 12 to18-month period, which means you do need all the capital at once. The best scenario is where things take off fast, so the business self-funds most of the costs. It is a sweet pipe dream, but not one you can reasonably count on it to happen.

When you have them by the wallet, their hearts and minds will soon follow.
— Japanese proverb

How then does one spend $100,000?

Six-pages trade advertising	$18,000
Tradeshow space and costs	$30,000
Publicity	$6,000
Printing art	$12,000
Promotional materials	$2,000
Business expenses	$1,500
Shipping expenses	$3,000
Salaries and benefits	$45,000
Total	$119,000

Obviously, there is much latitude in each of these numbers as there is no way to assume that every artist jumping into self-publishing will produce the same number of images to be printed, sell them at the same rate and price, or have someone working unpaid, but full-time later, and so forth. There is no end to the different number of scenarios that can arise as you begin to put together your plan and your budget. It will end up being what it is, and whatever you make it.

While the other items mentioned above are straightforward, the $30,000 for tradeshow expense perhaps needs some clarification for those who have not gone through the process. The $30,000 includes travel for two people, including airfare, hotel, cabs, meals and miscellaneous expenses. It covers booth rental for two booths and expenses on the show floor for labor, electricians, carpet cleaning and so drayage forth. Drayage is a big cost in exhibiting. This term describes the physical unloading of your crates, moving them to your spot, reloading them for storage and then the reverse on the move out.

Other tradeshow expenses include printing and framing enough work to fill the booth, building crates to ship your goods, and shipping your booth crates to the show. Advertising in the show directory and other promotional items are part of typical expenses. You can see the numbers add up quickly. Yes, you might get off with less than $30,000 to do a show, but it will probably come at the cost of eliminating something you later wish you had done.

Can you start a self-publishing company for less? Absolutely; thousands of successful artists in the print market have. The above scenario is the near perfect, ideal package. While I am not deluded enough to think it would be the norm for most artists seeking to make a significant move in the print market, it is my wish for you reading this book.

The critical thing about financing is to build your expectations around your situation. If you scale back on what you can put into the business, you have to scale back on what your expectations of how much you will make from it and how long it will take you to get the reward and recognition that represents your long-term goals.

What Does it Take to Launch a Successful Career in the Art Print Market Today?

The question emerging artists in the second decade of the 21st century need to ask is, "Does a tradeshow exist that is worthy of dropping $30,000-plus on exhibit fees for, especially for an emerging artist?" In 2010, with the industry's premier show, ArtExpo New York moving to a new and less desirable venue on Pier 94, there is no easy pat answer to the question.

In 2005, I held the conviction that a well-executed plan of advertising and tradeshow exposure, in conjunction with direct mail, publicity and professional follow-up, would create the solid foundation for an artist to build a substantial dealer network.

Such a network primarily consists of retail galleries set up to promote the artist with the intention of continuing to sell the artists' new editions as they became available. In the print market, there were many more galleries just five years ago than today and there were far fewer online venues for art print buyers to shop

Market conditions now are much more different than in any previous times. Factors contributing to changing the landscape for the art print market include the following:

- The rise in usage and importance of the Internet.
- The increase in number of e-commerce sites, such as art. com, allposters.com and others too numerous to mention, and their market penetration.
- Changing consumer habits and home building designs.
- The proliferation of big-box retailing.
- The flood of cheap Chinese oil paintings.
- The declining number of independent art retailers.
- The demise of art trade publications and art tradeshows.
- The explosive growth of social media sites, including Facebook, Twitter, LinkedIn, YouTube, Flickr and many more.

When you consider the above factors, it is not difficult to understand why a previously reliable formula does not work in today's market environment. The formula I provided in 2005 was just that: a formula. Many successful artists in the print market commonly used it; however, it was not all inclusive, as many other artists managed to build successful print market careers using a modified version. Just as when you look at a roadmap to a destination, there are many options to get to the same place; and the same is true about building a successful career as a visual artist.

In the first edition of this book, I strongly encouraged readers to attend ArtExpo. This is because I believed there was no better place for you to get smarter fast about your future in the business than by immersing yourself in the experience of ArtExpo. For more than 30 years, it has been the single most important marketing event for artists and publishers seeking a share of sales and national spotlight in the print market.

The show, like the industry in general, has been on the decline in the latter part of the last decade. It opens a new decade with yet another new owner and a new venue. In March 2010, ArtExpo New York has relocated from the Jacob Javits Center to Pier 94 on the Hudson River. I warned about the show losing its dates at the prestigious Javits in my Art Print Issues blog [www.artprintissues.com] in 2008. Unfortunately, that prediction came to be true.

While I will sadly say that ArtExpo does not carry the same importance for artists, publishers or collectors as it once did. I will also say the state of the industry is such that, despite being trimmed down in size and with a less desirable location, there is no real challenger to ArtExpo. That said, the show proved in 2010 it can still deliver for artists and publishers with the right look and price points. Basically, it has traded its "sure thing" status to "hedged bet" for many artists and publishers.

If anything, today's market place provides artists with more ways to build a career. The primary difference I see now is that using my formula, or any formula, with the intention of building a career that leads to national prominence as a visual artist would be difficult to devise and harder yet to execute. Because of the new factors listed above, the fickleness of consumers, a weak economy and a fragmented marketplace, working to build national prominence as an immediate goal is not as feasible now as it was in the past.

This is not to say it is impossible for an artist to build a national career in today's market; I simply do not consider such a goal as the best approach to attacking the job of building a successful, profitable career in the print market at this time. While I still consider gallery distribution as a practical way to get one's work to market, I also hold the strong belief that visual artists should diligently work to control as much distribution of their art as possible. In other words, they should have has many direct sales channels as they can reasonably build and manage, which puts them into competition and conflict with galleries.

The question then becomes whether visual artists have both a viable gallery network and have multiple direct distribution channels? The answer is complicated, and there is no single solution. I do believe it is possible to have it both ways if an artist chooses to do so, especially for someone whose work is most desirable. For others, whose work is still evolving, choosing to focus on galleries versus direct distribution arguably may be the best plan in the early stages of building an art print career. Since we will discuss distribution channels, including galleries, in a future chapter, we will leave the debate and decisions about what is best for you until then.

The formula and budget I provided in 2005 was, I believe, both simplistic and realistic. It intentionally did not explore other available options, because to do so would have overcomplicated the process. I knew then

– as now – that my readers would absorb the advice and then make their own decisions. I did not then, nor do I now, harbor delusions that artists would follow my advice without alteration.

Since I do not have as straightforward a formula now as I did in 2005, it is more difficult to employ the S.W.A.G. Factor to come up with a round figure of annual expenditure for jumpstarting an art print career. If the available multiple factors and choices were complex and intimidating then, they are modest by today's standards.

Undaunted by the challenge, I will offer some ideas on the amount and type of expenditure that an artist seeking to break into the print market today should expect. Previously, a building a dealer network primarily consisted of finding retail art galleries, some dealers, and picture framers to work with.

In the past, building such a dealer network was the only way for an artist to sell enough art prints annually to create a full-time career. Today, that is still a laudable goal to pursue. However, with the diminished number of retail art galleries that sell art prints, building such a dealer network is more difficult than in the past. Moreover, I believe those remaining galleries will be more fickle, harder to deal with, and less likely to take chances on unknown artists.

Given that the gallery distribution method is more difficult and less predictable for success than before, it can be argued budgeting purely to build a dealer network may not be the best solution for emerging artists today. This is especially true now that artists have the technology and tools to help themselves in ways never before possible. This means your planning should include working with galleries while also seeking to develop your own solely-owned direct marketing vehicles. The big decision for emerging artists is whether to attempt to do these things sequentially or concurrently. Only your own needs, desires, instincts, resources and circumstances can guide you in this decision.

With the above outlook in mind, I will again incorporate the aforementioned S.W.A.G. Factor and offer the following budget considerations for those attempting to launch an art print career. We will use an aggressive but realistic goal of establishing ten galleries in the first year while simultaneously establishing one or more direct sales channels. The point is to develop attainable goals to assist in establishing a logical budget.

In this scenario, I will assume you are planning to grow locally and regionally, as opposed to attempting to launch nationally. Doing so will help you hold down your costs and avoid the diminished ability of national trade magazines and tradeshows to deliver as in the past. You should consider it a natural outcome that your expenditures will be greater than your income in your first year, and likely into the second or possibly third year.

If you find the reality of losing money in your first years unacceptable, you should plan on keeping your full-time job for now and working on your art career in your spare time. When you realize the vast number of famous artists who supported themselves as illustrators, teachers or other occupations before they moved on to full-time careers as visual artists, you will also understand there is no shame in growing slowly.

Although the following budget is designed for those ready – both professionally and financially – to begin working full-time as visual artists, it will be just as informative for those who are taking a part-time approach to a permanent visual artist career. As was the case with the 2005 budget, the full amount is not required upon launch.

It would be good to have the full amount below as a cushion to start, but if this were necessary, it would kill many otherwise lucrative art print careers. These figures are from the S.W.A.G. Factor, and as such they leave out many other budget items, such as insurance, shipping, and payroll. The point is to get you thinking seriously about what it is going to take to get your career off the launch pad.

How much should I budget to launch a full-time art print career now?

Preparing and printing art	$15,000
Promotional materials	$2,500
Business expenses	$3,000
Shipping expenses	$4,000
Professional e-commerce website	$500
Regional travel	$5,000
Publicity	$6,000
Online advertising	$2,000
Total	$38,000

Raising Money

Whether or not you are tradeshow bound, you will likely need to raise money for your art-publishing venture. In order to raise the funds and properly start your business, even if raising money is not an issue, you should know about break-even analysis. By demonstrating that you not only understand the concept but have also developed a realistic analysis of your business model using it, you will go a long way towards gaining confidence from investors and making them much more comfortable with you as a businessperson.

Let us get into some of the pricing that goes on in the industry. To start, having a good understanding of how posters are priced through the various channels into the retail market will help you make better decisions about what you want to do with your art and will assist you in making good break-even analysis forecasts.

I am not suggesting that you get into the poster-publishing business. With all the changes in the marketplace for posters and publishers, it is far too risky to consider. Planning to make a full-time living with a poster publisher is not realistic for any artist at this point. In today's poster environment, some versatile productive artists who have a knack for creating art preferred by volume buyers are able to produce a decent cash flow, particularly if they are also in the print market utilizing some other distribution model. Overall, however, it is a tough road to follow. Under ideal circumstances, it would take several years of collaboration with a publisher to reach the point of steady income – but there are no guarantees it ever will reach this point. Nevertheless, it is both eye opening and instructive to learn about wholesale poster pricing.

Typical Wholesale Poster Volume-Pricing Scenario

A typical discount for a buyer to request from a publisher is for a 50-50-20 deal. You should be aware of this kind of industry idiosyncrasy discounting. Translated, the jargon means the buyer is requesting a reduction in retail price of less 50%, less another 50% and finally less another 20%.

Using a $40 retail poster price, here is how honoring a 50-50-20-discount request turns into a publisher's final wholesale net price of $8 per poster:

$40.00 x .50 = $20.00 (First Discount @ 50%)

$20.00 x .50 = $10.00 (Second Discount @ 50%)

$10.00 x .20 = $8.00 (Third Discount @ 20%)

If you self-publish, do not be surprised when you find buyers who are not really volume buyers asking for similar discount. Many people in the industry do not think twice about trying to put publishers or artists on their knees with regard to pricing. Some have legitimate reasons for asking, while others are trying to bully you for a lowball price. Unfortunately, the above scenario does not get to the lowest price publishers will provide for some high-volume buyers. It is a harsh business these days, especially since there is no such thing as a lock on subject matter, content, themes, sizes, et cetera. There will always be competitors who can produce a similar look.

Keep in mind that the mom and pop galleries and frame shops that sell prints and posters are small businesses that, on average (according to DECOR magazine's regular reader surveys) generate less than $300,000 in annual sales – and that is average. When you deduct rent, product, salaries, benefits, marketing and other costs, all paid from that amount before profit, you can quickly see why some have to be hardnosed on pricing. For them, it is the difference between profiting or not.

There is a lesson here in that being sensitive to pricing and costs are things that should be important to your own business, so it should not be a shock that many of your smarter customers have the same concerns. How they come across when they ask for discounts is often the difference between wanting to work with someone or not. Unfortunately, like every other business, this one has its share of those who are difficult. The good news is they are more than offset by those who make doing business with them a pleasure.

What you need to do is figure out in advance what your bottom line is for as many scenarios as you think you might encounter. There is nothing worse than not being able to respond with authority to a tough question when a deal is on the table. If you have done your homework, including your break-even analysis, and you know your costs and inventory, then you can quickly calculate your reply to discounting requests. You will be even further ahead of the give and take if you have anticipated certain requests and have a reply ready.

To keep things real, as mentioned above, I do not believe self-published artists should consider posters as their medium of choice. Here is more detail on why:

First, the market has been changing for years, with volume buyers becoming increasingly important to publishers. The number of independent shops continues to dwindle and those that remain are careful about what they stock. This gives new publishers fewer openings to establish themselves with repeat buyers.

Second, selling posters these days requires having a great Rolodex full of potential volume buyers. Without important buyer contacts, a new poster publisher is faced with nearly insurmountable odds of getting to market.

Third, volume buyers and consolidators, such as Liebermans.net, [www. liebermans.net], will not consider publishers who lack a deep line of images. The same is true for expecting representation on Art.com and Allposters.com, the Internet behemoths that dominate the online, open-edition art market. The days of starting with eight or ten images and building a line around them are long gone for self-published artists and publishers attempting to break into the poster market.

As an aside, Art.com was in the news in 2007, touting itself as being in pre-IPO (Initial Public Offering) mode. I examined the situation and challenged the reality of it in a blog post titled "Is the Art.com IPO for Real?" which also provided an interesting historical look at the development of the company. You can search on www.ArtPrintIssues.com for the title to find it in the archives.

While the cost of getting into the poster publishing game has become prohibitively expensive, margins have become slimmer than ever. It is a business now where only the strong survive. Industry observers note that new poster publishers are not coming on to the scene any longer.

In my first edition of this book, I wrote that there was a consolidation of publishers. Bentley Publishing Group alone has acquired Aaron Ashley, Rinehart Fine Arts, Art Folio West and Leslie Levy Publishing in the past few years. The company also provides distribution for Grand Images Posters. These are all publishers with large catalogs and impressive buyer lists. While their reasons are not all the same for selling their businesses, all would agree that increased competitiveness and the changing landscape helped them decide to sell. Since the first edition, Bentley Publishing Group has also acquired Joan Cawley Publishing, one of the top southwest art publishers.

Late in 2009, one of the industry's most influential and largest poster publishing operations, Bruce McGaw Graphics, announced that it had been sold to Jack Appelman. He is the CEO of Applejack Art Partners, a leading poster and print publisher and art licensing company. Just a few years ago, this would have been unthinkable, because Bruce McGaw Graphics has been one of the industry's largest and most important poster publishers for decades. The name of the new company is McGaw Graphics.

I predict that the next few years will see further consolidation and major ownership changes in the poster business. It has not been a fertile market for startups for some time, and prospects for a change in course are not on the foreseeable horizon.

Will Your Self-Publishing Art Print Business Make Money?

You will not have a chance of knowing that without doing some calculations, and one absolute must is to prepare a break-even analysis before doing the more detailed work on your overall business plan.

While you cannot know with utter certainty that your business is going to be profitable, you can get much closer to a realistic idea by analyzing the financial accuracy of your concept. Perhaps the most basic research you can do is to prepare a "break-even analysis" for your business. This, along with a few other financial forecasts, will give you – and potential investors – a more clear determination of whether your business will succeed.

A break-even analysis shows how much revenue your business will have to generate to cover its expenses before profits. Your obvious goal is to promptly surpass your break-even point so you are not only covering expenses but generating what is called cash flow, or what's left after expenses. You quickly need to bring in more than the amount of sales revenue required to meet your expenses. By doing this, you significantly strengthen your odds of seeing your business prosper.

You will find that both well-informed investors and entrepreneurs employ a break-even analysis as their main tool to sift through ideas for new businesses. They look for projected sales revenue that surpasses their costs of doing business, because they know it's crucial to get this kind of financial justification from their break-even forecast before taking the next step of writing a full business plan. Since having a break-even analysis will be an integral part of your business plan, you can give yourself a head start on getting that important piece of pre-launch planning done.

Can you skip on this work? You bet you can, but "bet" is the operative word, because it is an enormous gamble to launch a business without proper financial preparation. Remember, sophisticated investors will not allow you to forgo doing this important prep work; not having it prepared will negatively influence their impression of you by showing you have a significant lack of business skills and attention to detail. You can fly by the seat of your pants with your own money, but you will not get off the ground that way with investors. If this is sounding like too much work, not fun or in some other way not worth doing, it is a sign that you should be seek to work with a publisher instead of self-publishing.

Steps to Prepare a Break-Even Analysis

To start with, you will have to use a system better than the S.W.A.G Factor mentioned earlier to hone in on what your expected expenses and revenues will be. This will require some intense – but valuable – research from you. It should include a competitive market analysis, which is an investigation of companies in the market place and, in particular, what their pricing strategies are, at least as best as you can ascertain.

Unfortunately, since the art business is nearly 100% privately owned, you will not find much in the way of published sales figures and revenues to base your own projections on. To a great degree, you will have to wing it on this one. However, by doggedly asking questions and by getting help from the right individuals, you can come up with a realistic projection on the business.

Needing facts, it will serve you well to befriend knowledgeable people in the business. Get to know other artists who are already enjoying success. Talk to art publishers, editors, sales reps or anyone you and your organization should cultivate. Look for all who can give you the information to help formulate a good overview of your competitive market, particularly while you are in the formative stage.

A good source rarely tapped is the moulding rep. They know who is buying the quantities and often have insights into the businesses, which are their customers. If they cannot tell you specifics, they ought to be able to generalize in ways that will still be helpful to you. Find out who are the reps for Larson-Juhl, Roma, Max Moulding or any of the other top moulding companies in your area and then contact them. Reverse the tables and treat them to lunch; they can be an invaluable source of all kinds of industry news and insights for you.

You do not have to know details about all the businesses, but it helps to know as much as possible about those who you see as your main competitors. You will find that knowing your competitors is not just a way to spread industry gossip; it will help you make critical decisions that can help your company grow.

Getting a copy of any of the latest research by industry publications like DECOR, Art Business News or Art World News would be about the best source you will find to help you begin your market analysis. The Internet remains a great source of information, and using all available industry contacts can be useful, too.

You will also need to determine your own projected sales volume and your anticipated expenses. It is a worthy idea to spend some time and money on books about business planning. Some excellent software also is available to teach you how to make reasonable revenue and cost estimates. In addition, you can find remarkably good free advice and help on this and other startup questions through SCORE (Service Corps of Retired Executives), which is a non-profit organization that is part of the U.S. government Small Business Association. You can find your local chapter online at www.score.org

Break-even analysis is critical to a start-up business. You will need the following figures and calculations to complete this analysis:

Fixed costs – Overhead is another way to describe costs that do not vary much from month to month. They include rent, insurance, utilities, and other set expenses. You should also put in a line for miscellaneous costs, which should be around 10% of the total of your other fixed costs, to help cover expenses you cannot predict.

Sales revenue – Total all the money your business will generate in sales each month or year. Please do not let your enthusiasm or desire to make your numbers work out influence you or drive you to avoid being brutally honest in evaluating your sales potential. It will come back to haunt you like a bad dream. You have to base your forecast on the volume of business you can truly expect and not on how much you need to make a good profit.

Average gross profit – Sales revenue is the remaining balance after you pay the direct costs of a sale. (Direct costs are what you pay to provide your product or service.) Here is an example: If your giclée print costs $100 to produce, and you sell them wholesale to a dealer for an average of $300, your average gross profit is $200.

Average gross-profit percentage – This calculation works off the figures you pulled together for your average gross profit per sale. It shows how much of each dollar of sales income is gross profit. To get the answer, divide your average gross profit figure by your average selling price. From the above example, you would take your average gross profit of $200 for your giclée' print and divide by the average sale price of $300, which would result in a gross profit percentage of 66.7%.

Calculating your break-even point – Now that you have done the above calculations, it's simple to figure out your break-even point. Divide your estimated monthly fixed costs by your monthly gross profit percentage to learn the amount of sales revenue you have to generate to break even.

Staying with the example of the wholesale giclée business, let us presume your fixed costs average $4,000 per month. By applying your anticipated profit margin of 66.7%, your break-even point is $6,000 in sales revenue per month ($4,000 divided by .667). Therefore, you must have monthly sales of $6,000 to cover your fixed costs and direct (product) costs. If you want to eat and grow your business, you have to make more than that, because that $6,000 does not include a profit for your company or a salary for you.

You would not be the first brave entrepreneur to go through this financial exercise only to be sadly surprised that you did not hit a break-even point. If you find it is higher than your anticipated revenues, you will have to go back to the drawing board to see if you can change parts of your plan to reach a break-even point.

Here are some things you might be able to do to cut your costs:

- Charge more for your work.
- Find a less expensive supplier or buy in larger quantities to get your costs down.
- Cut down on personnel costs, maybe you don't need someone full-time right away.

- Work from your home or share space somewhere instead of paying rent.
- Use your creativity to figure other ways to cut down overhead.

Cutting costs should be the core part of your business fiber, regardless of how successful you are. You will find few, if any, top executives at any company (in art publishing or otherwise) who are not extremely sensitive about keeping costs in line. As the wise saying from Ben Franklin goes, "A penny saved is a penny earned!" If you start with this as an integral part of your business plan and actions, you will give yourself greater chances for success early and better profits later.

If you have massaged the numbers and your break-even sales revenue still is not working out satisfactorily, it might be time to back away from your business plan. If this happens, it is not end, nor the worse outcome. Imagine if you did not do the calculations and ended up blowing a lot of your money, and maybe even the investments of your friends and family, who may not have required hardheaded planning and forecasting before passing the hat for you.

Success takes more than a good break-even analysis. If your forecast shows you will generate revenue beyond your break-even point, you are fortunate and are moving in the right direction; but now you will need to figure out how much profit your business will generate, and whether you'll be able to pay your bills on time, when they are due, and more. Your positive break-even forecast is a great start, but you will need a more complete analysis before moving from hypothetical to actual when it comes to putting dollars into your art business.

Here are some other necessary projections to complete your financial picture. Since they also will be an integral part of your business plan, they are especially worth completing:

Profit-and-loss forecast – This is a month-to-month projection of net profits from your business operations.

Cash flow projection – This projection shows how much actual cash you will generate each month to meet your expenses.

Start-up costs estimate – This shows the total of all of all expenses incurred before your business opens.

You can make these projections by hand, but you will find it easier to make changes if you can use a spreadsheet program such as Microsoft Excel. A suggestion for business planning software is included below. It will take you the process in an automated way.

There is more to financial modeling and business planning than what you find here

Do not take what you learn here as all you need to know about business planning. There are many great books and resources, including those listed below, to educate you further on this topic. Besides giving you a primer on finances and business planning, I hope you come away from reading this chapter with a clearer understanding that you are embarking on a serious business venture. The more you treat it as a serious business, the greater your chances for success.

Business-Plan Resources

There are many resources for finding out more about completing a business plan and conducting the exercises to get accurate financial projections for your business. Here are some suggested titles:

Getting to Plan B: Breaking Through to a Better Business Model by John Mullins, Randy Komisar

The Successful Business Plan, 4th Edition: Secrets and Strategies (Successful Business Plan Secrets and Strategies) by Rhonda Abrams

How to Write a Business Plan by Mike McKeever

The Entrepreneur's Success Kit: A 5-Step Lesson Plan to Create and Grow Your Own Business by Kaleil Isaza Tuzman

The Art of the Start: The Time-Tested, Battle-Hardened Guide for Anyone Starting Anything by Guy Kawasaki

The E-Myth Revisited: Why Most Small Businesses Don't Work and What to Do About It by Michael E. Gerber

A great suggestion is to get the bestselling business planning software: Business Plan Pro by Palo Alto Software, Inc. The software receives high marks from numerous reviewers. I have used it myself and found it to do all I expected and more.

I went into the business for the money, and the art grew out of it. If people are disillusioned by that remark, I can't help it. It's the truth.
— Charlie Chaplin

Chapter Six
Exemplary and Successful Self-Published Artists

Art is never finished, only abandoned.
— Leonardo da Vinci

Why Would an Artist Choose to go the Route of Self-Publishing?

There are basic points regarding both the merits and the pitfalls a visual artist should consider when deciding to self-publish. These include the following:

Self-publishing merits

- You can maintain artistic control;
- You can make more money;
- You can produce at your own rate;
- You make all the choices about what to paint

Self-publishing pitfalls

- You will need financing;
- Your art – i.e., your passion – will become a business;
- You will need strong motivation to stick with a successful style;
- Your available time and desire to be involved in most (if not all) aspects of the business will determine your early success.
- You do not get any input from an informed publisher on what to paint, e.g., content, colors, sizes and so forth

Study successful self-published artists and you will find that most use a combination of all the possible ways to market their images. Nevertheless, there are those who gain success despite not incorporating every available element into their marketing schemes. This shows that if you execute your marketing well in enough in some areas, you can forgo another marketing element or two and still get grand results.

I always recommend using every means available because I believe it is best to make as many positive impressions, from as many angles as possible, on your target market. While I cannot deny the success of some artists and publishers who avoid marketing opportunities, I wonder how much better they would fare if they were to include more forms of communication and promotion.

Regardless of whether or not successful self-published artists use all the marketing tools available to them, they all share what I call Self-Publishing Essentials, including these common traits:

Common Traits of Successful Self-Published Artists

- art that resonates with the buying public
- a business plan to create and sell the art
- a dedicated marketing/sales maven to make the business run
- an artist willing to prodigiously create in the same genre or theme
- financing
- a clear understanding of the primary business they are in

Just as with the marketing mentioned here, there are artists who successfully manage their careers despite lacking one or more of the points above. I include this information because I know that realistically many reading this book will assess their own situation and conclude they also lack one or more of the points, and this is okay. To some extent, it simply comes down to whether the artist has the ability to create compelling art, and shows initiative and ambition. A serious dose of a few traits will overcome a shortage in other common traits of successful self-published artists.

Coincidentally, one of the artists covered in this chapter is someone who abandoned exhibiting at art tradeshows at a time when they were one of the predominant means of attaining new dealers. She is Pat Buckley Moss (more commonly known as P. Buckley Moss). I refer to her several times throughout this book because she is an art-print marketing hero to me. Honestly, I have many marketing heroes in the art print business, but her compelling story demands to be told.

When it comes to understanding that the business you are in is building and nurturing a dealer network, no artist does it better than Pat. Others may have made more money or have more dealers, but I believe none have earned the deep loyalty of dealers and collectors as she has.

To my reckoning, her level of personal involvement with her dealer network exceeds all other artists in the print market. Although I have never met her, I would consider it an honor and privilege to do so. Despite never calling on her company for ad sales, I worked closely with colleagues who knew her from her early years and had watched her career develop. From them, I learned much about her, including that initially she did exhibit at tradeshows; but as her dealer network grew, she put her time into them instead.

What did more time with her dealers mean? In her case, she annually appeared at 100 or more one-woman shows for her dealer/galleries. Remarkably, she maintained this grueling schedule for more than 15 years running. You can understand, with such a travel schedule, why she had no time for tradeshows. For her, the effort paid off in a level of loyalty from her dealer network as strong as any artist has ever enjoyed, and this has led to fabulous sales results.

The following story exemplifies how her efforts produced dramatic results for her galleries. When I worked for DECOR magazine, I spent many years at its St. Louis home office. One morning, I found a story of great interest to me in my local newspaper, the St. Louis Post Dispatch. The article detailed how P. Buckley Moss had come for an appearance for one of her dealers in Collinsville, Illinois. Collinsville is a suburban bedroom community, about 12 miles across the Mississippi River from downtown St. Louis, which at that time had a population 16,000.

The article reported that her collectors had lined up to meet her and get signed prints, posters and collectibles. The event lasted eight hours and resulted in $100,000 in sales. That is a phenomenal one-day take for any small business, much less a suburban art gallery that sells prints and posters. Do you think the owner of that shop would walk through walls for this artist? I know I would if she had produced those results in my gallery.

The article also reported that Pat has dyslexia and that she donated a part of every sale from the gallery to local charities. She graciously contributes a portion of her proceeds from every show to help children with reading disabilities. It is another way she connects with her audience and uses her celebrity to make a difference. Surely, her goodwill comes back to her in increased publicity and popularity.

But Pat's marketing effort goes well beyond personal appearances for her galleries. She and her marketing-maven husband have had the most regular, consistent and ambitious advertising schedule – in both consumer and trade publications – of any print artist for more than two decades. I realize that a demanding travel or advertising schedule is not possible or likely for many artists reading this book, but you can still learn much from understanding how she created a loyal following among her dealers and collectors. My advice is to learn from her and follow her example on your own level.

Since Pat and her husband have a definable niche, they use that to their advantage and advertise in the lifestyle consumer magazines, such as Country Woman. These are publications the artist's collectors are most likely to read. For her, consumer advertising is a way to help her dealers by creating awareness for her work and driving sales to them. It is another way she helps others and herself in the process.

If you can follow the way Pat has worked to build a dealer network and keep it enthused about you and your art, you are on the way to certifiable success. It is not easy, but little in life worth achieving is, as I am sure you agree.

Perhaps you cannot spend that much time away from home to be able to support your galleries with personal visits. Then you have to start thinking creatively about what other ways you can support them and encourage them to sell your art when customers are in their galleries. If you want to be important to your galleries, find ways to be their marketing partners.

You could be thinking to yourself, "I would like to follow the example of P. Buckley Moss, but I have so many other obstacles and distractions that keep me from concentrating my energy on my art business." If you tell me that, I will believe you. I also will tell you there are artists who have achieved – and are achieving – enormous success in the art business today by virtue of overcoming greater obstacles than most artists can imagine.

A prime example is Cao Yong [www.caoyong.us]. You can check out his vibrant international city, sea and landscapes on his website. Cao is a Chinese immigrant who came to the U.S. in 1994 and could not speak English. Picture that challenge.

Although he previously had a successful art career in China, learning a new culture and a new language is still a huge hurdle for anyone to overcome. Can you imagine moving to China to make a go of it with your art career? The reverse is exactly what Cao faced. You can read his biography on his website and learn even more about the many hurdles and hostilities he faced before he got to the U.S.

In a move that is quite typical, Cao Yong first worked with publishers Aaron Ashley and Fortune Fine Art before emerging on his own as a self-published artist. As you can judge from the number of works on his site, he is a prolific painter.

Kudos to Cao for his ability to tap into what his collectors want. This is something you want to aspire to in your career, and you can learn much by studying him and other artists. It is always a good idea to try to discover all you can about how other successful artists are handling their work. Their websites are often a great place to start. While Cao began with works published as serigraphs, it appears from viewing his recent works that has given his print business over to the giclée medium. Moreover, in the case of his earlier giclées, he was selling the same image in two editions at separate prices. It appears as if he has abandoned the multiple-size editions for now.

At the time I wrote this book's first edition, Cao had more details on his website, including number of pieces sold out and his retail prices, than he currently provides. I was able to surmise that he had sold, at retail, work valued at more than $2.5 million, all from a series of 14 paintings done in 1998 (this was without all the editions in that series being sold out). I used it as an example of the kind of income a prolific and popular print artist can generate.

The lesson here is that you should be a student of your competition. I guarantee that if you start selling well, you will have many people studying what it is you are doing to be successful, and some will be trying to copy you.

A word about knockoffs: sometimes knockoffs are blatant and are obviously illegal, but other times the artists will simply have borrowed your "hot" theme or look and incorporated it into their line. While the latter will infuriate you, get used to it. It is a part of the business. It is also a way you will know for sure you are in the big time when you discover you are being "knocked off." However, there is a fine line between "creative borrowing" and outright copyright infringement. I will tell you later on how to protect your intellectual property rights.

Copy from one, it's plagiarism; copy from two, it's research.
— Wilson Mizner

Cao's biography indicates he has been a regular ArtExpo exhibitor for more than a decade. I am sure he found the effort and expense of being there rewarding or he would not have continued to invest in the show. The visibility dynamic in this business is extremely important, and for many, ArtExpo has always been worthwhile for learning about the art print market up close and personal, even for those who need to travel from outside New York. Just to walk the show and see the works and marketing efforts of Cao Yong and other top-selling artists has been enormously helpful to many emerging artists.

With the art business suffering the same economic woes as the real estate business, and after the move to Pier 94, ArtExpo is not the sure thing it was in the past. It is, however, still the best chance to see how top-tier art publishers and self-published artists present their work and work their booths.

Another popular artist you are likely to encounter at ArtExpo is Yuroz [www.yurozart.com]. He has a distinctive modern style that some say is a derivative of Picasso. He has been the model for what happens when a serious fine artist is deemed too commercial. This occurs when museums and institutions that would ostensibly ensure the reputation of an artist long after he has sprung off the mortal coil choose instead to ignore him.

You can read an incisive and well-written 4,100-word cover story from the February 2, 2002 issue of the Los Angeles Times Magazine titled, "Never Mind the High Praise. How About a Little Ink? His Work Is Priced as High as $150,000. He's Been Commissioned to Paint by the U.N. But There's No Place in the World of Fine Art for Yuroz and Others Like Him," by David Ferrell.

There is a small fee to download the whole article from the LA Times website. [www.latimes.com]. The article offers a thoughtful view of this artist's work and his successes and anguish over being ignored by the museums he wishes would collect his work. I highly recommend reading it as part of your art print education.

The article title just about says it all. Here is an artist who has enjoyed tremendous success after starting out dirt-poor and homeless. As with Cao Yong, Yuroz is an immigrant to the U.S., originally from Armenia. While he has enjoyed the success many of his contemporaries would love to experience, for him it is bittersweet. As the article states, with his desire for acceptance by museums, he probably overstayed at ArtExpo. At the time the article was written in 2002, he had exhibited at the show for 14 years running.

The gist of the article is that Yuroz, by taking the path of making an extraordinary income in order to create a great life for his family and make them as comfortable and as safe as possible, might have let the chance at art immortality pass him by. In addition, he had to accept there was no guarantee museums would have afforded him the attention he coveted even if he had been less commercial.

As it turns out, Yuroz has managed to put the indignity of the magazine article and the stigma of being "too commercial" to rest. His work is now in several museums, and he has recently had impressive commissions from the Vatican. He is proof that if you keep to your own vision and work hard, you can have it all: success and acclaim on your own terms. Well done, Yuri!

Will you have to make a choice between posterity and prosperity? I hope you do, for it can only happen if your art career is in a steadily ascending arc. With odds stacked against them, most struggling artists should be so lucky. However, you did not choose to be an artist because it was the road more traveled; it is more likely that the path chose you, and you have simply followed it. No matter how you found yourself on the path, you should not ignore the chance to prosper from being on it.

Another way of distinguishing artists who earn huge amounts of money from those who are vetted into museums, often without large incomes, was characterized in an August 30, 1999 article in Time magazine. The piece was titled "The Art of Selling Kitsch. Don't Look For These Creations at Your Local Museum. Instead Try Your Local Mall." For a small fee, you can download it from the Time magazine archives.

I will paraphrase the first paragraph from the article:

> [Seven years ago, struggling artist Thomas Kinkade sat in a secluded gallery well past closing time, determinedly propounding the virtues of his luminescent garden-and-cottage scenes to a young couple. He told this couple he was going to give it a few more months and if he couldn't earn a living, he'd close up shop and move on.]

According to the article, Kinkade went on to become the top earner of more than 30 "palette-to-paycheck artists," who were multimillionaires and quite the opposite of starving artists. In the process, they earned the scorn of art historians and the toniest fine art galleries, who characterize these artists as populist artists.

I don't know about you, but I am not ashamed to admit I like a lot of the work that these top-selling print artists create, and I don't care if it is populist as opposed to museum quality or not. Still, some of the stuff that is passed off as fine art astounds me. Despite all the rationales that sycophant critics and art elitists come up with about the multi-layered deep meanings of certain works, some of it escapes my interest and comprehension.

Given the choice between a pile of broken glass on the floor, a solid blue canvas titled "Blue," or a Steve Hanks image of children languishing on a dock, I will take the latter every time. In this regard, my tastes most likely mirror the tastes of potential buyers for the art painted by readers of this book. So, take heart and paint on!

I will take privilege here to modify a couplet I read by the "Wizard of Ads," Roy H. Williams here. "When you create for the classes, you live with the masses. When you create for the masses, you live with the classes." Certainly, the 30 palette-to-paycheck millionaire painters mentioned in the Time article typify the saying.

Art is really about your choices and the choices of those whom would be your customers. Once you have zeroed in on who they are, you can quit worrying about those outside your target range, even if that means ignoring museums, critics and Manhattan galleries.

The Time article ends with a poignant quote from Wyland, one of the top selling limited edition artists of our time.

The art snobs frown on any marketing or business, but the old masters weren't successful until they were dead. I didn't want to wait that long.

Where you come down on this debate of being too commercial, or getting in a museum, is a purely personal decision you have to make. I believe that – just as with the trio of choices I opened this book with regarding being full-time, part-time or a hobbyist – there is no wrong choice here, only the one right for you.

Wyland might not get into any museums of note either, but that has not stopped him from gaining tremendous exposure for himself and for his cause: creating awareness for and preserving our oceans and marine wildlife. The amount of good he has accomplished through his whaling walls program is remarkable, astute and amazing. His goal is to paint 100 murals depicting whales and other marine wildlife on buildings worldwide by 2011.

The whaling walls are a stroke of promotional genius and work on multiple levels in creating awareness for himself, his art, and his cause. You can see some stunning pictures of him at work on these murals on his website [www.wyland.com], which he claims more than one billion people have viewed. Think about the price of reaching that many eyeballs if he had had to pay a print publication or television station for the same exposure. His whaling walls personify the best in publicity, in thinking big and in acting on the thought. In painting these magnificent murals, he has set and broken his own record for largest ever, and I will give odds that he has done more to further his cause than nearly any so-called fine artist has done.

In addition, Wyland has become a multimillionaire along the way (the Times article pegged his as a $50-million business back in 1999). Meanwhile, he enjoys what he is doing in bringing joy and a love of the ocean to people. Who could criticize his work; and more importantly, does he care if art snobs and critics ignore him and Time magazine calls him a populist artist? From my encounters with him, I would say I am sure he never worries about it.

Another artist whose work I greatly admire was Richard Earl Thompson. He was one of the great American impressionist artists of the 20th century, who had the misfortune to be born at a time when abstract art and expressionism were all the rage. He passed away in his 70s in the mid-1990s after having created some 1,500 beautiful paintings in his lifetime. As with many of his generation, he started out his career as an illustrator in a time of Underwood typewriters, block type and zinc engravings. He was one who transformed from a self-published limited edition artist to selling primarily open edition prints (his work can be found at www.impressionistprints.com and www.thompsonsfineart.com)

Richard Thompson embodies a long line of illustrators who crossed over to find themselves pursuing their true passion in the field of fine art. The history of art in the 20th century is laden with examples of extraordinary artists who learned and worked the craft of an illustrator, only to use it as the foundation for another means of creative output that would reach people on a different plane. However, the craft of an illustrator is nearly a lost art in today's Mac and Photoshop environment.

Richard Thompson's splendid originals regularly sold for $30,000 to $60,000 and higher, with some selling for well into six figures. In his lifetime, he was featured a record number of times on the cover of JAMA (Journal of American Medical Association), a feat that is considered in fine art circles and by art aficionados as prestigious as getting on the back cover of Readers' Digest. Recognition from either of these publications is a huge career booster and worthy of your highest aspirations.

Richard, who was the son of a painter, had the good fortune to have a son and daughter-in-law – and eventually grandson – who all loved his work and had the ability and desire to promote it. Together they built a terrific family business, which they operated out of their Maiden Lane gallery just off Union Square in San Francisco for many years. Entering it gave a person a glimpse of visiting a gallery filled with Monet paintings at a time when the master lived.

In addition to selling his original works from the gallery, they also formed a publishing company that initially sold offset limited edition prints of Richard's work. This was also during the aforementioned time when paper-borne limited edition prints were very popular. It was before the introduction of the giclée format and the bursting of the offset limited edition bubble.

Some say artists are more sensitive than others are, and that by carefully observing them you can get a glimpse of the future. I think Richard foretold the decline of the limited edition bubble when he told his son, despite the company doing quite well, that he was done with limited editions and no longer wanted to take the time to sign them. He would rather spend the time painting. How prescient was that for him? It helped his publishing company get ready for the next wave of marketing that would sustain them through the downturn of business in the limited market in the early 1990s.

Thompson also wanted more people to be able to see his work and preferred to sell his prints as open editions, allowing all who wanted them to be able to purchase them. His masterpiece, his best-selling image, and his highest-priced original are all one in the same, "Bellingrath Gardens."

You will find a beautifully framed print of it on a wall in my home. The print has sold in the tens of thousands on paper and in the canvas-transfer format. Had it been a limited edition print, only a few hundred people would ever have had the great pleasure of owning and enjoying this print. I am one collector who is grateful that Richard Thompson made this decision.

His son had a great marketing mind and, as a former ad sales rep, knew the value of advertising. He used it well over the years to promote the line of images. The family also worked many of the Decor Expo tradeshows on the Decor circuit and effectively used their direct-mail lists. In many ways, their company was a model to emulate for those starting out.

With the elder Thompson's death in 1991, and then his son's in the early 2000s, the business has slowed, although it does continue to market his work. It is a perfect example of how enduring an artist's work can be decades after they have passed away.

There are countless stories of self-made self-published artists – far too numerous to mention in this book, much less attempt to provide anecdotes about them or their business models. Nevertheless, no matter how many of them you study, they usually encompass those same self-publishing essentials detailed earlier.

Another of my favorites is Arnold Friberg [www.fribergfineart.com.] Like Thomas Kinkade, he painted backdrops for motion pictures. Friberg is famous for creating a series of monumental works that toured every continent in the late 1950s to help promote Cecil B. DeMille's epic motion picture, "The Ten Commandments." Other great examples of artists whose careers began as an illustrators include N.C. Wyeth, Norman Rockwell, Bob Timberlake and Andy Warhol. Look around and you will find many more.

Bob Timberlake [www.bobtimberlake.com] is perhaps not a household name to some, but to the legions of collectors throughout the Southeast, he is a revered artist. His influence and style was picked by the home furnishings industry and was secure long before Thomas Kinkade and others were licensing their look and style for home-decor manufacturers.

Timberlake's art propelled him into creating and licensing all manner of home furnishings in masculine Americana pieces. The source for many of his licensed pieces was his personal collection of art, accessories and furniture in his North Carolina cabin. For many years, Lexington Home Brands painstakingly recreated and sold these pieces with his name licensed on them

At one point, Lexington, at their factory showroom in High Point, North Carolina reconstructed his cabin to display the whole line. When I visited there some years ago, I felt I had entered a time warp at Disney World. The complex housing the showroom is a modern steel and glass building; however, when you went up a flight of stairs, crossed the wooden bridge over the gurgling stream to his cabin, and heard the crickets chirping, you quickly lost that exterior modern perspective. It was fascinating to see the extended reach and influence one creative person can have over so many areas that stretch well beyond art on paper. Therefore, no MOMA shows are likely for Bob Timberlake, but no regrets are likely either.

Sadly, this story is not ending well; in 2008, Timberlake took legal actions against Lexington for a variety of reasons, including failure to promote his line and order pieces from it. A court ruled in favor of Lexington in late 2009, and both parties agreed to honor the current contract through to December 2010. Regardless, what a wild experience it must have been for Bob Timberlake – one that most artists cannot imagine happening to them. Timberlake's story proves how far some visual artists are able to influence the world around them.

Successful self-published artists come in all stripes. One, who crosses over many boundaries in the business, is in what I would consider the decorative arts field, but nonetheless is also a print artist with a fine career. Her name is Mary Engelbreit. [www.maryengelbreit.com]. She is from St. Louis, and I confess that due to my own tastes and biases, had I not lived there for many years I might never have known about her. That is not to say she has a small following. Quite to the contrary, she became a lifestyle maven with her own magazine, Mary Engelbreit's Home Companion, sported a half million subscribers at its peak before succumbing to declining advertising revenues, which is the bane of all print media today. Regardless, it is a remarkable feat and measure of success!

While the subscribers were still there, the economic conditions that ravaged many home-decor magazines finally took its toll on her home decor advertiser base, Worry not for Mary Engelbreit or her company. It has licensed some 6,500 items with a lifetime retail sales volume of $100 billion.

The kinds of images she creates are cute, colorful, whimsical and homey, which is not what would normally catch my eye. Yet despite a personal lack of interest in her style, I still find it fascinating that the art business is so vast, with so many entry points. Here was a visionary leader in her field and a licensing phenomenon doing $100 million in annual sales, who was completely off the radar of an otherwise seasoned and sophisticated art-marketing type – namely, myself. Were it not for her retail store in a suburban mall in St. Louis and occasional coverage about her in the St. Louis Post Dispatch daily newspaper, she might still be a mystery to me.

Perhaps the reason she was off my radar brings up an interesting point. She bypassed the traditional means of getting her artwork to market, including all the concepts that I preach and that form the basis of this book. She does not advertise in any of the art and framing trade publications or exhibit at any of the shows. She started out in greeting cards and grew her art publishing-and-licensing business in the gift industry.

As you know from my previous statements, I believe artists should pursue all available opportunities; and were I a rep for DECOR in St. Louis, I would be making my case for her company. I think it is missing a great chance to open new markets in the DECOR magazine and Decor Expo markets; although with $100 million in sales, it is not as if the company needs the income. So why have I gone to the trouble to write about her when she flies in the face of my best advice and succeeds tremendously against it? I am glad you asked. Two reasons come to mind:

1. To remind you that this book, while definitive when it comes to outlining the traditional means of building and marketing an art print career, cannot cover every contingency for getting an artist's work to market;
2. When someone is this successful, it is inspiring and worth noting.

The licensing market includes many other licensing phenoms who enjoy enormous success. Unfortunately, I do not have space to detail them all here. A few examples include Flavia Weedn [www.flavia.com], Jody Bergsma [www.bergsma.com] and Stephen Schutz [www.bluemountain.com]. Stephen Schutz and his poetry-writing wife, Susan Polis Schutz, have long since sold their business for millions, but no one can deny the tremendous success they have had with their careers.

Paul Brent is a noteworthy licensing success because, unlike the others mentioned, he followed the traditional pattern of marketing that I outlined in the first edition of this book. That is to advertise frequently, attend as many tradeshows as possible and create as much publicity buzz as possible, and then repeat until a large dealer base was developed.

Brent followed that prescription faithfully for many years. Along the way, he built a very profitable and distinguished successful self-published artist career. Now, his $30-million-annually licensing business has grown to the point he no longer partakes in trade advertising or tradeshows. Nevertheless, for those of us who travelled the circuit in the heyday, we will always be able to say we knew him when.

It is certain none of these artists with enormous licensing careers are likely to find their works courted by topnotch museums, but I doubt it is a concern for any of them. Ultimately, your description of success and how well you achieve is all that matters.

To get back to Mary Engelbreit, her success is undeniable in terms of reaching people, using her talent and making great use of her creative abilities. A couple of her quotes prove what a plucky person she is. Here is what she said in describing how she launched her own greeting-card company when she was eight months pregnant:

Proper timing is overrated. There's always a reason not to do things – it's too expensive, or it's not the best time, or this, or that – but I believe there are wonderful opportunities sailing by, and you have to be ready to grab them.

Her second quote neatly and succinctly wraps up the sentiment in terms of a true American success story: "I believed in myself, and now I'm living my dream."

If, through reading this book and – much more importantly – through believing in yourself and applying your talent, you find you someday are living your dream, I would be proud if something you learned in these pages had a small hand in guiding you there.

Chapter Seven
Finding and Working With a Publisher

True art is characterized by an irresistible urge in the creative artist.
— Albert Einstein

From experience, I know that many readers have already decided the self-publisher role is not for them. As with most options in this book, that decision is neither good nor bad. It comes down to what is best for you and your situation. No matter how you arrived at your conclusion, if you have determined that working with a publisher is your choice; I applaud you for having made the decision. For most artists, it is the easiest, best, and safest – and sometimes only – course of action.

Regardless of whether or not you yearn to own your own publishing business someday, even if you are not ready right now, the information you find in this chapter will help towards success with an established publisher. Although getting started with a publisher will, for some of you, be a step towards eventually publishing your own images, for now having someone else mind the myriad of details involved in publishing art is the best path.

While working with a publisher is far less expensive and complicated than publishing your own work, you still need to work hard at first to find the right publisher and then to maintain the relationship. If that sounds liking find a life partner in marriage and making the arrangement work for the long term, you are right. There are definite similarities; and as with a marriage, the more you work at it and keep communication open and honest, the better the result will be.

As with any relationship where each party needs confidence to rely on the other, you will find there are both merits and pitfalls to working with a publisher. Here are some of the major points to consider:

Merits of working with a publisher

- You get feedback and advice on what to create.
- You can concentrate on creating art.
- You get recognition and sales through expensive marketing efforts.
- You get access to the dealer network.
- You get access to the licensing contacts and established business relationships.

Pitfalls of working with a publisher

- You get feedback and advice on what to create.
- You make much less money, typically 8 to 10% on the wholesale price.
- You are in a stable of anywhere from a few to dozens of artists.
- Your publisher has established stars that pay the bills; and if you aren't one of them, you might have to struggle for recognition.
- Your fate is tied to the overall profitability and potential of your publisher.

Of course, as with any good debate among intelligent people who have a difference of opinion, you and others might take issue with these points. Unlike a former tradeshow director with whom I once worked, I welcome questions and debate. That director had a sign on his desk that neatly summed up his opinion about negotiating and debate; it read: "Be reasonable, do it my way!"

The reality is that while there are countless stories of artists working in concert with publishers and making sizable incomes from the revenues the publishers generated for them, there are many more for whom the revenue from publishers is a mere steady trickle. For your sake, I wish I could accurately account for the difference between the stars and those back in the pack. Unfortunately, that is not any more possible than predicting lottery numbers.

If pressed, I would again call upon my always fallible S.W.A.G. Factor and say that most successful artists who work with publishers instead of self-publishing share common attributes or traits, similar to those of the self-published artists we discussed in chapter four.

To refresh your memory, successful self-published artists have these things in common:

- talent
- art that resonates with a large group of collectors
- financing
- personnel, usually in the form of a spouse, devoted family member or close friend
- willingness to prodigiously continue to create art within the same thematic range in order to continue to supply the dealer and collector base
- ambition

If you review the list, it is obvious that having personnel and financing are items not as critical to success when working with publishers. Those two factors are at the heart of why many otherwise capable artists end up working with a publisher. Achieving your goals in publishing results from believing in yourself and your talent, and working hard at all the aspects of the business you can control.

As with most facets of publishing, success in working with a publisher comes down to talent, luck, ambition and timing. Not all of those facets are completely within your control. You can't control whether or not you will encounter someone who will make a huge difference in your career or like your work, although being ambitious surely can help in that regard.

When I think of artists in other fields, I sometimes wonder how they would do in other eras. For instance, look at the incredible career of Bob Dylan. Dylan was a scrawny 19-year-old kid from Minnesota when John Hammond plucked him from obscurity and changed his fate. Was luck involved? Of course, Hammond could have thought – like many others at the time – that Bob Dylan was a Woody Guthrie copycat. Instead, he acted on his finely-tuned instinct spotting talent. Hammond is noted for discovering or helping further the careers of Benny Goodman, Billie Holiday, Count Basie, Big Joe Turner, Pete Seeger, Aretha Franklin, George Benson, Leonard Cohen, Bruce Springsteen, Stevie Ray Vaughan and many others.

I admit to being an unabashed fan with the utmost respect for Bob Dylan. His contributions to rock and folk music and his towering influence over pop culture and other recording artists in the 20th century seems almost as unreal as his lyrics sometimes. Admiration aside, I doubt if Dylan were to come onto the music scene today – an industry dominated by hip hop and slick pop, where there is little room for singer/songwriters – that he would have found the same success or been as influential.

Destiny and kismet are always at play, and against these you can only strive to do your best. To some degree, you have to have the right look at the right time and get connected to the right people – as in, publishers – to get to the top of the heap in art print publishing.

This does not mean you will suffer in despair if you settle for a position somewhere further down the ladder. I suppose with his enormous talent and ambition, Bob Dylan would still have carved out some kind of rewarding professional career as a musician and songwriter or lyricist if he were starting out today. He previously has commented that he should have been a manager. With his drive and belief in himself, I am certain he would have been great at it had he taken that path.

Your control over your success depends on how you position yourself and how you manage your business and the opportunities that present themselves to you. You can enjoy a nice living as a print artist if you apply yourself to being as successful as you can by keeping as many of the above-listed traits working in your favor.

If working with a publisher is your first decision, your next is in what medium you wish to see your images reproduced? That is, what format best suits your images? Sometimes this requires serious contemplation on your part. With the dominance of the giclée digital print medium, the decision is set for most, but not all, artists.

Sometimes the content or size will help guide the decision, and knowing that your work relates to a certain theme or style will also help dictate format and publisher choices. For instance, if you are a wildlife artist, you are probably looking at offset limited edition prints and giclées, which is where the bulk of this market is found. For starters, you'd want to look for publishers such as: Mill Pond Press, [www.millpond.com]; Wild Wings, [www.wildwings.com]; Hadley House, [www.hadleyhouse.com]; or Greenwich Workshop, [www.greenwichworkshop.com]; among others. This list is far from inclusive, and you will find many of these listed publishers offer more than the wildlife genre.

When it comes to working with a publisher, you need to be as proactive as possible in making decisions; it is your career after all. Yes, you are putting your career in their hands, but you need to maintain as much control as possible. This means deciding beforehand what medium you want to see your art reproduced in, and whether to make it limited or open edition and so forth.

Ultimately, you may not be able to dictate choices and there may be cases where you are asked to reconsider your adamant decision. You can decide at the time what is best for you. Try to be as flexible as possible. Forming your own strong opinion honed by your instincts and investigation long before you begin contacting publishers should negate much potential controversy.

This sounds like a no-brainer, but I'll say it anyway: if you know your images are really best suited for a poster catalog, you should focus on those publishers who primarily or exclusively publish posters. These are publishers more likely to be found in a source such as Lieberman's Wholesale Prints & Posters, or supplying sites such as www.art.com and www.allposters.com.

If you have determined that your images belong in the limited edition market, which can mean anything from offset lithography on paper to giclées and serigraphs, you should narrow your search to those publishers whose emphasis is on that end of the market. At one time, a division existed in the limited market between offset lithographic limited-edition print publishers and giclée publishers, but it faded away.

There also was a time when you could find publishers who exclusively published serigraphs, but this is rare today. Most publishers that offer serigraphs are also in the giclée market. They just cannot resist the better pricing and inventory options available when publishing giclées. When you consider that an edition size of serigraphs run in 100 colors can easily top $50,000 or more to produce, it becomes clear why few publishers will risk such upfront money when giclées are available and sell well with no inventory headaches.

The downturn for ArtExpo New York, as discussed in Chapter Five, should be proof positive that artists, now more than ever, need to carry their own water as much as possible when it comes to getting their work to market. In other words, be your own sure thing.

In the first edition, I told readers that if posters were their medium of choice, then the Decor Expo Atlanta show should be the first place to go, followed by the Decor Expo New York show. Since then, the Decor Expo New York show has ceased to exist and the 2009 Decor Expo Atlanta show was put on hold in order to give its new owners a chance to regroup and retool for 2010. New dates have been announced for September 2010.

The revamped show will be back in the Atlanta Gift Mart, running concurrently with the Atlanta Gift Show. Since the show began in that location and it was with the synergy of the gift show dates that helped the previous Decor Expo Atlanta shows grow into a huge powerhouse international show, for a brief time anyway, I hope the new arrangements help it regain some of its former glory.

If you plan to attend New York or Atlanta, give yourself enough time to absorb the shows. Underestimating how long you will need to even walk these shows, much less to try to meet people, is a mistake many people make. Spend as much time as you can if you are walking the shows. Of course, if you don't have the financial budget or time to allow such a luxury, you will have to work smarter and try to see only what is most important to you for your personal growth and knowledge base needs.

If you cannot get to New York or Atlanta, don't stress over it. Sometimes things are not possible, even though we know they ought to be. Keep in mind there are plenty of successful artists, especially those repped by poster publishers, who have never set foot in any tradeshow. It is not a do-or-die criterion for the advancement of your career – especially now that you can no longer count on seeing most of the biggest and best poster publishers under the same roof at any one show – and you can find your path to publishing success in other ways.

If you haven't had the chance to peruse the websites of some of the better-known publishers in the industry, this should be on your must-do list. Another option is to find a local gallery that carries works of artists you admire and then spend some time there looking through its catalogs.

At the time of the first edition of this book, it was not as feasible to see the catalogs of most poster publishers online as today. The only way to get into a catalog back then was to get a physical copy and pore over it in person. These days, you are much more likely to be able to find a publisher's website and peruse it at your leisure, on your own schedule.

Some galleries still carry catalogs, especially now that they and their publishers have found that relying on digital copies and websites in order to hold down the heavy price of printing catalogs has reduced their business. So, in some cases, it might still be a worthy exercise to visit a gallery that carries posters and review the publishers' catalogs. However, I offer that suggestion with the following caveat: having spent time working in a gallery, I can tell you that many owners find the visits by artists using their galleries for personal field trips as much as a museum to be a nuisance. Keep in mind that galleries are there to make money, not to entertain artists who aren't really prospects for them. So, be respectful of the time and space, and don't put on ruses as a buyer so you get personal attention from a salesperson. Politely ask if you can quietly review the catalog in question.

If you are visiting poster galleries, typically they are accustomed to having people take time to go through their books, but, that doesn't mean you shouldn't have the same respect for them as you do for original or limited edition galleries. They all need to eat, and someday one of them might have your work in its shop. As you can imagine, if a customer came in who was a great prospect for your work, you would not want the owner or salesperson distracted by another artist with no intention of buying. I cringe at making these suggestions, but since I also realize there are few ways to get your hands on a catalog, I do it with the admonishment to be very respectful of the gallery in the process.

In 2005, I wrote that many publishers would not entertain any dialogue with collectors or consumers and typically redirect them to the most convenient gallery that carries their work. They know the quickest way to gain the enmity of their coveted dealer base is to begin to compete with them. Today, more artists and publishers have distribution schemes that create conflict between their dealers and their direct sales to consumers. Thomas Kinkade has many company-owned galleries, for instance. Channel conflict has not been the norm in the art-publishing arena, as most publishers preferred to concentrate on their work as wholesalers in support of their dealer base.

The decline in the number of galleries and the rise in importance of the Internet, along with continued improvements in print-on-demand technology and the proliferation of online sites that specialize in selling art, have changed the business. The rules are changing even as this is book is being written, and I expect that by the time a third edition comes out, they will have changed even more.

You have greater means and discrepancy with how you decide to handle the distribution of your work than artists from any other era. This presents problems and opportunities. We will discuss your options in more details in a future chapter. For now, keep in mind if you plan to work with publishers, you will need to make decisions on how much you want to control getting your book to market.

Fortunately, the Internet makes everything easier these days, especially for sleuthing to gain intelligence on companies that you want to work with. While viewing a high-quality, four-color rendition of a print or poster is a much richer experience than the maximum 72 dpi images you see online, you can still gain a good understanding of the offerings from various publishers by viewing their websites.

A most important task for art publishers is to constantly look for new artists with fresh ideas and images. Go to any tradeshow and listen as buyers come into their booths. The first question is usually, "What's new?" It doesn't matter if the old stuff is still the greatest thing since sliced bread and is carrying the company and its dealers with 80% of the sales; everybody wants to see the new stuff. Moreover, a publisher never knows when the next big thing just might appear.

Some years ago at the Atlanta Decor Expo show, a couple of artist friends approached me for help. They had been working the show trying to find interest in their work. I took them a publisher's booth and introduced them to the person who was the point person for the company when dealing with artists. She took an immediate interest in the work of each of them.

I would love to provide more details about the publisher and the artist, but then I could not tell you the outcome. One of these artists had a unique and stylish take on high style type of imagery. It was perfect for the market at that moment. Working with input from volume buyers and from the publisher's rep, the artist developed a series of images that caught fire, and over the following 12 months the images had wholesale revenue of more than $500,000. The effort netted the artist $50,000, and he kept all the substantial licensing rights. Due to the subject matter being somewhat trendy, and because volume buyers are always seeking fresh looks, it could not sustain sales, but did help the artist establish a name for his look, and he is still capitalizing on it today.

Publishers realize a serious part of their job is to be ready to look at new work and almost all have formal policies and methods for reviewing the works of new artists. Just having the understanding of how much importance publishers place on finding artists should fuel your confidence in your efforts to land a contract with one.

Publishers also have criteria for what they would consider the ideal artist. What follows is a composite of talking with many publishers over the years to ascertain what qualities they seek in an artist.

Publisher's artist wish list

Publishers wish to work with an artist who:

- has work with commercial appeal
- has work that is consistent
- is easy to work with
- works on deadlines
- is coachable on specific design requests
- is dependable and reliable
- is available and easy to contact
- is flexible and versatile

Do those attributes accurately describe you? If you can honestly say yes to all of them, congratulations! Your success is all but signed, sealed and delivered. However, the reality is that for a multitude of reasons, few artists can live up to every item on the list above. Publishers are aware that their wish list and reality rarely coincide and accept what they find in the best and worst qualities of artists with whom they work.

If you have already tried approaching publishers, you have probably received a variety of responses. As with life in general, it takes all kinds, and that means you will run into publishers who are friendly and gracious and those who are less than that. Don't be put off by anyone who is not receptive or friendly; your goal is not to make friends. Your first goal is to get an audience, and your second is to be accepted by one of your top choices.

Don't Fall in Love with Your Work

If the above statement sounds contradictory, that is to be expected. Nevertheless, in the world of poster publishing, it is a truism that can help you if you understand what it means and embrace it. While there has always been a certain element of truth and accuracy in this statement, for those artists seeking to get large amounts of their work in the market place it has never been truer than now.

There is nearly always some natural friction between an artist and his or her publisher when it comes down to deciding what an artist should produce. That is, colors, sizes and subject matter are open to debate. The artist comes at the work from a personal vision, while the publisher looks for the work has the best chance to sell well.

Over the past decade, a third and powerful element has made its presence felt in the open edition market. This is the volume buyer: someone who represents large, national, big-box retailers, or who is a middleman sourcing paper art and framing materials to assemble as ready-to-hang pieces. Unfortunately, these buyers have risen to great importance in the market place, and as a result they control what publishers will actually print. I know many publishers who lament finding great artists but not being able to use them because their volume buyers will not place orders for the work.

To some extent, the artists who manage to get regular royalties from their publishers are those who are the most willing to produce what a volume buyer seeks. It is a production job, not unlike being a graphic designer who completes work on assignment. It is for this reason that you read the bold statement above about not falling in love with your work.

If working under these conditions is unacceptable, then seeking work with poster publishers may not suit you. Alternatively, if you can paint quickly, you can teach yourself to get a quick return on work that you may not have to even sign with your real name.

The holy grail is to spend less time making the picture than it takes people to look at it.
— Banksy (famous British graffiti artist)

Submitting to Publishers

My friend, Jason Horejs, is a successful second generation professional art business entrepreneur. His father is a highly regarded painter who, along with the business acumen of his wife, has managed raising a family from the fruits of selling originals as a full-time painter. Jason followed in the family business by establishing a well run and successful gallery. He is also the author of "Starving" to Successful: The Fine Artist's Guide to Getting into Galleries. This is one of the most straightforward and informative books for advice on working with galleries. I give it my highest recommendation! Jason also conducts webinars and in-person workshops on a regular basis.

One of his suggestions is to avoid trying to solicit a gallery by sending materials or phoning. He believes artists will have greater and much more immediate success by cold calling the galleries they target. Walking his talk, he encourages artists to contact him in this manner. Since Jason has watched this approach work for decades for his father and he has built his own substantial experience on the gallery side, it is difficult to argue the point otherwise.

When it comes to approaching publishers, you may find they are more insular; they are not setup for meeting with the public, and as such, I do not suggest cold calling on them. Tradeshows provide the one exception to this rule. I advise against bringing a huge portfolio into a show. Rather, have samples that are 5" x 7" or no more than 8" x 10" in size to show.

You must be respectful of a show exhibitor's time. If they are busy with a buyer, the last thing they want is to be interrupted by anyone, so make sure any attempt you make is done at a time when the booth is empty and you will not be competing with their attention. If they become engaged, offer to step back and get out of the way, or ask if you can come back.

Personally, I would prefer to hang around in that situation, but not interminably. Be your own judge about this. If it appears to be a brief conversation, take the time to look at the art in the booth. If it looks like an order writing or otherwise serious conversation is ensuing, then come back later.

The Formal Submission Policy

One thing all the best publishers do have in common is an established means of how they want to receive artist submissions. Many conveniently have their submission standards posted on their websites. A typical clear cut example of how publishers offer submission information can be seen on the website of one of the industry's top poster publishers and distributors, Image Conscious

[www.imageconscious.com]. (I would leave the full URL to the submission section, but these addresses change. Dig into the menu on any publisher's site to find the submission link.)

In this case, the staff at Image Conscious have provided you with all the information your need to submit. They have made it easy for you to submit your work by telling you in advance all the details on how they like you to submit your artwork. You simply need to follow the guidelines and then hope for the best.

If you have questions that are not covered on a publisher's website or in the submission materials, you should not be shy. Call and ask for clarification. That could include how you can follow up on your submission. There is nothing wrong with following up. It can be construed as professional if done in a polite, even and persistent manner. You can, on the contrary, also be viewed as highly unprofessional if you just become a relentless pest.

If you let your eagerness or anxiety push you over the line into the pest category, you will damage your chances of success at getting your work published.

It is a good suggestion to take a few deep breaths and practice what you want to say before you make those follow-up calls.

Obviously, if you follow the guidelines publishers provide for you, you are going to have a better chance of getting a favorable reception. Always be courteous and remember that following the rules won't help if what you paint is not what they are looking for. If you have done your proper analysis before submitting, you will cut down on both the number of places you submit and the number of rejections you receive. Not all publishers have as clear submission information on their websites as Image Conscious.

With some, you will have to contact them to request the guidelines be sent to you.

Do not risk everything on one endeavor. You should not submit to just one publisher because you admire some artist in the line, or for any other reason besides thinking there is a fit. By submitting to several publishers at a time, you give yourself greater odds of having success. Be patient. It can take weeks, if not months sometimes, to get replies from publishers. Some publishers review for new artists only at certain times of the year.

In some cases, a publisher may say you are in the running, but there will be more decisions and things can drag out for agonizingly long periods. Knowing this is the nature of the business before you get started may tone down some anxiety in waiting.

With regard to submission standards, whatever you find out from a publisher that you have targeted, pay close attention to them and follow the instructions. How you respond can show the publisher you are both eager and professional. Giving a hint that you are someone who would be easy to work with is always in your favor.

Being a prima donna will only work for you if you are in a position to deliver images that are going to be instant top sellers in the market. Otherwise you'll find that being difficult will end up getting you less attention. This is especially true where a publisher is putting out a thick catalog with potentially hundreds of other artists represented in it; because from their perspective, there are always other options for coming up with a similar look but without the hassle.

How Do I Find Art Publishers?

In the days when trade magazines and tradeshows brimmed with poster publishers, it was relatively easy to find them. They were all visible in the market place and still are, to a lesser degree, today. If you are not in the custom of reading the industry trade publications, you should make it a high priority habit. Even in their diminished capacity, trade magazines are your windows to what is going on in the business.

In our digital age, it has become easier to review back copies and read current ones. You do not need to subscribe to the paper edition. Given the reduced cash flow situation trade magazines are experiencing, it is advisable to access them via their online versions. Both Art Business News [www.artbusinessnews.com] and Art World News [www.artworldnews.com] have digitally archived issues. This gives you a chance to go over past issues to help you spot trends on colors, sizes, prices, and subject matter, and to learn which publishers are aggressive in today's economy.

Because it is so important, this thought bears repeating: in order to succeed in this business, you need to be a student of it. You need to learn how things are done, who is doing them, and why. Trade magazines are full of this information. Not just the articles, which are aimed at the primary readership of dealers and include ideas and suggestions on how to operate their retail businesses; but also the editorial columns and advertising, which are full of useful information for you to glean about the activities of publishers and artists.

To start with, many of the top publishers are frequent, if not monthly, advertisers in the trade publications. The primary trade publications for artists to be reading are DECOR [www.decormagazine.com], Art Business News and Art World News. The latter is an independent publication, while the first two were acquired by Next Step Media. Next Step Media was formed by Kim Feager, the longtime publisher of DECOR and Art Business News.

I worked with Kim Feager for nearly two decades and am very happy she managed to salvage not only the magazines, but the Decor Expo Atlanta show as well. Through her efforts, she was able to keep the previous investment-banking firm ownership from abandoning these venerable products while they had their attention on the also-struggling, but much larger, financial-services operations. It would have been a travesty to see these media vehicles go away.

Once you start to read and carefully review the content of these publications, you will begin to understand which publishers are most likely to be the best candidates for your images. You'll see some that publish a variety of artists, and others that specialize in one or two. As discussed earlier, not every publishing company follows my prescription for success by using a combination of trade advertising, tradeshows, and publicity and so forth. That means there are good candidates for you to be submitting your work to that aren't regularly featured in the advertising pages of the trade magazines – some not even on an infrequent basis.

You will find some of those who are missing from the magazine-advertising pages in a few other places. The Internet is one place you can look, but it can be a tedious task. It would require much patience and determination. Still, if are enduring enough to wade through the first 50 or more pages that result from search-terms such as art publisher, poster publisher, fine art publisher, giclée publishers, limited edition publishers and so forth; you will uncover companies with no presence in trade magazines and tradeshow directories.

The annual Artist's & Graphic Designer's Market is a directory with many useful listings. Most artists only buy it periodically, if at all. My most recent version had many outdated listings in it. Apparently, the editors do not update every listing every year. Nonetheless, you will find publishers and leads for other wholesale art buyers in it.

By now, you know my biases. I believe in using all the tools available to get a product to market. It is hard for me to understand why you would want to eliminate from your plan opportunities to get your message in front of your best prospects. My advice is to try to hook up with the more prominent publishers, because they normally are the ones using all the tools.

Here are some resources to help you find art print publishers:

Art trade shows

- ArtExpo New York [www.artexpos.com]
- West Coast Art & Frame Show [www.wcafshow.com]
- Spring Fair Birmingham, UK [www.springfair.com]

Licensing shows

- Surtex [www.surtex.com]
- Licensing International Expo [www.licensingexpo.com]

Trade magazines and directories

- Art Business News
- Art World News
- DECOR
- DECOR Sources Online [www.artandframingdirectory.com]

- Artist's & Graphic Designer's Market
- Art Business Today [www.fineart.co.uk]

National art consumer publications with art print interest

- Southwest Art [www.southwestart.com]
- Wildlife Art News [www.wildlifeartmag.com]

Home furnishing and contract design shows

- International Home Furnishings Center [www.ihfc.com]
- High Point Market [www.highpointmarket.org]
- World Market Las Vegas [www.lasvegasmarket.com]
- Hospitality Design Expo [www.hdexpo.com]
- NeoCon [www.neocon.com]

Assuming your work has commercial appeal, you should be able to find many suitable publishers for it by poring through the above resources. I have mentioned attending tradeshows as a way to jump-start your art print marketing education. A valuable item you'll come away with from any of these shows is the show directory. These days, courtesy of the Internet, it is often possible to drill down to the exhibit segment you seek without leaving your computer.

The show directory conveniently tells you the name of every company exhibiting at the show and gives all their contact information. Not many will include the name of someone to contact, but everything else is there for you to begin building your own publisher database. If you aren't able to view the directory online or make it to the show, contact the show producer as soon as it is over to inquire about purchasing a copy of the show directory, as their remaining supplies of these directories will be limited.

By reading trade magazines every month and noting the various publishers who advertise in them, you will begin to build up a general idea of which are the best prospects to approach. The same holds true for the tradeshow directories. These are invaluable sources for your research on which publishing companies to contact.

DECOR publishes an annual Decor Sources directory. It is also available (and more robust) in its online version [www.artandframingdirectory.

com]. You can use it to find those less visible publishers – the ones who neither advertise nor exhibit at tradeshows. You might think, why bother? Do not be fooled. Some of these publishers have great contacts and work completely out of the limelight.

There are just two consumer art magazines on the above list. While there are numerous other consumer art publications, the two mentioned are the best prospects for finding art print publishers. Although these others may have editorial content you find compelling, you will not discover many prospects for publishing companies to approach in their pages.

When approaching the top echelon of publishers, remember you will be competing with many artists for visibility, attention and space in their marketing materials. For instance, once accepted, your images might only be shown once a year – if at all – in their trade advertising, but that wouldn't mean members of their sales staff aren't hustling your images to appropriate buyers behind the scenes. For many publishers at this level, trade advertising compares to window dressing for a department store. It highlights the new fashions, but the real shopping only begins when a buyer enters the store, or, in your case, opens the catalog.

The largest poster publishers, those with hundreds or thousands of images, primarily rely on their sales and marketing staffs to send samples of new suitable works to their best customers and prospects. Even though the mom and pop retailers might not see your image in the latest ad from these less-high-profile publishers, many of the volume buyers and top dealers will be sampled with your work as soon as they are available in proof format.

Publishers know what they are doing, even though many new artists really have to wonder if they are getting any exposure at all from their relationship. Unless publishers know they have a certified winner with some image or line of images on their hands, they know they need to work on building awareness for you and your style of art.

In some cases, things won't work out and you'll feel the need to move on once your contract is over. Keep in mind, however, that it can take a while for your images to break through and establish a initial following with the dealer base and buying public. Patience in these situations is required, although understandably, it can be tough. This is where having a professional and courteous relationship with your publishing company personnel will work in your favor. Developing and maintaining these relationships is the best way to be kept abreast of your circumstances.

Publishers typically pay 8 to 10% (sometimes higher for top-producing artists) of the net wholesale price they receive for a print. That means if they sell your image at a $40 retail price with the typical 50-50-20% discount, as previously discussed, they end up with $8.00 and your take is $0.80 (10% commission) per piece.

Seeing the economics broken down to such a fine point and relatively minuscule point can be demoralizing to read. However, take heart, because plenty of artists working with publishers are doing nicely when you consider they are also licensing the images through them as well. We'll discuss licensing in a later chapter. For now, keep in mind that it can be an important source of income for you, and when you layer it with the publishing royalties, it will be lucrative.

To help augment your income, you may have to self-publish some of your work in giclée or some other format and seek sell it on your own website or through one of the many one online art venues. Other means to distribute your work might be through local galleries or by exhibiting at local or regional shows. This is where having an entrepreneurial streak can help. If you are fortunate and do not need the income from your art to pay your bills, you can be patient and let things develop through working with your publisher.

You could realize you have dual careers going at once: one aimed at the fine art originals gallery or art show market, and another aimed at the poster and print market. The previously mentioned examples of how Arthur Secunda and Richard Thompson prove this is possible; they are just two of many artists who have accomplished this feat. Another approach is that some poster publishers have artists painting for them under an assumed name.

While personality is important in the marketing of a limited edition artist such as Wyland, Steve Hanks, Thomas Kinkade or P. Buckley Moss, it is really far less important to publishers that represent the work of many artists. Most poster publishers do not have their artists making personal appearances for them. You can retain anonymity from the public with a poster publisher.

Having a theme attached to your work will help you in the marketing of it. When working with a publisher, once you are established, it doesn't hurt to let the publisher know you have the capability and desire to paint in other themes. This is especially true if you are willing to take direction and be coached by the art development team.

If you can help them fill a need in a product line without them having to discover yet another new artist, you make yourself that much more valuable. This multiple hat scenario isn't going to work out for every artist, but it's something to keep in mind as you develop your relationship with a publisher.

Depending on your needs, you could consider working with less prominent publishers on what could be called the second level. Working with a less visible company doesn't necessarily mean you will make less money with them. Some of them are connected to the contract design market: the commercial side of interior design.

Contract design involves interior designers who work on commercial buildings, including hotels, office buildings and hospitality operations. The contract design market needs and orders vast amounts of artwork at one time. Some have direct connections with volume framers and bypass the retail section of the market, while others have found a profitable niche that allows them to operate without competing head-to-head with larger publishers.

Finding less visible publishers is more difficult, although some do surface at the larger tradeshows and in directory listings. If you are using the publicity columns of the trade publications, or are advertising or exhibiting yourself, they may find you instead. Typically, they have smaller booths at tradeshows, use less advertising and have an overall lower profile than industry leaders. It is easy to figure out who is who through mere observation or by learning how many artists or images they publish. Do not forget, it is the job of every publisher – regardless of how large or small – to look for new artists.

This book is aimed at dealing with the middle and lower tiers of art being sold. Often, it will be tougher to crack second-tier publishers' lineups than the open edition and poster publishers on the bottom tier. This is due to second-tier publishers working with fewer artists. Therefore, when bringing on new talent, they can be fussy in reviewing for it. You will find these publishers advertising primarily in Art Business News and Art World News and exhibiting at ArtExpo.

In some cases, gaining a reputation for yourself in the print industry or art arena will be helpful as often it will lead to relationships with people who are in a position to introduce or recommend you to someone else. Over the years working with DECOR, I made many connections for artists with publishers, an example of which was the artist mentioned earlier in this chapter, who I introduced to a publisher at a tradeshow.

Another way to gain visibility with potential publishers is to exhibit at shows where publishers might be on the lookout for new talent. One show is the SOLO show, which is part of ArtExpo New York. For some artists, this is a great opportunity to gain exposure to the market and, in particular, to introduce their work to publishers who will be attending ArtExpo. Given the change in location to Pier 94 in 2010 and underlying economic conditions, I advise walking the show and talking with SOLO artists there before deciding to do the show in subsequent years, or until the economy and art market improve dramatically.

Do you recall the Time magazine article that derisively referred to populist artists as palette-to-paycheck artists? That article noted 30 artists who were millionaires or multi-millionaires. If you thought they were all self-published artists, you would be wrong. Some of them work with established publishers who do the printing, marketing and sales of their work.

Here are a few examples of high profile, high-income artists that have worked or do work with publishers:

- Bev Doolittle – www.greenwichworkshop.com
- Robert Bateman – www.millpondpress.com
- Steve Hanks – www.hadleyhouse.com
- Thomas Pradzynski – www.palatino.net
- Royo – www.royoart.com
- Carl Brenders – www.millpondpress.com
- Charles Wysocki – www.hadleyhouse.com
- Warren Kimble – www.wildapple.com
- Bob Byerley – www.wildwings.com
- G. Harvey – www.somersetfineart.com

Access to information on what the actual income is for any of the above artists is not available, but I can say with confidence that each one has done very well from the financial relationship they have with their publishers. Some undoubtedly are millionaires or multi-millionaires through those relationships.

Most on the list are working with publishers who specialize in limited editions as opposed to posters and prints. Nevertheless, there is variety in that some of the publishers listed have a number of artists, while others are single-artist publishers, such as Royo at Royo Art, or represent just two artists, for example with Pradzynski and Manuel Anoro at Palatino Editions.

There are cases where artists working for poster publishers earn substantial incomes, especially when the royalties from the licensing of their images is included. Licensing has become an important aspect of art publishing revenues and has flourished into a full-fledged portion of the operation of many art publishers. This subject is important enough that it will be discussed in more detail in a later chapter.

The Artist-Publisher Relationship

Let us assume you have gone through the steps of targeting publishers and contacting them and have found one that wants to publish your images. Congratulations! You've taken a giant step towards making your art career full-time and prosperous.

This is a timely place for this quote:

A verbal contract is not worth the paper it is printed on.
— Louis B. Mayer

When it comes to dealing with a publisher, you will find that reputable ones will have legal documents. They are designed primarily to protect the publisher and – to a lesser degree – you. It will bind both parties for a period of time. Take heed from the Louis B. Mayer quote and do not deal with anyone on a handshake.

Sure, there are stories of people who have had fabulous and lucrative relationships based on nothing more than a promise, but when it comes to your career, you cannot afford to take that chance. My advice is to find a good lawyer who has experience in contract law and who insists on getting EVERYTHING in writing.

If you are scraping by on a starving artist budget, an alternative often suggested is to seek legal help through pre-paid legal programs. They offer legal advice at rates far below a typical lawyer's. Most advice they dispense can be deemed reliable for simple transactions, such as wills, some divorces, or creating a corporation and so forth. However, I do not recommend that you settle for this kind of legal advice when it comes to reviewing a potentially complex contract that affects your future and your livelihood.

A good lawyer will not tell you whether to sign a contract. They usually take the stance that their job is not to tell you whether to skate on the pond, but rather how hot the blades, how thin the ice, and how cold the water is. It is left to you to make your own informed decisions.

A quality lawyer also will admit that if their clients listened to every cautionary detail of possible negative outcomes from engaging in any given contract, there would be no contracts, just stalemates with all parties unable to agree. This means that after you have heard everything your lawyer has told you, you have to weigh the potential positive outcome against the negative and engage in good faith bargaining with your publisher.

Here again, understanding the art of negotiation and mastering some basic skills will lead to more favorable results for you. Obviously, seasoned publishers dealing with an artist ready to sign their first publishing and licensing contract have a huge advantage. If you come into the negotiations with demands the publisher views as unreasonable, they can assume the position of "take it or leave it."

If you only ask for what you think you might get, you are likely to be scaled back from what you wanted. However, if you ask for more than what you truly expect, you might get more than you estimated you would. There you have Lesson One in negotiation techniques. Imagine your improved results if you studied and polished your skills for such a scenario.

Even as a newbie, you always have rights, and you should do your best to make sure you keep as much control over the negotiation process as possible. I mentioned before that being a prima donna is not the best way to get good cooperation with the staff of your publisher. That doesn't mean you can't insist on maintaining the integrity of the art you are submitting or that has been approved for publishing.

For instance, if they would want to add graphic elements or type, or pump the red, or whatever the issue, you should maintain the final say on whether or not that will be allowed. Keep in mind that publishers are operating a business that is – to a degree – fashion and trend oriented. When they make suggestions for changes, it is because they believe those changes will lead to more sales.

Therefore, if it is your masterpiece, you might want to refuse to allow it to be altered. On the other hand, if it is something you don't mind seeing altered, you are probably going to enjoy seeing more money in the form of commissions by being agreeable. This is why I stated earlier, "Don't fall in love with your art," especially when it comes to cranking out a large body of work for a publisher. However, at the end of the day, it is your choice, and that's how it should be stated in your contract.

Since you are being paid on the sales of your images, you also should have some right to review the portion of the publisher's books that contains records of the sales of your prints. This is not to say you should feel the need to audit your publisher's books annually, but that merely by having the contractual right, you help keep the playing field more level.

The following is a summary of the things to consider when entering into an agreement with a publisher:

- Pre-register your copyright at www.copyright.gov.
- Get it in plain writing that the artist holds the copyright.
- State the number of copies the publisher is authorized to sell.
- Set a time limit on how long the publisher can advertise and sell works.
- Maintain some control over reproductions whenever possible.
- Ask for conditions whereby your contract can be broken (contracts are made for divorces, not marriages).

Expect to have the images you and the publisher agree to license to be tied up for a minimum of three years. If publishers are going to take a chance on you, they need to know they have enough time to earn a profit from the deal.

Anything else you can get into the deal to help sweeten it for you is worth asking for, or at least using as a bargaining chip. If you have done your homework, you probably already know at least some of the means your potential publisher uses to market images. You'll want to ask:

- whether they have a catalog and how often they update it with supplements;
- where and how often they advertise;
- at which shows they exhibit at;
- whether they have a licensing division;
- what portion of their business is with the volume-production market and how often they sample them;
- what they do with other marketing tools, such as direct mail and fax blasts, or website and email marketing, and so forth;
- what their plan is for breaking out new artists.

Depending on the nature of your relationship to start with, the openness of your publisher to share details and, to some extent, how eager they are to publish you will decide how much of the above list they will be willing to share with you, Mr. or Ms. New Artist on their roster. Do not consider it your inalienable right to demand answers to these questions, but it doesn't hurt for them to know you are interested in how their marketing process works and how it will affect the sales of your images.

It is unlikely a publisher will commit a timeframe as to when your images will appear in any given issue of a trade publication or be displayed as a framed print in their booth. However, they ought to be able to give you some assurances and, in some cases, even concrete details how they intend to market your images.

More On Contracts

There are two basic ways publishers pay artists: either by royalty or a flat fee. Royalties take much longer as money comes in only as inventory is moved. Most publishers are going to want to pay you in royalties; it's to their advantage. You can always attempt to negotiate an advance against royalties. If you are successful in getting the advance, try to make it non-refundable. Perhaps you can use the second point to give away in a negotiation to get the advance. Sharpen your negotiation skills; they really will come in handy more often than you imagine.

You need to get into the contract the specifics of your deal on items large and small. Who pays for shipping and insurance of your original work to and from the publisher? If you have provided other valuable materials, such as 4" x 5" transparencies, framing, et cetera, make sure your contract states they will be returned to you and when.

This is a good place to recommend a couple of books. The Legal Guide for the Visual Artist and Business and Legal Forms for Fine Artists are both authored by Tad Crawford for Allworth Press. Both contain much useful and valuable information to help artists maintain legal control of their work and how it is sold by third parties.

You will sometimes find that proofs produced without the intention of being sold are marked as H/Cs, which is short for the French term, Hors d' commerce. This is used more often in "elite printmaking," such as etchings and serigraphs. It means that before the sale, H/C is used for proofing purposes and sometimes in promotion to help create interest in the finished prints. All proofs and prints need to be accounted for in number and disposition (how they were used.)

How H/Cs will be used and disposed should be clear in your contract. This is especially true in the case of limited editions that are more expensive than posters.

Sometimes, H/Cs are denoted as P/P, which stands for "printer's proofs." This is more common in offset and giclée printing.

At a recent West Coast Art and Frame Show, I visited the Epson booth. It was there to promote its line of fine art digital printers. It has collaborated with artist Michael Godard, "the Rock Star of the Art World" [www.michaelgodard.com]. There were many examples of his work in the booth. Each one was clearly marked "NFS" to denote "not for sale."

Your contract should state that all such proofs not used or destroyed should become your property, and it should also state who will pay insurance and shipping costs to get them to you. Likewise, if printing plates for example etchings or serigraphs are used in the production of the prints, they need to be canceled and saved with proof– or the actual canceled plates – provided to the artist.

If you determine the income from a publisher is not going to be adequate, you ought to think about getting your originals into galleries and finding other ways to market your work. Some publishers require an exclusive with you, meaning they don't allow you to shop the work they decline with other publishers. Some do not make this distinction. Remember my advice on learning some negotiation skills? You can see from this instance alone why it would be good to have worked on them before starting to seek a publisher.

I am certain all publishers would love to assure all their new artists they are going to experience unqualified success with their imagery. Unfortunately, it's not that easy. Publishing is a fashion- and trend-oriented business. As such, neither your publisher nor you can be certain what is going to work. With their experience, publishers have good judgment about what prints will be hot, but they are sometimes surprised when a particular image gets legs and swamps the sales of similar images from a line.

Having a print or poster get legs, or having an artist that takes off with a whole series of images that fly off the shelves and result in endless licensing deals, are what makes the publishing business profitable. Those winners pay for lots of dogs that won't hunt. What you hope and pray for is your art turns up in the winner's category.

The facts are that it's nearly impossible to predict what is going to happen once art is created and ready to be marketed and sold. This is also true in other areas of the arts. Consider this quote from a February 23, 1993 article by Bruce Haring on www.Variety.com

Eric Clapton, the legendary rock guitarist/singer long deified by his fans, ascended to Grammy heights, capturing six prizes, including album, song and record of the year, to highlight the 35th annual Grammy Awards last night at the Shrine Auditorium.

Clapton, whose single "Tears in Heaven" detailed his heartbreak after his young's son's accidental death, admitted when he accepted his album of the year award that he was convinced that his award-winning "Unplugged" album" wasn't worth releasing.

"I didn't want this to come out," he said, "then finally agreed to it coming out in a limited edition. Then it sold a few, a few more, and I thought, 'Why not give it a try?'"

I do not know about you, but that beautiful, haunting, evocative song can still well me with emotion when I hear it more than a decade after it came out. Yet, at the time, this giant recording artist was unable to recognize the power and reach of the melody and lyric he had composed and performed. Perhaps it was because of his grief and the personal nature of the song having been written after the tragic death of his young son.

Whatever blocked Clapton's vision for the potential success of this work, it pointedly serves as a reminder to artists that you never know how things are going to work out. Whether you are unsure or positive that your newly submitted pieces are going to set fire, don't cash any checks until they arrive, and accept that sometimes things don't happen the way you would desire. And think of Eric Clapton when, in your mind, you are unsure of the value of the commercial appeal of your work – you might be surprised.

Over the years, artists have often asked me my opinion on whether their images were ready for market. Most often, I could or would not reply one way or the other. Naturally, I liked some more than others, and there would be some that, regardless of whether they appealed to me personally, I could see had the "right" look for the current market trends.

I will tell you how I responded then, and would now, to the question of whether your art sell. "The only people whose opinions matter are those who are willing to fork over some dough to buy your images." Just as with Eric Clapton – he couldn't tell whether his single was worth releasing, but once the album was recorded, his fans resoundingly voted with their pocketbooks. They sent the message to him through sales, which led to the industry's top awards for achievement by a recording artist.

Everyone else – you, your publisher, the retailer – can work hard to make the right impression and influence the buyer, and all the activity will help; but in the end the consumer has to want what you have created.

Building a dealer network one at a time is what creates the selling base. That base forms the platform for an art sales phenomenon to take off. When the phenomenon takes hold, it is driven by measures outside the control of the marketer. It takes a life of its own. In his bestseller, The Tipping Point, Malcolm Gladwell explains how seemingly insignificant incidences or a series of them can lead to phenomena beyond your imagination. The book is an interesting, and recommended, read.

Marketing success and sales phenomena are the reason word-of-mouth is the most important aspect to the success or failure of motion pictures. How else can you explain why, in the same summer, the quirky and relatively low-budget indie film My Big Fat Greek Wedding became a blockbuster, while the big budget Steven Spielberg and Tom Cruise thriller Minority Report was a bust.

For those of you who wish to learn more about how word-of-mouth marketing can be applied, check the Society for the Word of Mouth [www.theswom.org] and the Word of Mouth Marketing Association [www.womma.org]. The latter is geared towards larger companies, but you can still find practical information on its site.

In the end, the buyer is in control, and no amount of high-profile appearances or marketing dollars will make a huge effect on people's opinions. If you are lucky enough to be painting the daisies or angels just as they become all the rage, you are going to see some good sales result from the effort.

The early bird may get the worm, but the second mouse gets the cheese.
— Stephen Wright

The stories in the industry abound with artists who claim to have been the first to come up with a concept or theme that then takes hold in the popular market. Take For example, the well-known marine artists such as Robert Lyn Nelson, [www.robertlynnelson.com], Christian Riese Lassen [www.lassenart.com], and Wyland may debate and lay claim over who was the first to portray the thematic over and under-ocean-view concept. Nevertheless, it is more likely true that California artist George Sumner [www.sumner-studios.com] was the one who actually pioneered that theme. While the debate over who fathered the idea can rage, the reality is that the former three artists all have benefited financially from the concept, far more than George Sumner has.

The previously mentioned quote from the Time magazine article about Thomas Kinkade thinking about throwing in the towel on painting cottages seems shocking given the man's eventual record-breaking success in the print marketplace. It is interesting to note then that California artist Marty Bell began with the concept of painting romantic cottages for a collector society many years before Kinkade decided to emulate her.

Sadly, Marty passed away a few years ago, and her partner in life and business, Steve Bell, has since retired. Still, if you research the dates on her first cottage prints and look at her subject matter, you will clearly see the influence she had on Thomas Kinkade. In true second-mouse fashion, Kinkade decided to paint cottages and build a successful collector society around them, just as Marty Bell had done before him. The results of that decision made him the most financially successful print artist ever.

Finding a popular trend and putting your own spin on it is a time-honored tradition. For instance, if you notice low-slung pants for young women is in fashion, you can bet every pants manufacturer whose market is young women will have that look in their lineup as soon as possible. Why then should it be any different in the decorative art business?

It has been said that since Shakespeare there have been no breakthroughs in the basic concepts of writing plays; e.g., comedies, dramas and so forth. In one way or the other, all writers since have been creating permutations of his writings. I am not a Shakespearean or English Lit scholar, but the point is that all artists borrow in some way and all have been influenced by artists who preceded them. We do not live in a vacuum.

It is understood your art comes from a deep personal creative well and, as such, you do not want others tapping from that well. Who would? What happens though is that your art becomes part of a larger thing, around which a business is organized. It is ultimately recognized not just for its beauty and aesthetic quality by those who purchase it, but also as a fashion look and a potential cash flow generator for marketers, in the form of competing art publishers, to imitate.

What does this mean? Being the creative force behind a new look or trend is not a guarantee you will be rewarded for your efforts. It depends on how fast your competitors start knocking you off, or whether some of them are able to refine your look and make it even more popular than the original. It also means you can be on the other side of the equation and take cues from your competitors and your publishers to create and be influenced by what you see in the marketplace.

You can bet any publisher worth his salt is constantly on the look out for what is "hot" so as not to miss some market share when the next "angels," "daisies," "urns and ferns," "martini-themes" or whatever takes off. You also can anticipate that when publishers see something that looks as if it would fit into your style and capability, they will suggest it to you to see what you can come up with for them.

If your vision is strong enough and your creative output prolific enough, you can own a look regardless of how many copycats come out of the woodwork seeking to take a share of your market. The great Americana artist, Warren Kimble, whose work has been a stalwart for years for poster-publishing-industry juggernaut Wild Apple Graphics [www.wildapple. com], has spawned countless imitators. Some undoubtedly have crossed the line, only to realize how vigilantly Wild Apple defends its copyrights. Yet none of them have come close to approximating Kimble's ongoing and storied success.

If you are going to work with a publisher, you really could not do much better than aspiring to define and own a look for years on end, as Kimble has done. The trick is that he is an original, and being able to do what he has done with yet another look and style is difficult. Still, one can look at Kimble's work and see the influence of Jasper Johns and other artists whose works helped shape and influence him, and yet his work retains its own distinctive and recognizable look.

Artists who wish to work with publishers are faced with the same advice as for would-be self-publishers, which is to take a brutal assessment of your talent and capabilities. By keeping that assessment in mind when you begin to envision how you see your own success in working with a publisher come to fruition, and by establishing realistic and attainable goals, you give yourself the best opportunity to fully enjoy the results of your efforts.

Take the attitude of a student, never be too big to ask questions, never know too much to learn something new.
— Og Mandino

Chapter Eight
Copyrights and Certificates of Authenticity

There is no short-cut to art, one has to work hard, be open and flexible in your mind, keep the child alive inside you, and through a whole lifetime be ready to learn new things and, of course, be mentally prepared for a hard punch on your nose – especially when you think you are doing well.
— Bente Borsu (actress)

To start, let me clearly state that I am not a lawyer and am not qualified to dispense legal opinions. When it comes to legal matters, my advice is to hire the best, most qualified attorney you can find. Disclaimers aside, you will find worthy suggestions and resources here.

Think of this book as a door opener to ideas and concepts. If each were to be fleshed out, you would be holding a 1,000-plus-page book. This chapter is to help you locate the necessary information and sources to learn some basics about protecting your intellectual property with copyrights, with the understanding that you need will need additional resources to know everything pertinent to your copyright protection. You will also find information on the use and importance of Certificates of Authenticity (COA) for your artworks.

There are entire books on legal issues for artists, and there also are many lawyers who specialize in advising and creating legal documents to protect intellectual property rights for individuals, companies and visual artists. Some of the biggest legal fights carried on by Microsoft, other software developers, multi-national corporations and the entire entertainment industry are centered on the efforts to keep rogue nations and individuals from pirating and abusing copyrights.

Of course, the fight is closer to home with the recording industry's Recording Industry Association of America and the motion picture industry's Motion Picture Association of America organizations aggressively taking on the freeloaders who illegally download music and movie files from each other. Some of the worst abusers are now being dragged into court and face stiff fines and even jail sentences for their actions.

These powerful associations have successfully sued Internet Service Providers, including Earthlink and others, to provide them with the names and other data regarding the activities of the persons they wish to pursue in courts. The actions taken by these organizations are part of a rising awareness in the public, and in the creative community, that intellectual property rights can be aggressively protected. You might be thinking, "I'm just a little guy, and how's this affect me?" Despite your size, you need to be aware of your rights, and how to protect them.

In the art industry, you will find there are those who will blatantly attempt to steal your images and market them as if they were their own. There are things you can do about this, which we will explore, but first let's establish some basics. What follows is taken directly from the U.S. Copyright Office website, at: www.copyright.gov.

What is Copyright?

Copyright is a form of protection provided by the laws of the United States (title 17, U.S. Code) to the authors of "original works of authorship," including literary, dramatic, musical, artistic, and certain other intellectual works. This protection is available to both published and unpublished works.

Section 106 of the 1976 Copyright Act generally gives the owner of copyright the exclusive right to do and to authorize others to do the following: to reproduce the work in copies or phonorecords; to prepare derivative works based upon the work; to distribute copies or phonorecords of the work to the public by sale or other transfer of ownership, or by rental, lease, or lending; to perform the work publicly, in the case of literary, musical, dramatic, and choreographic works, pantomimes, and motion pictures and other audiovisual works; to display the copyrighted work publicly, in the case of literary, musical, dramatic, and choreographic works, pantomimes, and pictorial, graphic, or sculptural works, including the individual images of a motion picture or other audiovisual work; and in the case of sound recordings, to perform the work publicly by means of a digital audio transmission.

In addition, certain authors of works of visual art have the rights of attribution and integrity as described in section 106A of the 1976 Copyright Act. For further information, request Circular 40, "Copyright Registration for Works of the Visual Arts."

The U.S. Copyright Website is the best place to begin learning about how to best protect your own copyrights. I suggest you invest the money to copyright each piece of art you plan to reproduce or license to give you the strongest legal standing in the event you need to take action against a company or individual who is violating your copyright. It will only cost you $35 per piece to give yourself the best safeguards for your intellectual property rights. You can register at www.copyright.gov/register/visual.html

Some artists correctly believe their work is protected without going to the expense of registering a copyright for each piece they create; however, there are compelling reasons to register your work with the copyright office. It is my understanding (do your own research or consult an attorney to know for certain) that without a copyright, you are limited in seeking damages and can only use a non-registered copyright to force an offender to cease and desist from using your images. Take the time to educate yourself on this important subject. Your images are your lifeblood and your copyrights are their safeguard.

An outgrowth of political activism by and on behalf of artists began with efforts in the 1980s to regulate fair treatment for artists in the course of art trade. The most noticeable outcome of that movement was the Visual Artists Rights Act (VARA) of 1990; title VI of the Judicial Improvements Act of 1990, Pub. L. No. 101-650, 104 Stat. 5089, 5128, enacted December 1, 1990. You can learn more about it on the U.S. Copyright Office link above.

This act contains some of the strongest safeguards yet for artists. It was put to use in 2004 when the artist Wyland, who was introduced in chapter six, took issue when his whaling wall mural in Detroit was to be painted over first to make room for an automobile ad and then later to be covered for a period of two years with some other ad. Wyland was able to invoke his rights and, to my knowledge, the mural still exists.

I know from a personal conversation with Wyland that he would strenuously fight for his rights as an artist to keep all public murals he has painted from being destroyed or violated in some other way. He told me about a challenge he faced with his mural on the Long Beach Sports Complex when the Aquarium of the Pacific, which was opening nearby, attempted to have the mural removed because they thought it confuse the public. They feared too many people would mistake the Sports Complex for the Aquarium because they were only a couple of blocks apart. The Aquarium backed off when he stood his ground, and the mural remains on the Sports Complex today.

You also should avail yourself of some of the better books on the subject of legal right for artists. As previously mentioned, Tad Crawford has written several books for artists including, Legal Guide for the Visual Artist and Business and Legal Forms for Fine Artists, both of which should be in your library. Another book to consider is Electronic Highway Robbery: An Artist's Guide to Copyrights in the Digital Era by Mary E. Carter. Daniel Grant in his excellent book The Business of Being an Artist gives the subject of artists and law extensive review and coverage. The volume is one of the most comprehensive books regarding the art business in my library.

There is more to understanding and acting responsibly on your own behalf regarding copyrights than reading a few books or merely registering your images with the Copyright Office. For many years, subscribers of Art Business News magazine have been given great legal advice in a regular column by Joshua Kaufman, Esq. He is a partner at Venable LLP in Washington, D.C.

If anything, I am a realist. Having been around artists for decades, I know that many reading this book will choose not to hire an attorney and not to pay to register for a copyright on their original work. The reasons are many and include a combination of finances, lethargy, lack of time and a general wishful notion that nothing bad will happen if they decline to register their work.

For those who feel the need for some help, but lack the finances to bring on an attorney, the online legal resource site NOLO [www.nolo.com] is one solution. It has a Protect Your Artwork e-form kit among many other useful and affordable documents available for artists. It also has a number of very informative free articles on copyrights and other useful topics.

Your Copyright Does Not Extend to Derivatives

You should know that if you give "someone" your original to photograph, scan or print, and "that someone" makes a derivative version of the original in the form of a photograph, digital image or other form, you do not own the copyright to that derivative unless "that someone" has signed an agreement with you, acknowledging your ownership of that derivative version.

Sure, you trust your photographer or your printer, but if you have a monster image that gains tremendous sales and the derivative falls into the hands of an unscrupulous person, you have a serious problem on your hands. You need to protect yourself by having vendors sign releases of any copyright ownership for any work they may do on your images.

Legal Issues Regarding Fine Art Multiples

As of this writing, there are no less than 14 states with laws regarding the sale of reproductions or multiples within their borders. The states with "multiples" laws include California, New York, Arkansas, Georgia, Hawaii, Illinois, Iowa, Maryland, Michigan, Minnesota, North Carolina, Oregon, and South Carolina. You are bound to abide to those state regulations for sales made via the Internet when your art is delivered to collectors within those states

As you can imagine, the laws vary from state to state and require different terminology regarding disclosure. Some research suggests that the laws of California and New York are the most stringent. Again, doing your own research is the only way to be certain you are in compliance.

The Importance of Certificates of Authenticity

Some artists, with good reasons, provide a COA with their original work as well as with reproductions. Besides helping to establish provenance for future owners by including a COA with your original, you also establish and reiterate your copyright on it. That is, although you have sold the original, you maintain the copyright for the image and as such maintain the sole right to reproduce or publish the artwork or any facsimile of it in any medium.

The facts are that the average collector buying an original is clueless as regards to the ownership of the reproduction rights of the piece. This should not be surprising when obtaining such knowledge is difficult, and it is made more complex because it may not seem immediately logical to some buyers. That is, without being expressly told, they may make the assumption that they have bought the rights to reproduce the work with the original.

The following is a list of items you should include on your COAs. The list may not be inclusive of every necessity for compliance in the 14 states with laws regarding multiples. It may also be more extensive than necessary for your needs. Check your own legal resources to be certain. Only those in a position of authority should produce a COA. This would include artists, the artist's publisher, and the artist's agent, with the originator clearly stated.

Ideally, your Certificate of Authenticity should include:

- Full name of artist;
- COA originator if other than the artist, including their relationship to the artist;
- Title of the work/print;
- Signature (include the artist's signature whether the artist personally signed the print or whether it was stamped by the artist's estate, or made by another person or source);
- Address;
- Phone;
- Medium of original;
- Dimensions of original;
- Year the original was created;
- Description and/or photograph of print;
- Dimensions of the print;
- Year printed;
- Medium of the print;
- Number of prints (indicate whether prints are signed or unsigned, or signed and numbered with a limit, or signed and numbered with no limit);
- Number of proofs (indicate number of proofs, whether signed or unsigned, or signed and numbered);
- Edition size;
- Restrike edition?
- Posthumous edition?
- Status of artist's signature;
- Edition if a part of a series of editions (HC [NFS], artist proof, press proof, etc.);
- Name and location of printer;
- Status of the plate or master (destroyed, on file, etc.);
- What printing techniques were employed;
- Type of paper or substrate used for the edition, and what

weight, if appropriate;
- Archival status of substrate and ink or dye;
- Any protective coating used;
- Workshop where print was created;
- Name of the master printer;
- Date of edition;
- Plate or matrix cancelled?
- Date of signing, if different;
- Additional information;
- Certificate-of-Authenticity model.

In addition to helping artists and publishers abide by state laws, Certificates of Authenticity provide collectors now and future buyers with the provenance, or proof, of the work. In today's digital environment, where the art making process can be altered in innumerable ways to achieve a final state to print and where identical prints can be made endlessly, it is all the more important to offer as much detail as possible.

These facts should include details about the artist's identity and clearly define the artist's participation in creating the print. If others are involved in the creative process, whether in the makeup of the digital information before going to press or afterwards in highlighting, embellishing or otherwise working on the print to produce its final outcome, it should be duly noted.

In the case where prints are made from the same original, making the number available in the market is strongly suggested. If there was any unusual process used to create the print, or if any other useful information is available, this should also be included.

A statement about any photomechanical, photographic process used to create a multiple of an image produced in a different medium, for a purpose other than the creation of the multiple being described, and a statement of the respective mediums should be provided. You are not only making a statement for the first buyer, you are also making a statement for future collectors and creating a clear paper trail for the provenance of your art.

In addition, include information about whether the artist was deceased at the time and when the master which produced the multiple was made.

In my 15 years with DECOR and Decor Expo, some of the most vitriolic exchanges (and there were some good ones) I witnessed among exhibitors, and even with the management of the various tradeshows, were over the question of allowing certain companies to exhibit. Most often, it involved the legal status of companies who sold inexpensive, assembly-line-produced, imported oil canvases.

While tradeshow management explained they could understand the frustration these exhibitors felt, they contended they could not restrain a company from an equal opportunity to exercise free trade without some legal standing to keep them from exhibiting. In other words, produce an order to cease and desist or some other legal means, and then we can get something done.

The growing problem of cheap imported oils that mainly originate in China has been the subject of columns in the Wall Street Journal and featured on national nightly news programs in the U.S. The negative impact of this trend is one of many that have converged on the art market in the past decade. Some artists, such as Thomas Arvid, have been successful in fighting cheap, illegal copies of their work. Famed Canadian artist, Robert Genn, also led a fight to keep illegal copies of his and other artists' work from brazenly appearing in online catalogs that promote cheap copies painted in overseas art factories.

On one hand, you cannot be too vigilant in protecting your intellectual property and copyrights; on the other, you cannot expend all your energy to fight battles on these fronts. There has to be a balance you can find. You can look at the career of legendary rocker, John Fogerty, as an example. He spent years locked in legal battles with his recording company over the rights to his music. It cost him dearly in many ways, without much in the way of victory to show for his efforts.

Fogerty eventually moved on and his career blossomed once again, but not to the same degree as it was previously. I think he might have been better off to concentrate on building his career and moving forward than stepping out of the limelight to fight a battle with huge odds against him.

One thing to keep in mind before you begin to worry about battling copies is that you have to have built a substantial body of work that is already selling well in the marketplace for copies to begin appearing. That is, copycats do not typically bother to knock off work that is unknown or unpopular. So, whether it is cheap Chinese oils or others in the market just emulating your look, if it happens to you, you will know you have arrived.

What you do next will affect your career in many ways. I suggest having good legal advice, defending where financially possible, and, most importantly, just keep innovating and producing. If your style is constantly evolving, you will always be ahead of anyone seeking to gain by copying you.

Who are you going to believe, your lying eyes, or me?
— Groucho Marx

Chapter Nine
Trends and Inspiration

There is no abstract art. You must always start with something.
— Pablo Picasso

To be frank, it seems presumptuous to have a chapter titled "Trends and Inspiration" in this book. This is because I don't think I can tell you where to find true inspiration. Inspiration is at the most elemental level of the soul of being an artist.

I can give you a great example of how I think being creatively inspired is not the same in every person. I good deal of the clarity I gained around this notion came from my observations as a fine woodworker.

For two consecutive years, I was president of the St. Louis Woodworkers Guild. There, I found many members who were as talented at their craft as any I have seen. However, while the talent level was high, there was an obvious division among how members approached their serious hobby, although it was never openly discussed. Nevertheless, it was discernible by those paying attention.

Many of our members, who were capable of building anything from wood, had no interest or confidence in designing their own projects. They would scour the woodworking journals and plan books for ideas of things to build. They would borrow plans or sketch and measure pieces, and recreate them; but you never saw an original design from this faction. They seemed completely content to be busy at projects knowing the final result would be nothing short of excellent.

Meanwhile, others were always busy designing their own projects from scratch. Once the pieces were finished, the origin of the design was not an issue. The interest was in how the piece looked when it was finished and what went into its construction. If you will recall the woodworker's comment in his letter to the editor, "The first one was fun to make." Obviously, he got more satisfaction from the creative challenge of making his furniture from new designs than he did from rebuilding and finishing more of the same piece again.

I have heard several art publishers also make comments about this difference in approach. They know some artists who are talented and can paint in a variety of styles and mediums. The catch is, while they possess the technical talent, they lack the vision to know what to paint.

Most publishers are looking for artists who can bring them a look. However, you should not be surprised if a publisher loves your look and then requests changes to it. Poster publishers in particular often ask the artists whether they can alter images to give them more commercial appeal. Study publishers and you will find they are rarely publishing the work they most admire. They are responding more to input from buyers, dealers, galleries and collectors. Of course, when they ask, the choice is always up to you. Ultimately, it is your copyright and property.

The bottom line for you as an artist is that it is very beneficial for you to develop a recognizable style so your collectors, galleries and other buyers can grow an appreciation for your work. Some of you might already have found the style that is – or will be – your hallmark. Others of you are searching for something that you can hang your hat on.

Finding that "something" is what this chapter is about. Where do you look for trends and inspiration? The good news is you already know most of the sources. You already have learned that being an early adopter is sometimes not the optimal place to enter the market. It doesn't hurt to be an early adopter if you have just the right look and can harness the marketing to make a move with it. If you do adopt early, try to emulate the terrific slogan employed for years by the Panasonic Corporation, "Slightly Ahead of Our Time." It is perfect for the art business, too.

Pioneers get the arrows, settlers get the land.
— author unknown

For those of you who are looking for trends, then trade magazines and tradeshows – despite their diminished capacity – remain great inspiration sources. You will discover what your competitors believe are the hottest looks in color, sizes, prices and content. These resources could not be more specific in terms of being helpful. This, once again, reaffirms why I encourage you to be a serious student of the business.

You need to go beyond the art print business to really become immersed in what is happening in the world of color. A great resource is the annual report published by the Color Marketing Group [www.colormarketing.org]. It bills itself as the premier international association for color and design professionals. Its mission is to forecast popular colors for the coming year for major industries such as home furnishings.

What you often see happen is the colors they predict actually start to gain traction with consumers about a year later. The furniture industry relies heavily on this group's forecasting to help them make choices about what colors will be going into their products. If you visit a major design center, such Las Vegas World Market, or the IHFC in High Point, NC, during market, you will see the colors and patterns you will find in retail showrooms in the near future.

If you were creating art for the poster and open edition print markets, as you plan your images, you would be wise to take your cues from this group. You see, by the time the furniture manufacturers respond to cues from the Color Marketing Group, as well as from other influences, and get the ideas into production and finally to your local showroom, it can easily be a full year later.

Have you ever wondered why grape and chameleon neutrals are coming back or why sea foam green and peach were on the crest, or why jewel tones had their time as a "hot" color? It is often because color professionals have determined these shades are what will bring in the best return for manufacturers of furniture and home accessories. Wall decor, as it is known in the furniture business, is a part of that mix.

The more your imagery matches in color with what those buyers are looking at for the rest of their line, the better your chances are that a volume framer will put in a large order in for your work.

If you are thinking your art transcends the couch and you are above being influenced by mundane things, that is an artistic decision; but it's also a business decision. Even if you are creating art intended for higher priced giclées or serigraphs, it can still help to know what influences are driving consumer buying habits.

You don't have to include mardi grape into your palette just because it is popular, but it won't hurt you to let the knowledge of it influence your work in some subtle ways either. On the other hand, if you are after the wall decor market, you want to dial in the right color combinations. As with all the advice proffered, it's your choice.

Unless you are averse to shopping, or even window shopping, you can make a working field trip out of visiting the big lifestyle retailers such as Crate and Barrel, Pottery Barn, Pier 1 Imports, Macy's Home Stores and Z Galleries. Add in visits to your better local furniture stores to round out the excursions.

Other great sources are the catalogs from Horchow, Gumps, Ballard Design and other top home-furnishing catalog merchants. All these influences will be a huge benefit to your ongoing trend education. Now you can stop throwing away all those catalogs without looking at them and take some time to observe what the color trends are, especially those for clothing, home furnishings and accessories. Other areas that affect color marketing are paint and apparel. Paint is more of a following trend, while fashion apparel is a leading trend.

A good way to see what is popular is to take some time to view the model home decor in your area. The designers who put together those sales house showcases are usually right on top of what is hot in the business. Often they are taking their cues from industry publications and showrooms.

Designers also are reading shelter books, as they are known, including Architectural Digest, Elle Decor, Dwell, Home and Garden, Metropolitan Home, House Beautiful, In Style, and more. You don't need to subscribe to all these books; you can review most of them in libraries for no charge. Many libraries will let you check out past issues.

Big-box retailers jumped in the home fashions market some years ago. Today, it offers affordable and stylish home decor fashions from hot-shot designers such as Thomas O'Brien, Michael Graves, and Isabelle de Borchgrave. With the help of these designers, Target has put fashion and color trends into the mainstream, so you can even look for ideas the next time you're shopping for a 48-pack of Charmin.

You can find trend indications from the mainstream by watching some of the top rated sitcoms and dramas on television. These examples are somewhat dated, but still prove the point. Miami Vice with Don Johnson and Phillip Michael Thomas outfitted in pastel with their office and the show lighting also done in pastel, reflected the colors and helped define the look of the 1980s.

The mega-hit show Friends, with its prominently displayed vintage poster on the set every week, helped fuel the rage for that look and format, which peaked in the late '90s. The Cosby Show helped Black Art go mainstream when the cast visited a gallery that exclusively carried world class art by Black Artists. Due to fragmenting media offerings these days, broadcast no longer has the sway it once did with mass audiences. But, it is still worth tracking for the shows or events that pull us all together to watch.

A surefire way to catch on to trends is to watch any of the cable shows on designing for the home, such as those seen on the House & Garden channel (HGTV). These shows are loaded with ideas on topical design and color themes – the same things that are influencing buyers at the retail level and at the volume-framer (OEM) level.

Keep your eyes open for any remodeling of local malls, or the construction of new hotels, malls and office buildings. Observe what is being done with them in terms of their style and color schemes. This mindset can make some everyday things that would normally go unnoticed turn into something that can be fun for you to monitor.

Content or subject matter is always going to be easier to pick out of the pages of your favorite trade magazines than from the decor of your local mall, but there are still other resources to consider. One terrific source is Lieberman's Gallery, [www.liebermans.net]. It is the largest wholesale distributor of art prints and posters in the industry. It is known as a consolidator.

Its business model works this way. Typically, poster publishers in particular have minimum orders in terms of number of units or price before they will accept and ship an order. If Barney's Poster and Frame shop needs one or two copies of the latest Jack Vettriano poster distributed by Image Conscious in the U.S., it might either have to make a larger order than it needs to make the minimum order with Image Conscious, or forgo ordering until the minimum order can be met.

What Lieberman's does is allow small shops to order one or two prints, or even one or two prints from several different publishers. It then places a consolidated bulk order with its publishers, receives the items, and repackages them to be sent out to the retailers. The price is the same to the retailer because Lieberman's gets a volume discount the retailers can't attain. Everybody wins in this scenario: the retail picture frame and poster shops can keep selling one print at a time from their catalogs without having to stock things they don't have the money or confidence to put into inventory; the poster buyer gets the order filled sooner; and the publisher moves another unit out of their inventory.

This remarkable business model has become so successful that Lieberman's is a most important customer for many publishers. This means it not only aggregates orders; it is also in the unique position to know what is selling best. Conveniently, the company occasionally updates its website with information about what the bestselling images are, so you can see what is popular. It's another source for you to work with when you are looking for trends and inspiration.

Art.com and its sister company, Allposters.com are the largest art retailers worldwide. You can visit those sites to find out which images are the current top sellers. Doing this kind of research can be a great way to get yourself out of a rut, or to just be inspired by what other successful artists are doing now.

When you begin working with publishers, they will be able to help you with ideas, as their resources are greater than yours. Often, their staffs attend the IHFC shows in High Point to look for trends and for new possible volume customers. When you put it all together and start thinking strategically about what you want to paint and what you think will have an impact in the marketplace, you are getting closer to obtaining the success that is possible from this end of the business.

If you can find a way to regularly read some of the trade publications that serve the home furnishings field as Design Trade [www.designtrade. net] and Home Furnishings News [www.hfnmag.com] and so forth, you will have yet another valuable source of inspiration for trends and ideas. Design Trade has an online issue to make it easy to quickly page through for inspiration.

Another favorite source for me is the British online publication N.E.E.T. Magazine [www.neetmagazine.com]. It is a treasure trove of great indie fashion design. While my age and gender put me well beyond personal interest in the funky vintage and trendy clothing, jewelry, purses and crafts, I admire the creativity expressed in the magazine, especially in its cutting-edge graphic design. It is all the more impressive to know the publication is the brainchild of its entrepreneur owner, Stephanie J. She is sole editor who manages the book and personally lays out each issue.

The Artful Home [www.artfulhome.com] markets through its website, direct mail, print catalog and email. It is another visual treat and should be a source of inspiration for you. It is also a place where you can submit your art to be considered in juried fashion for inclusion in its offerings.

I have no data yet. It is a capital mistake to theorize before one has data. Insensibly one begins to twist facts to suit theories instead of theories to suit facts.

— Sir Arthur Conan Doyle (Sherlock Holmes)

Chapter Ten
Business Marketing Basics for the Self-Published Artist

Art is making something out of nothing and selling it.
— Frank Zappa

As with any business venture, the best advice is to begin with the basics. There is no more fundamental need than to be able to clearly answer the question, "What business are you in?" In this chapter, we will help you answer that question and will delve into specifics on basic business tools for self-representing artists, including:

- trade advertising and tradeshows
- artist business and contact-manager software
- direct mail
- promotional materials

Future chapters will discuss using email, websites, social media, publicity, promotion and other business tools for managing the marketing of your career.

To begin the process of becoming a self-published artist, you must first have a good understanding of your target market. If that piece of advice sounds elementary, it is. Nevertheless, it is crucially important for you to know and understand your target market – to have in mind the person who will be buying your prints.

Best Buy once did a study of its customers that caused it to change its business practice. The electronics retail giant realized that 20% of its customers were responsible for 80% of its business. It also found that many of its customers added little to the bottom line. In fact, another 20% were the cause of much wasted employee time, consumed much of the company's promotional budget, and were the least profitable in terms of sales.

The company refocused its advertising and retrained the employees to cater to that precious 20% of the market, and as a result they saw sales improve by more than 20% in a matter of months. While you might not have the resources of Best Buy, you can still take a page from its book and work at learning to identify your target customers. When you know who they are, you can figure out how to cater to them.

If you are the Snap-On Tool Company, you know your primary target market is men ages 21to 55. You manufacture tools and your marketing to appeal to them. It's not to say art and mechanics' tools have much common, although I do find a sculptural value in many well-made tools. (The woodworker in me comes out again.) To reiterate an earlier point – keep in mind that although your art is beautifully created with loving, passionate care; it is still a business if you want to earn a living from it. I believe the way you market your business easily make a 20% difference in your results, regardless of your size.

You know what the subject matter of your art is, and you probably already have a good feel for who the dominant buyers are. If you don't know this information already through your research, experience and instincts, you need to figure it out; because it is vital to have a clear-cut vision of the niche you are going after. Who are you painting for; who is your buyer? If you can't describe your target audience, finding buyers is going to be difficult.

The more clearly you can see your prospective collectors, the more likely you are to create imagery that will appeal to them. Is thinking about marketing your art a way of selling your artistic soul? It doesn't have to be. It depends on how you conduct your business. Finding a comfortable way to feed your artistic body does not require selling your artistic soul.

To ensure your success, you should strive to become a student of your collector base. Start to study them, and when you begin to understand why people might buy your art and also understand what is it about your art that appeals to them, you are getting closer to honing your success. Don't take the S.W.A.G. Factor approach by doing your research anecdotally; use a facts-based system and accurate measuring. Be aware that your mind can play tricks on you, because it will default to your own prejudices if you don't track the information about your buyers as you receive it.

Find a way to keep score of not only who buys, but also who shows an interest and who doesn't. While you are sleuthing away, also track what it is that is selling and attracting interest. You will see patterns evolving from this activity. It will tell you what images in your line are working. Continue to refine and use the information to determine if it is content, size, color, price or some other combination of those that is generating sales and interest.

When you have face-to-face encounters, make it a point to ask questions about which pieces your potential buyers like and why. Be honest and ask for their help. Explain that you are doing informal research. Sometimes in a direct sales situation such as at an art show, approaching a buyer in a non-sale, non-threatening manner gives you an opportunity to talk about your art without showing your eagerness to make a sale.

This soft-sell approach can lead to sales as your prospects relax with you. Your opening could be as simple as this: "You seem interested in that piece. I'm doing some informal research on my work to find out what it is about certain images that appeal to people. Would you mind sharing with me what drew you to the piece?"

The purpose of doing personal market research is to learn which of your original paintings you should consider turning into fine-art prints. While you must know what to paint for your audience, you must also be able identify what niche you are aiming at with your art. With the data you gather, you will make informed determinations about what your target audience expects in terms of pricing, as well as content, color and so forth.

Gaining a clearer picture about these things will provide the support for your decision with regard to the best reproductive process for you to pursue; i.e., poster, limited edition offset prints, canvas transfers, giclées or serigraphs.

Here are some things to consider about your target audience:

1. Where is your target audience located?
2. What is the age range of your target audience?
3. Do they know anything about you or your art?
4. What would you like them to think about you and your art?
5. How will you attract them to your art?
6. Who else is competing for their loyalty and devotion?
7. Are you targeting business or consumer sectors?
8. How affluent is your target audience? Are they vulnerable to changes in economic conditions?

While gathering data based on all the above questions will be useful, there are other ways to consider targeting art buyers. One of the smartest advertising persons ever is Roy H. Williams, aka the Wizard of Ads. He is the author of three best-selling books on marketing, including The Wizard of Ads: Turning Words into Magic and Dreamers into Millionaires. Always a contrarian, he has this to say:

If you want to grow your business, don't target age, sex, income or education. Target according to buying motives. The question isn't, "Who is my customer?" but rather, "Why does my customer buy my product? What does it do for him or her?" The answers to these questions will tell you exactly what to write in your ads.

So, What Business Are You In?

Many businesses don't know how to correctly answer that question, and they pay a hefty price for it. Ray Kroc became a billionaire with McDonald's because he realized he was in the real estate leasing business. If he had thought he was in the hamburger or restaurant business, he would have made many errors in judgment on how to build his business model.

Granted, Kroc also took standardizing fast food preparation to a completely new level, but had that been the business model, he would not have enjoyed the same success. By buying real estate and leasing it back to his franchisees, he created a completely separate source of revenue from the franchise fees from an asset gaining in value as it aged. Likewise, if you consider yourself in the "art" business, or even the "art publishing" business, you are off on the wrong foot and headed up the wrong path.

In the first edition of this book, I answered the question about which business you were in as below, because it was the decades-old method of building a successful art print business. With the continued improvement and acceptance of digital art and printing, and with changing consumer habits, including the growing reliance on e-commerce and the explosion of social media, it is no longer the only avenue to a successful career in the art print market. Nevertheless, the original answer is still valid, just to a lesser degree than before. Here it is.

You are in the business of building, nurturing and replenishing a dealer network. It is through that network that your artwork will flow to the end consumer. It is business of the art retailer to romance your work to "their" customers. Their customers then become your collectors via your wholesale network. The primary job for your publishing business is to find and romance art dealers.

Think of it this way:

- Build
- Nourish
- Replenish

Put another way, it means Job One for your business is to come to work everyday with the goal of building that distribution channel of art retailers and art dealers. If you are a poster publishing company, you will also be focusing on the volume-art-buyer market.

Today, this is still a good business model – in part. Due to changing market dynamics, the likes of which we have previously never witnessed, it is neither the only model to pursue nor the best strategy to focus on in a single-distribution system. Because building a dealer network is still a legitimate method of creating a growing art-publishing business, I will stay on point here with building a dealer network. You will find new chapters in this book on alternative distribution methods and social media.

Before digging into the specifics on building a dealer network, I believe it is imperative to state a strong conviction here – one I have developed in the ensuing years since I wrote the first edition. I believe it overrides in importance the dictum about growing a dealer network. In fact, the statement below encompasses the old answer about the nature of the business you are in.

It is vital now, and for the foreseeable future, for all artists to control as much direct distribution of their work as possible. This means you are now in the business of building your own distribution channels, which may include a dealer network.

I am not advocating that artists turn their backs on building a dealer network through galleries, because there still is potential for strong repeat sales from them. Rather, I emphasize that new opportunities and distribution channels are present as never before, and current economic conditions (among other industry developments) are such that being able to fully trust in systems outside of one's control is not prudent. You might call it defensive opportunistic optimism.

If you want to learn from an artist who controls both her marketing and her distribution, while working well with those galleries that appreciate what she brings to the equation, study the career of Hazel Dooney [www.hazeldooney.com]. She puts incredible effort into communicating directly with her collectors and admirers, which results in her work being in demand. Smart gallerists seek to work with her because they know her work will sell, and she has already done much of the heavy lifting when it comes to marketing

While I believe the gallery system continues to offer artists opportunities to get their work to market and for steady repeat sales, the possibility looms over the galleries that they may backslide or go out of business as never before. With our soft commercial real-estate market and other economic factors, the actions of others could cause them to go out of business. There has never been a more apropos time than now to live by the saying, "Don't put all your eggs in one basket."

Okay, back to the burning question: If building a dealer network is important to my business, how do I do it?

The answer is simple, but easier to say than do – one at a time. There are arguably somewhere between 8,000 and 12,000 art retailers in the U.S. that sell some format of art reproductions. These retailers are opposed to fine art galleries exclusively dealing in originals. If we take the lower figure in the range and imagine you as the artist could add 1% more dealers annually, you would be gaining 80 new dealers a year – and would be doing a smash up job.

Let's look at this scenario: suppose you were promoting reproductions of your work as giclées, and you had a dealer base of 80. Make a further supposition that each dealer averaged one sale a month for you. That means you'd be shipping nearly 1,000 prints to them annually.

Based on a subjective $300 wholesale price point, 1,000 prints sold would bring you $300,000 before any expenses. Of course, this is not your break-even figure. But, if you deduct printing costs of say $100,000, you would still be left with $200,000, which (using the example I provided earlier as an estimate of annual running costs for a publishing company) would more than cover the $119,000, (with $15,000 budgeted for printing)..

The admonishment, "Your results may vary," applies here. These are example figures, and every situation is unique. Your pricing could be much higher or lower than $300. For most, gaining 40 new dealers in the first year would be a major accomplishment. However, if you sold them each two prints per month, you would have the same total sales as the original example above. So many variables come into play it makes it difficult to know in advance what your results will be.

The popularity of your art depends to some extent on how in tune your images are with market trends. However, with that as a given, your results are going to depend on financing, marketing execution and follow up. Although some visual art helps define – or is defined by – a period, other styles are transcendent of time. I believe it would be a natural goal to aspire to the latter, but I also know much art-print gold has been mined in the former.

As an artist if I could control it, I would want my look to be leading the pack. Not necessarily the first one in, but one that was able to take ownership by producing an easily attributable and totally unique style that defined a look or movement. If you do find yourself at the cutting edge of a trend, keep these immortal words in mind:

If you're riding' ahead of the herd, take a look back every now and then to make sure it's still there.
— Will Rogers

Sometimes things such as the dreadful 9/11 attacks knock the sails out of the best-laid plans. Ask any of the hundreds of companies who were devastated by that event. Many were looking forward to one of the best shows ever in Atlanta (scheduled to begin September 14, 2001) only to see it cancelled in the wake of the attacks on that day of infamy.

More than four years later, many of those companies had still not fully recovered from the losses of that show's cancellation, nor from the repercussions that rippled the economy in its path. You see, for many of the companies that exhibit in Atlanta, it was Christmas for retailers. They had come rely on it for a large part of their annual sales and for the invaluable contacts generated there each year.

But no one in the business who was still reeling from the aftermath of the cancellation of the Atlanta Decor Expo show could imagine how other factors were bearing down to change the business even more. These included the churning ownership of media and tradeshow properties, changing consumer habits, the growth of e-commerce, big-box retailing patterns and the flood of cheap oil paintings from China.

The convergence of those factors rocked the art print market. So much so that in 2009 Summit Business Media LLC (the latest and last investment banker owners of Art Business News, DECOR magazines, and the ArtExpo New York and Decor Expo Atlanta tradeshows) was prepared to shut down those businesses.

These once venerable properties were salvaged by top-level employees not ready to let them slip away. You should be grateful – as I am – that they did. Had they not, the job of building a dealer network would be much more difficult. Although the trade media properties serving the art print market are far from robust and unable to deliver as in the past, they remain useful and important to the growth of the business and as vehicles for artists to connect with dealers..

The situation was such in 2009 that Next Step Media LLC had no other choice but to cancel its fall show in Atlanta. The company had been formed by former longtime publisher, Kim Feager, to purchase Art Business News, DECOR and Decor Expo. Her decision was done to give her new ownership group and its employees time to regroup and come back with a workable plan for Decor Expo Atlanta in 2010. Overall, the industry gave her high marks for her level head and her tough decision to forgo the show for the year.

Unfortunately, the 2010 Décor Expo Atlanta show was canceled due to lack of support from exhibitors. As I said in the blog post noting this sad development, the show is all but lost for the foreseeable future. Even a show with as much history as the this one cannot sustain after being canceled two years in a row. I do not predict a replacement show to come along as the investment and risk are very high at this time and in the difficult economy of late 2010.

ArtExpo New York is now produced by Redwood Media Group, LLC, a new company formed in July 2009 by Robert Reeder and Eric Smith, who is an art business veteran and the former Vice President of Summit Business Media. Summit Business media was the leading worldwide producer of art shows and art-related trade publications, including ArtExpo Las Vegas, Art Miami, Art Business News, DÉCOR and Volume.

It is under Redwood Media Group that the ArtExpo New York show is moving Pier 94. But despite downgrade in terms of location, the show will be in good company... as it follows both the Armory Fine Art Show and the Architectural Digest shows at the same location. Finding these other shows there is another indication of how things in other markets have been affected by changing market forces.

The ArtExpo Los Angeles show also was canceled as getting a viable venue there was made problematic. It was replaced by a show to be held in Los Angeles. This show was also canceled. The handwriting is on the wall that art tradeshows are quickly fading as prime vehicles for helping artists get their work to market.

Let's return to the original premise of building a dealer network, which it is done one at a time. The facts are that it takes a combination of coordinated marketing components to effectively move the sales dial in your favor. You and your marketing-maven partner need to gain a good understanding of how these various components work and learn how to blend the use of them into a seamless marketing strategy for your art business.

The more planning you put into the details, the less likely you will be managing by crisis. Even though this all might sound overwhelming, I assure you that being in the position of constantly being late or missing marketing opportunities is even more overwhelming. As of the writing of this book's first edition, there just were a few ways to get to market. They included:

- advertising
- tradeshows
- publicity and promotion
- direct mail
- email
- websites
- reps

In the first edition, the items above were listed in a hierarchy of their importance. Obviously, there are other marketing factors to consider. However, because they were far less effective than the items listed, they were intentionally left out. Regardless, you should be thankful then – as now – that you do not have newspapers, television and radio to contend, as do marketers in other fields.

With the changes in the market now, there are now other factors to consider, such as social media, specialty marketing and alternative distribution. You will find these factors addressed in future chapters. Also, you will find information on publicity and promotion, websites, email marketing and reps addressed elsewhere in this book.

Trade Advertising

Just as tradeshows have come on hard times, so have trade magazines. It would be difficult to say which are doing worse vis a vis their glory years. It is my estimation now that advertising in trade magazines for most artists, especially emerging artists, is a large gamble with not good odds.

Although it saddens me to say so, I would have to advise against trying to use trade advertising as a means of establishing an art print career. There may be some valid reasons for investing in trade magazines, but for most it is an expense best left off the budget until there is some marked improvement in trade magazine results.

Having just advised against trade advertising for most artists at this juncture, it is tempting to edit out the following information about how to best go about laying out a trade magazine strategy. I am leaving it in because there is good information that can be used in other ways, and because there is a remote chance trade advertising will get back on its feet before this book sees another edition.

You already know I sold advertising for DECOR magazine for 15 years, which naturally predisposed me to believe it is the most important in the marketing hierarchy. But I also sold tradeshow space, direct mail lists, websites and more. I learned from first-hand experience with all methods what worked best for my customers.

Moreover, every bit of research I have ever seen any trade publication serving the retail-art industry conduct with their readers has indicated that magazine advertising is the most influential of all the ways dealers use to find new companies and new images. With their monthly reach, magazines are the most important sources of information for buyers. While the above is accurate in today's economy, trade advertising has slipped in importance for art print publishers.

If you asked me what you should do with regard to advertising versus tradeshows, my answer would be to do as much as possible of each, along with any other marketing channel that appears opportunistic. I believe you should do as much as humanly and financially possible. Doing so is the best way to get the maximum exposure in the least amount of time.

Mass marketers measure their impressions in the millions and know that getting enough exposure with the right message will move product. You have the same task on a smaller scale. You want to make as many impressions, from as many angles as possible, on your target audience.

When you begin to plan your advertising, you should start with the idea of using it for all its purposes. If you think of it as vehicle merely to show your latest work, you are shortchanging yourself and your advertising's potential. Learn to use it to support messages streamed to your customers and prospects in other ways.In your planning, use the four C's of advertising:

1. Clarity
2. Coordination
3. Consistency
4. Continuity

Clarity – Don't complicate your message. Be clear about who you are and who you are not. You don't have to cram every aspect of your business plan into each message. Be concise and clear and keep it simple.

Coordination – Use advertising to coordinate the message, look and feel of your entire marketing efforts, including logos, direct mail, websites, email, et cetera. For example, ads for Coca-Cola may be strikingly different from each other, but there is never a doubt as to whose ads they are. The same is true if you get coupons, postcards, or emails promoting Coke. Maintain a coordinated appearance in the integrity of and look of your company image and brand as they do.

Consistency – Decide what your message will be and maintain a consistency with it in all of your advertising. The impact of your advertising becomes exponential when it is consistent over time. Your customers and prospects will not only see your latest offerings, but be reinforced with your message.

"Nobody doesn't like Sara Lee,"

"Budweiser: The King of Beers,"

"Burger King: Have It Your Way."

Those tag lines or slogans don't necessarily dominate every ad from those brands, but they have appeared often enough that they are instantly recognizable because they have been consistently present in message after message from their marketers.

By maintaining a consistency in your advertising, you lay a foundation and build upon it. The ones that come before support each succeeding ad, strengthening and consistently reinforcing your message to your customers and prospects.

Continuity – When millions of people can sing your jingle or repeat your advertising slogan, isn't the battle won? Why would McDonald's continue

144

to advertise when they have enormous visibility in great retail locations, millions of customers coming into their restaurants daily and so on? It is not because they want you to enjoy the free programming you see on your television; they are not that altruistic. It is because they know that their message needs to be repeated in a consistent manner in order for them to continue to capture market share. The adage "out of sight, out of mind" applies to mass marketers as much as it does to growing publishing companies and hopeful artists.

Deciding to run one or two ads to see what happens before you commit to more is throwing your money away. Your prospects in trade magazines are retailers who are used to regularly seeing new artists and publishing companies coming into the marketplace. By virtue of their longevity, they have seen advertisers come and go and these are not the type of companies with whom they want to do business. The best are waiting for more than two ads to see what kind of sticking power you have.

Dealers want to see more than an ad with beautiful artwork displayed. They want to see commitment that the advertiser believes in its work and message. The last thing they want to do is commit their time and effort to bring in a new artist only to sell a few pieces and then find out the artist has abandoned the print market. One of the best ways to convey your conviction alongside your fabulous images is to use continuity and constancy in your advertising.

Research in various media over the years has shown it takes as many as six exposures to a message before someone will react to it and respond. This is why I would put a minimum of six ads in the proposed budget for a new advertiser.

If finances are thin, you can of course do less, but you will have to realize your effectiveness is going to be diminished. If this is the case, you should scale back your expectations to fit your budget. The other thing to do is to work harder at publicity and promotion to help balance out a reduced schedule.

There is always jockeying among advertisers, particularly frequent advertisers who demand that their insertion in the magazine be placed in a FFRHP (far forward, right hand page) position. You'll notice in many publications that some advertisers have franchised a certain page upon which they appear every month. They normally get this placement by agreeing to advertise every month and paying a premium on top of their regular ad rate to retain that position.

My opinion on premium positions has always been that you can negotiate for some decent placement without paying a premium. While you may not get a specified page, you might be able to swing a right hand page in the first one-third of the book by agreeing to a multi-issue contract. This way, the money you save on a premium position can instead be used to buy more space.

For example, if you are saving a 10% premium, that means you could run 11 ads for the cost of 10 (with 10% premium) – give me the 11 ads over position every time. Of course, the longer your contract, the better your negotiating position; but a six-month contract ought to be enough to get you some consideration. Again, your negotiation skills will come in handy here.

Sometimes, pages that are adjacent to some of the best-read copy in the publication go begging with little or no demand for them. This situation happens because often there are departments, table of contents, masthead, columns and clusters of competing facing full-page ads all vying for upfront positions, even though the feature copy that is usually most important to readers is farther back in the publication. And, unlike aggressive competitive advertisers, readers aren't keeping score of whose ad appears where in the magazine.

A well-executed ad will pull a better response than one slapped together regardless of where either is placed in the magazine. There have been tests to show that placement is overrated, and I agree. I still prefer a right-hand page facing a full page of editorial in the first feature section of any magazine in which I am advertising. Since the fiercest competition is for the front and cover spots, you can often land this kind of position by asking (negotiating) for it.

A word about well-executed ads: they don't just happen. There is rhyme and reason behind how well some ads pull over others. It was always frustrating for me to work with artists who designed their own ads and had no clue what they were doing. They may have agreed to pay $2,500 per ad to get into a publication, but to save some money they decide to put the ad together themselves using a limited – or no – background in graphic arts. I have seen this scenario often and it often yields less than satisfactory results.

The advent of the PC and the Mac, along with the arrival of Illustrator, Photoshop and other desktop publishing software, gave everyone who could work those programs the idea they were a graphic designer … wrong. Being blessed with artistic skills doesn't mean you naturally have great graphic art skills. Even if you have the sensibility of an artist, unless you can couple that with the training of a graphic artist, you are probably not going to be able to do the best job designing your own ad. Besides, you are probably too close to the subject matter to be objective about it anyway.

There is more to putting together a good ad than including a graphic of some beautiful image you painted. Just being able to understand typography and type placement is huge. Knowing how certain colors reproduce in magazines can be huge. Knowing why certain color combinations work better in some ads is helpful. Knowing how to properly create a proof can be huge. And the list goes on from there in lost opportunity to put your best foot forward by doing it yourself.

Do yourself a favor: hire the best graphic designer you can afford and have them work with you to pull together your whole graphic style – not just for ads, but for logos and all the other elements that make up awareness for your company. Check their resume and portfolio before you hire and make sure the portfolio is really theirs. I wouldn't compound the situation by hiring someone who is self-trained unless they had extensive experience, a great sample book and references. I don't have anything against self-trained people, many are capable, but in a world where there are many qualified and educated people to do the job, why take the chance?

Some advertisers look upon magazine advertising as a beauty contest, especially in the art business. This is not limited to art magazines. You still see high-powered Madison Avenue agencies concocting clever memorable television ads that do everything but help the viewer recall the advertiser or product. Your ad should not just display your art, it should convey a sense of your company and sell something, or ask for the order.

These folks running beauty contest ads are not properly answering the question, "What business am I in?" And certainly they are not answering Roy H. Williams' poignant questions: "Why does my customer buy my product? What does it do for him or her?" They think they are in the art business when they should be concentrating instead on using trade advertising to build a dealer network. You should be happy that they are helping you out by not taking full advantage of their advertising dollar.

David Ogilvy, who was a giant figure in the development of advertising in the 20th century, taught that every ad should sell. He championed the concept of quality in visual taste and literate copy in advertising. You could do no better than to follow his simple and powerful advice for your own advertising: "Always give your product a first-class ticket through life."

I'm telling you this because I have noticed through my own observations over nearly two decades that often the ads that pulled the highest number of reader responses weren't necessarily the prettiest. Many had multiple images in the same ad (they were showing their product … gasp!), although most weren't neatly lined up like tombstones in a military graveyard. Rather, they would be overlapping at attractive angles or set in other interesting layouts. Don't be afraid to show the product. Do it, as David Ogilvy advises, "first-class."

Trade publications in this field have done away with what were called "bingo cards." Those were the ever-present postcards with rows and columns of numbers on them. Readers were instructed to circle on the card the corresponding number found at the bottom of any ad they liked, and then return it, postage paid, to the magazine to be compiled and forwarded to the advertiser.

Bingo cards were always faulty. Ask yourself, how many good prospects would use them instead of using the phone? And how much value you would receive from the many great literature collectors who were the primary users of bingo cards?

Nonetheless, they did give advertisers and publishers some independent means of measuring response. Now with toll-free phone lines, email, Web pages and even toll-free fax numbers, they have lost their usefulness and really only add unnecessary expense to producing a magazine; thus, the cards have now gone the way of the free meal on an airline.

Although bingo cards are gone, like so many other quaint practices, trade publications today still offer ways for readers to contact advertisers. You should investigate all possibilities and seek to take advantage of them. Your rep is not going to be paid to help you get freebies or extras, so make sure you ask what is available.

You can do some of your own research by training your staff who answers the phone to ask the person calling where they saw your ad. If you are in several publications, you can run different ads in the same months to help avoid confusion. Many new phone systems have extensions that can be keyed specifically to an ad in a publication. The more you accomplish being able to track responses, the better the better your results will be. Another suggestion is to offer different specials or challenge your creativity to come up with other bright ways to key responses to your ads.

The most important thing to do is to get a consistent reliable system in place to help you monitor your advertising, so you can track where your response is coming from. David Ogilvy would also tell you that if you continuously test your advertising, you would continuously get better results from it.

Some advertisers go to the extreme of entering the data in a prospect database to track not only what ads pulled in a new prospect, but also what ads pulled a response that ended in a sale. That's a lot of work and is beyond the scope for a new publishing business to go that far, but it is something to shoot for in time. Knowing how to best allocate your advertising budget gives you a tremendous advantage over less sophisticated competitors.

Magazines have to be more imaginative these days to come up with ways to help their advertisers get and measure response. One of your duties is to debrief your rep on everything the publication will do for you to help you in this regard.

I would ask my rep to let me know what ads pulled the best response in the last 12 months and whether they have any way of capturing information that will be helpful to you personally. It is not a sure thing you will get the research, but doing so will help you understand which ads pull best from a graphics point of view, as well as what works best in terms of content, size and color. Be curious and persistent in probing for information your vendors have to offer you. Knowledge is power.

Some publications have value-added programs they offer to advertisers. These are not always thrown on the table; you should make a point to always ask what is available. Will they do an email or fax broadcast for you? Will they give you use of their mailing list at no cost or reduced costs? Are there package deals you should know about? What tie-in editorial promotions do they have? Often, if you don't ask, these programs won't be revealed since most of this stuff is a nuisance with little return on investment (ROI) attached to them for the publications and reps.

Advertising is a mix of part art and part science. You want the finest looking, most creative and inspiring ad that will do the best job for you. You will have multiple purposes for your advertising, but "to sell" should always be part of the purpose. It will be your front line in helping you create a brand strategy for you, your art and your company.

If branding is your top priority, you might want to forgo the idea of placing a bunch of small ads that would try to maximize response in favor of something that is planned strategically to lift awareness for you and your images. The latter concept could be a follow up to a series of ads scheduled as branding – keep thinking long range. And if you are branding, then top-notch graphics are that much more important.

When Greg Bloch launched Triad Art Group Publishing [www.royoart.com] to sell the works of the fabulous Spanish artist, Royo, he spent far more on his ad budget than one normally would if using a typical 5 to 12% of annual revenue figure.

Bloch knew that running a slate of full-page and spread ads with Royo's dramatic, romantic images would leverage his brand and his artist and ramp up his sales at the same time. And he knew that this aggressive advertising would make his company seem larger and more important than it might otherwise have been perceived, given that it was a startup.

Greg came into this situation prepared with experience, financial wherewithal and an artist ready to catch fire. His results were nothing short of phenomenal. His advertising allowed him to compete with larger, established publishers and set the stage for his marketing efforts, which were heavily focused on selling pre-show and at-show at ArtExpo.

Because circumstances have changed so much since the early 1990s when he began plotting his strategy, I cannot say whether you would find the same aggressive approach from Greg Bloch today. I imagine if he were attempting launch Royo now, he would use a different combination with his advertising, tradeshow and marketing mix.

Regardless of what you may feel about aesthetics and the "art" business, don't allow it to get in the way of focusing on the core reason for your trade advertising, which should be to gain dealers. This means you should make it as easy as possible for them to respond to you. You should invite their response. This is not crass; it is good business. Asking for response can be done in a tasteful manner that still satisfies a need to have a grand, eloquent presence, if such is your goal.

Advertising rates should be called "advertising suggestions." That is, you may never have to pay rack rates shown on an advertiser's published rate card. To start, there is the standard advertising-agency rate discount that amounts to 15%. The rate was initially set up to help advertisers offset the costs involved in producing the ads for the publication. It is a rare art-publishing company that hires an outside advertising firm.

Some publications, especially consumer magazines, balk at offering this discount to all but recognized agencies, which are those who are listed in some specific directory or other as an ad agency. This would be opposed to your in-house agency with no such listings – don't be dissuaded from getting this discount. If you are creating the ad materials and providing everything in the specified format that an ad agency would provide – whether that is digitally or in four-color separations with a proof –you should be entitled to the discount as a recognized ad agency.

When you see an advertiser's rate card, it is usually showing you what are known as gross rates. These rates are those before the 15% agency discount. When the rates are taken down by the 15%, they are called net rates. As an advertiser in a trade publication, always work your deals off the net rate, not the gross rate.

Although publishers try hard to price advertising fairly, or at least competitively, they rarely – if ever – have all their advertisers paying the same rate for their earned insertions. Earned insertions usually come in at 6, 12, 18, and 24-times within a 12-month period. Sometimes you'll see a 3-time rate. An "earned rate" means the advertiser has, for example, contracted to run 6-times over 12 consecutive months and thus has "earned" the 6-time rate.

The advertiser can choose the months in any sequence. For example, six ads might be run consecutively, or on two and off two, or every other month and so on. The sequence does not matter, as long as they meet the requirement to run the agreed number of ads during the contract period.

You also can combine a smaller sized ad with a larger one in the same issue and each would count the same towards your frequency discount. While it is not suggested to go that route unless it truly makes sense for you, it is worth knowing.

The point here is that it is your responsibility to negotiate the best rate possible. You should make an effort to get to know and develop a personal relationship with your rep. This can be advantageous to you in many ways.

Reps are in contact with many of your direct competitors. Although you cannot expect them to give away proprietary information, they are hearing and seeing things that would be helpful for you to know. Reps are aware of opportunities long before you will be, and they can help you in both tangible and intangible ways to improve your business. It is in their best interest for you to succeed, but they are the same as everyone else: they are more likely to go the extra mile for those with whom they are comfortable – so treat them right.

If you have a problem with the publication, reps are the ones you will turn to first to straighten things out. I used to tell advertisers that printers and dry cleaners are similar in that if you give them enough chances, they will eventually screw something up. For instance, your ad might be left out of the publication or might not appear in the promised spot. If you have a cordial relationship with your rep, you will get a better, quicker and likely more satisfying response than if you have an adversarial relationship. It just makes sense.

If you are a frequent advertiser, it ought to be worth a good meal now and then. Taking time over lunch or dinner is a great way to get to know someone and learn more about the plans of the publication and tradeshows. Sometimes a little insight can be used in very advantageous ways.

To some degree, ad reps serve two masters in that they advocate for you to help you get the most from your relationship with the publication but are also paid on commission; the more you spend, they more they make. Normal advertising commissions for independent reps run between 15 to

20% of the cost of whatever you are billed. Usually, they are paid between 5 to 10% for tradeshow space. The good ones are well compensated, which means you don't have to feel guilty about asking for their help to get a better rate.

While good independent magazine reps do make a decent income, keep in mind that they are not subsidized in any way by the publications they serve. Other than occasionally receiving comped rooms at shows and a few meals on the publisher's credit card, they pay all their expenses (including health, retirement, travel, mail, office, and phone, and so forth) to get the message to you and help the magazine stay viable. Reps who are actual employees of a publication are under different compensation but most are primarily paid on commission.

Having viable trade magazines should be important to you. They serve the purpose of educating your customers. By helping your customers become better and smarter operators of their businesses, they in turn help make them better customers for you. They help introduce new customers and prospects for you, and they act as the voice of the industry in trying times when leadership is required. If trade publications ceased to exist, your means of getting to market would be sorely hampered.

Reps are loyal to the publication because that relationship represents their livelihood, yet they must also be loyal to their advertisers because participation and timely payment fund their livelihood. Understanding that dynamic will be helpful to you in negotiating with them.

Remember, rarely does a rep have the ability to make deals beyond a certain point, (for example, by moving a 12-time schedule to the 18-time rate without management approval). And by asking them to help you negotiate and advocate a lower rate for your advertising, you are asking them to make less money. Therefore, having a good relationship with your rep and the magazine management is always going to help you get the best rate and deals on ancillary products.

I do not suggest opening with the following strategy. Nevertheless, if I felt I was not getting the best rate, I would use my hardest-nosed method of getting to the bottom line. That is where I would ask my rep to tell me straight forwardly what the best rate anyone running a similar schedule (for instance, a 6-times, full-page, four-color), is getting. If there is any hesitancy at all, ask them to put it into writing for you. Many people will shade the truth in conversation, but far fewer will do so in writing. That is an example of hard nosed negotiating and I would only resort to it if truly necessary.

The negotiation should work this way. You, my rep, are asking me to sign a contract to complete a certain number of ads at an agreed upon rate within 12 months of the first insertion. I agree to this request. In return, I am asking you to warrant in writing to me that I am not subsidizing anyone else's lower advertising rate for similar schedules by paying more than they are.

While negotiations can become contentious, if you have established a rapport with your rep that shows you are honorable and you will complete your contract and pay on time, they should be agreeable to making sure you are paying the lowest rate possible for your advertising.

Fair is fair, hence you must be aware there could be other considerations included in a company's ad rate structure. There could considerations such as the length of time a company has advertised and the amount of tradeshow space they take. It also might include their participation in other promotions, or the frequent availability of their ski chalet in Aspen (okay, that last one was there to test if you are paying attention).

If there are discrepancies that could cause another company with a comparable ad schedule to get a lower rate than yours, you should know what aspects outside their earned rate helped them lower theirs in order for you to make multi-year plans accordingly. Knowing the rules, implied and otherwise, will help make you a smarter marketer.

Multi-year advertisers are the norm in trade publishing. These companies don't continue out of undying loyalty to the publication or the personnel. They do it because it helps them achieve their marketing plan. You should be thinking as quickly as possible to move from stressing out over making the payments on your ad schedule for one year to how your advertising will affect your business over many years.

You can build your branding and results by using flights of ads (which are a sequence of ads, with each one building on the message of the previous.) Implementing a complex strategy can take years. You have a finite number of issues in any year to advertise in, even if you are in every publication, but thinking strategically for the long term and the short term will help you employ tactics you might not otherwise have even considered. Never be afraid to think in big terms or for longer than the next show season in conceptualizing and strategizing your ad campaigns.

While you may not be thinking in terms of decades for planning, keeping the thought you are in the game for five to ten years is appropriate. Learn to use long-range planning to help you build brand wealth and name integrity along with other suitable attributes to go along with your continuous efforts to build your dealer network through advertising.

You will find that many times publications will be looking to offer you deals on ancillary products in lieu of cutting your rate. Sometimes these will work well for you. The majority of them have a list, as mentioned above, of value-added items to offer advertisers. The list can range from preferential treatment in certain editorial or promotional features to links or banner ads on their website, access to their mailing lists, reduced rates or free ads in their tradeshow directories and more.

You should take advantage of all the value-added items available to you. As with publicity, you'll see that many of the smartest and best marketing companies are using everything at their disposal to help them get their messages out. The interesting thing about advertising in trade publications is that it levels the field. Your beautiful full-page ad can be just as effective as one from a multi-million publishing operation.

When you use this tremendous dynamic to leverage your position against much larger companies, and at the same time participate in all of the value-added and publicity available to you, you are creating a mass of impressions and upping your visibility to the highest possible point.

Tradeshows

Tradeshows are wonderful because they are tactile. You can see the print or poster, usually well framed and lit, in person. It makes a difference when potential buyers get to see your work and meet you in person. A problem with tradeshows is that they are infrequent. There are scant few good national opportunities for tradeshows each year – not to mention they are expensive to undertake.

In glory days past, there annually were a dozen or more tradeshows to consider for exhibiting. Now only ArtExpo New York and the West Coast Art and Frame Show Las Vegas remain from among them. Art Business News magazine has partnered with the promoters for the 2011 Toronto Art Expo show held in April. This show has been around for awhile.

Toronto is a great city to visit, but it is not New York and I do not expect this show to replace ArtExpo New York. This is true even should ArtExpo New York fail to produce in 2011 or beyond. The nature of the business, recent history, and a location out of the U.S. all stack the odds against this show gaining the traction it would need to supplant ArtExpo

The nature of the business is ever changing. Tradeshows and their players continue to come and go. Hobby Hill Publishing produces the West Coast Art & Frame Show [www.wcafshow.com] annually in January in Las Vegas. It also publishes Picture Framing Magazine [www.pictureframingmagazine.com] for the professional picture framing audience.

The WCAF Show is the only show in the Western states since both Decor Expo and ArtExpo have both abandoned the region. It continues to please art publishers as a viable venue to business, especially for those domiciled in the Western states.

The Decor Expo shows started life as the Art Buyers Caravan shows. There were as many as seven regional shows in addition to its two large concurrent New York shows, Galeria and Frame-o-rama. In what would have seemed impossible only a few years ago, there were no Decor Expo shows anywhere in 2009. In a return to its roots, the Decor Expo Atlanta show was scheduled to run concurrent and co-locate with the Atlanta Gift Show. Unfortunately, as stated above, this show was canceled a second year in a row in 2010. I do not expect it to return.

As with my advice on how to best go about trade advertising, it is tempting to leave out the following bits of wisdom about making the most of tradeshow exhibiting. And, the same conclusion comes to play here. That is the information is valuable on its own merit despite the downturn in importance for tradeshows. And, there is still useful information to be gleaned from perusing the advice below, and so I leave it in for your benefit.

When it comes to any of these tradeshows, there will be lots for you to learn. The more you know before you go to your first one, the better the experience will be for you. Attending one in advance is ideal. As a tradeshow representative, I used to poetically tell my first-time exhibitors that their experiences would be as valuable for what they learned as what they earned.

Naturally, most newbies exhibit with high hopes and anticipation of great things, but they are still unaware of the many nuances only experience can provide. Most had to go through the experience themselves to understand what my poetry meant.

At shows, you will find those around you with more experience can often become great resources and fountains of knowledge for you to tap. There are friendships to be made, too. Yes, you are all there to sell to the same people, but in this industry, you will encounter many decent, helpful people.

As you get involved in booking your own show space, you'll discover there is an art to finding the right location for your company in the show. Many companies have strong opinions about where those best places are. As a new company without standing, you will have to get used to working your way up the priority list; but it will greatly help your cause if you and your marketing people plan in advance to work hard at establishing a great relationship with the show management staff and, of course, your rep.

Booths are generally assigned according to point rankings with the shows in terms of years at the show, size of your booth, whether you advertise and how frequently. This means the companies with the most points get first dibs on the choicest spots. This is the law of the jungle at work, and presumably it is fair. Nevertheless, you'll always find examples of companies in good spaces that do not seem to fit the qualifying criteria. If you investigate, you'll often find they have established a positive working relationship with those people who are in a position to do them some good (their rep and the show staff) when an opportunity arises.

Shows are dynamic things and booth assignments are changed for lots of reasons. Sometimes spaces open up for you that are normally not be available to a newcomer. So your relationship with show staff and your booth space rep can help if you give them a chance and a reason. Work on gaining their friendship and their respect.

A word to the wise ... making unreasonable demands on the show staff is, in the long run, self-defeating. If you want people looking out for your best interests, being an overbearing customer is not the way to do it. You can be forceful and polite at the same time.

Having personally attended more shows (as a representative of the show management) than most people go to in a lifetime, and having experienced bad behavior by people under pressure for all kinds of reasons, I can testify it rarely pays off. It's true you catch more flies with honey than vinegar in life, and it's true in tradeshows for booth placement and having special favors granted.

Of course, budget concerns dictate how much you can do, and that is where the concept of setting realistic goals comes into play. You need to determine how much you can put into the business in terms of money and personnel time. This will give you the best chance to meet rationally set expectations.

When you establish unrealistic expectations because your heart overrules your head, you are setting yourself up for both headache and heartache. Don't do it! The best way to crush your business and your enthusiasm is to believe bigger things than possible are going to happen to you, because you are special, different, lucky, star-crossed or blessed. Once the art is created, it's all about the marketing and the budget, and how effectively and efficiently you allocate them.

Below is some advice proffered from my friend and former colleague, Kim Klatt. The list and information have been embellished by me. Kim has been a leading tradeshow sales rep for many years. His list of clients and contacts and industry experience is extensive. He is a great contact for any artist to have as a friend and colleague.

Detailed below is a three-step advice plan for tradeshow attendees. Many of these items are invaluable and worth noting, especially for those of you who are ready to embark on your first tradeshow:

1. Pre-Show Activities
2. At-Show Activities
3. Post-Show Activities

Pre-Show

- Determine your objectives for the show.
- Plan on-site sales.
- Develop sales leads.
- Introduce new releases.
- Grow existing accounts or open new ones.
- Network.
- Conduct market research.
- Begin image building.
- Make plans for "Show Specials."

Make action plans to help fulfill your objectives

- Plan and plot the layout of your booth before you leave.
- Be prepared for unexpected occurrences, and for things to take longer and be more expensive than you imagine.

Have a checklist for everything:

- business cards
- sales literature
- bags or Kraft paper for on-site sales
- office supplies (ink pens, stapler, staples, rubber bands, and so forth)
- file folders
- clipboards for order forms
- order forms
- tape and tape guns
- copies of your contract and all paperwork
- address book
- candy and candy bowl
- punch or fish bowl for drawing
- medications
- extra glasses or contacts

If you think you'll need it, take it, so as to not waste time and energy tracking stuff down at the show. This list could go on for pages; hopefully these items will start you thinking of what is important for you to bring to the show.

What do you want to communicate at the show?

- the uniqueness of your art
- marketing plans to assist new galleries
- new artists for the company
- new products or types of prints
- artists or images you plan to highlight at the show

What do you want to accomplish at the show?

- sales
- sales leads
- possible new artist contacts
- new vendors for framing supplies
- new printer contracts
- new sales reps
- new ideas for marketing and selling
- impressions and suggestions for new art trends
- industry information and developments

Pre-show promotions are crucial and add zest to your results

- Send important buyers and prospects slides, photos, and samples.
- Begin trade advertising two to three months prior.
- Drop direct mail two to four weeks prior.
- Begin publicity two to three months prior.

Reasons pre-show promotion and preparation is important

- Your best customers and prospects are gathering at one time; they need to know you will be there.
- Most seasoned attendees plan their show in advance with a specific agenda – and you want to be on it.
- Your prospects will need your booth number, and directions to the show if they are coming for the first time.
- You can create awareness for "Show Specials."
- You can let certain buyers know that you are holding "special" pieces for them to see.

At-Show

- Arrange your booth in an open, inviting fashion.
- Don't block openness of your booth by putting a table between you and customers.
- Be inviting; you want buyers in your booth, not in the aisle looking in.
- Creatively use as much space in your booth as possible without making it look cluttered.
- Don't be shy about excusing yourself from salespeople, other exhibitors or anyone else who has your attention to talk with buyers who enter your booth.
- Don't let boorish, overbearing people command your attention when other buyers are come into your booth.
- Be ready to easily capture contact information, name, address, phone and email.
- Give everybody something for giving you their information: mini-prints, note cards, free shipping on their first order after the show, or a one-time upgrade to overnight shipping for the price of ground delivery.
- Use whatever ideas you have to be creative and have fun with your customers and prospects.

Always arrive at your booth early

- Walk the show to see your competition.
- Check lights and everything else is okay.
- Make friends with exhibitors around you.
- Bring some snacks and drinking water with you.
- If it's cold/flu season, bring an antiseptic, waterless hand lotion with you.
- Make a point of introducing yourself to the show and magazine editorial staff; it may be your only chance to meet them face-to-face.

Reasons selling at show are different from elsewhere

- Visitors are bombarded with information in a short time frame.
- Visitors are talking with your competitors at the show.
- Visitors are tired.
- Visitors give you precious few minutes to capture their attention, as opposed to a 30 to 60-minute in-person sales call

Timing of the actual selling encounters in your booth

- Engagement of prospect: three seconds
- Prospect profile matching: 30 to 45 seconds
- Qualification of prospect's needs: three to six minutes
- Communicating your message and the next step: 60 seconds

Keeping buyers in booth and getting be-backs back

- Have extra clipboards with order form ready to give to buyers if you are busy – ask them to begin filling in their contact information and noting the pieces they like; it will help keep them from leaving
- Think about having an unannounced be-back offer – if a buyer says they will be back, give them an otherwise out-of-sight pre-printed "special" offer that describes your art, gives your booth number and is good during show hours.

Post-Show

Three "must do" post-show rules:

1. Follow up
2. Follow up
3. Follow up

Additional post-show activity

- Be prepared to immediately enter the names and addresses of all those prospects and customers you met at the show. If you can bring a laptop and do it during down hours at the show, you are ahead.
- Send everyone you met at the show a postcard, email or personal note to thank them for coming to your booth.
- Offer an extension on your "Show Specials" for an extra 30 days
- Call your hottest prospects instead of sending mail.
- Don't wait. Your competition is seasoned and they will be taking sales away from you if you don't follow up quickly.

Bonus points

- While looking good is important, strive to be stylish in comfort.
- Take a pair of comfortable shoes for each day, as each spreads pressure points and eases foot pain from long hours of walking and standing
- Plan in advance to have some fun in the city wherever you are. You never know for sure when you will be back.

Let's take a break to talk selling concepts for a moment. If you grasp and buy into this concept, there may be no better laboratory to refine it than a tradeshow where you get so much exposure in a short time.

Here is a quick take on how every prospective buyer can be classified into one of just three categories. On a percentile basis, it most often breaks into a 30-40-30 split.

1. The first 30% will buy from you with little incentive; they are already predisposed to your images. They are what are known as the low hanging fruit. You will never be successful if you only sell to these folks.
2. The second 40% is interested, but needs convincing and hand-holding. They could be trying to decide between your images and your competitors, or have other reasons for dawdling on the decision. If you master the art of selling to this crowd, I guarantee you will be successful. They hold the keys to your prosperity.
3. The final group is comprised of the 30% who will never buy from you for whatever reason. That's life; you can't win them all and shouldn't knock yourself out trying to convince these prospects to buy from you. The trick is to know when to give up on them.

As you learn to master how to effectively sell to the middle range buyers, you also will begin to have a feel for when to give up on buyers who are not good prospects. We discussed earlier how the big-box retailer, Best Buy, had changed its approach to concentrate on the customers who represent the best margins and profit and realized a dramatic increase in profitability in a short time as a result. By learning how to close, convert, recycle or discard these three types of buyers, your business can emulate the strategy of a billion-dollar merchant.

Building a Client Database

Your mailing list is your number one asset.
— Alyson Stanfield, the Art Biz Coach

The foundation of your career's long-term success requires you to build a client and prospect database. It is the single most important task you can undertake to foster your career growth. You must make it an ingrained habit to gather names and other contact details of those who not only purchased your art, but also those interested in your art.

I worked for a time in a gallery on Main Street in Scottsdale, Arizona, a retail fine art destination known worldwide. The gallery owner maintained her spot there for more than 30 years before retiring. One of the first things I learned was how important a viable mailing list was to the success of the business.

We mailed photographs of new works in the gallery to every person who had expressed an interest in a particular artist. It was eye-opening to learn how many first sales came anywhere from 6 to 18 months or longer after a prospect's initial visit. Had the gallery not been vigilant about accumulating names and regularly communicating with its customers, it would not have succeeded.

While getting a first sale is important, building repeat sales to the same collectors is how your business will grow. Top selling artists and galleries create repeat business by maintaining contact and building relationships. This only happens if you steadily work to stay in touch with your contacts.

Getting started

Everyone you know should be on your list, including business people with whom you do business. Do not make the mistake of pre-judging who will buy your art. The gallery mentioned above had typical well-heeled customers, but it also had some repeat buyers who did not fit the stereotypical art buyer. Your pest-control person, windshield-repairer or auto-repair mechanic can fall in love with your work and become a repeat buyer.

You have more potential prospects for you initial database than you realize. Here are some suggestions to help you get a list together.

- Business cards – have you kept a stack of cards but never gotten around to entering them?
- Business contacts – if you buy goods or services from someone, they should be on your list.
- Personal phone books – most people keep one in their kitchen or desk drawer.
- Sales book receipts – do you have records of all your sales where you hand wrote a receipt for a sale?
- Business directories – are you now, or have you been, the member of some business or social organization? Go through and find contact info for all the names you know in each.
- Former or current colleagues – if you or your family members are employed, use the employee directory to find those with whom you have personal relationship.
- Guest books – have you put out a guest or visitors' book at shows where exhibited or during studio visits?
- Correspondence, Christmas card lists – search your computer documents and any handwritten lists to find names.
- Class reunions – do you stay in touch with old school chums? Add them to the list.
- Email addresses – make sure you thoroughly go through all the names in your email client so you capture those names and addresses.
- Online sales receipts – if you have sold your work online, you should have a PayPal or other type of receipt from the transaction.

- Social networks – this includes friends and colleagues from both online and offline associations and networks.
- Many publications will rent you a list of their subscribers. Contact them directly to get more information.

It can be tempting to build a large group of artist friends. After all, it is true that birds of a feather do flock together. Some artists are art buyers, but as a group they will not buy enough to support your business. Instead, work to expand your network and client database beyond artists.

A word here on email lists. It is not correct, or even legal per Can-Spam laws, to add email addresses of people who have given you a business card at some point. Do the right thing, ask for permission to put them on your list. It may be smaller, but it will be more effective. If you are diligent, you quickly will grow your list the right way anyhow.

Business Software for Artists

If you are going to enjoy long-term success, you must maintain a customer database and an inventory database. There is no excuse. Powerful computers are dirt-cheap and there are excellent contact manager/ database programs to help you. Some are generic business tools; others are artist-specific business tools. No matter what program you choose, you need to get started using it now!

The days of getting by with a phone, a file drawer and a Rolodex are as gone as 8-track tape players. You need to invest in proper technology to help your business compete and grow. The time and money you invest in purchasing and learning technology will be paid back to you many times over.

Here are two lists of resources for you to check out. The links are provided for your ease in locating them.* You will need to do your own due diligence on deciding which programs will work best for you.

Software for Artists

Archer Artist .... www.archerartist.com

Art & Craft Business Organizer .... www.jaminmark.com/acbo

Art Tracker from Xanadu Gallery .... www.xanadugallery.com/ArtistSvcs/ArtTracker

ArtAffair Software .... www.artaffairsoftware.com

Artist's Butler 3.6 .... www.lynndavison.com/lynnsoft

Artlook Software for Artists .... www.artlooksoftware.com

ArtSystem for Artist Studios and Estates............ www.artsystems.com/solutions/studioestate.htm

Artworks Artist Software .... www.artworkspro.com

Bento .... www.filemaker.com/products/bento

eArtist v4.0.0.. www.artscope.net/eArtist

Flick! 4.0.2 .... www.arawak.com.au/flick.html

Gyst .... www.gyst-ink.com

VamP Visual Artist Management Project .... www.vam-p.net

Working Artist .... www.workingartist.com

General Contact Manager and Bookkeeping Software

ACT! .... www.act.com

Prophet.. www.avidian.com

Contact Plus .... www.contactplus.com

Microsoft Outlook...

Bento for Mac .... www.filemaker.com/products/bento

FileMaker Pro .... www.filemaker.com

QuickBooks .... www.quickbooks.com

OpenOffice.org .... www.openoffice.org

Software programs tend to come and go and the URL to reach them changes frequently. You will find the most up-to-date resources at www.ArtistBusinessGuide.com

168

If you are in the market for free software to compete with Microsoft Office, check out OpenOffice.org [www.openoffice.org]. It is an open, feature-rich, multi-platform office productivity suite. The user interface and functionality are similar to other products in the market, such as Microsoft Office or Lotus SmartSuite, but in contrast to these commercial products, OpenOffice.org is like the best things in life, free with no strings attached. The software has been downloaded by millions and has been translated into 30 different languages.

Consider this. According to the National Sales Association, sales occur in the sales cycle in this manner:

- 2% of sales are made on the first contact
- 3% of sales are made on the second contact
- 5% of sales are made on the third contact
- 10% of sales are made on the fourth contact
- 80% of sales are made on the fifth to the twelfth contact

When you grasp that repeated exposure to your targeted audience is your ticket to success, you will understand the importance of having a systematic means of gathering demographic information; e.g., name, email address, address, phone number, sex, age, et cetera. You may start with just the first two items and build on your database as contact with your customers grows.

When you create repeated exposure in an organized manner by consciously planning layers of marketing-message impressions on your audience, you give yourself the best options for creating customers.

Direct Mail and Promotional Material

While there is no arguing that modern life is awash in technology and the Internet has changed everything, you will find direct mail and printed promotional materials continue to prove their value to smart marketers. Some poster publishers who tried to avoid the heavy cost of printing their catalogs by moving everything to digital found their sales slipped dramatically as a result. They subsequently reverted to using a combination of both printed and digital promotional materials.

Direct mail is important, and you should have a system of capturing contact information and the capabilities of using that data to follow up with people and promote to them at appropriate times. This is a critical function, and the better the software and more thorough your follow through on building your customer and prospect files, the better and more effective a marketer you will become.

An excellent time to use direct mail is before trade shows. If you layer timely advertising, direct mail and publicity around your tradeshow exhibition, you give yourself maximum exposure to your primary buying audience at the right time. You want to get your advertising in at least one month before a major show and preferably two. Your direct mail should be timed to hit in two to three weeks before a show. If you have done your homework, you'll have all the publicity possibilities laid out on a matrix, so you will know when you need to get the materials sent out.

Postcards are a great way to affordably help kick off your direct mail program. There are companies that specialize in printing postcards at low costs. Some offer help with purchasing direct mail lists, although I am not sure this is an effective way for artists to gain clients unless the list is for galleries or dealers.

Postcards are one of the best and most affordable promotional tools for artists. Select one of your strongest works and make sure you get the highest quality photograph of it. You will want your name on the front of the card. Use a type font that makes it clear and easy to read how your name is spelled. When I see advertising or direct mail with the artist's name obliterated by some weird font or blend into the image color, it is just annoying because I easily want to know the artist's name.

If it makes sense from a graphic design perspective, include the title, medium and size in smaller print below your name on the front side. Otherwise, just use your name on the front.

On the reverse side, repeat your name in large letters, and beneath that list all your contact information, including phone, mailing address, and Facebook and Twitter links. If there is room, add a brief bio beneath the address and phone number. Check your specs to leave enough room for your mailing address, including the lower section where the post-office bar code will be added.

A solid lineup of print materials can go a long way to helping polish your image with prospective collectors and dealers. Like advertising, it is an equalizer. Your promo materials can be as impressive as those coming from a large corporation. When you use striking images in a professionally produced promotion, you will go a long way toward establishing your reputation with your best prospects.

Keep in mind that your patrons are not impressed much by your awards and gallery notices; they are more interested in you as a person and about your motivations for painting. Show your appreciation for your customers. Give them special insights, gifts or rewards. I remember reading about the artist Linda Blondheim, who sends tea bags, bird seed packets and recipes in her newsletter. She offers referral rewards and forwarding rewards in her subscriber newsletter.

Promotional material ranges from your business card to slick four-color brochures. Some of the most successful artists I know always have something on them to help promote their work. If nothing else, they have a business card printed in four-color with a signature piece of work on it. They are not afraid to use whatever they have with them to gain another interested prospect.

Everybody is a prospect. It is not your job to decide in advance who will and will not buy your art. Whenever you give a card, flyer, or other promotional item away, make sure you get contact information in return. You can offer in return to send a special price offer or a link to a non-public page where you have specialty items or whatever creative idea you come up with to position you and your art in the potential buyer's mind.

I was inspired by a company called MagCloud [www.magcloud.com] and wrote a blog post on Art Print Issues about it. You can use their program to create your own print-on-demand, four-color magazine. While it is not as inexpensive as a mass-run press, you can still use it to create a catalog, opening night presentation, gallery presentation or lots of other uses. Additionally, you when you create an issue, you can make it public so it will be available online for anyone to view and — if you choose —to order their own printed version.

A great use of direct mail is to regularly follow up on sales to buyers. This will keep your name in front of your collectors. Sending a "thank you" note as a post-sale follow up should be a ritual. Get it in the mail within a week of the sale. To make it personal, handwrite at least part of the note. You might include a postcard from a previous mailing or news clipping about you, or to invite them to subscribe to your blog.

Chapter Eleven
Publicity, Promotion and the Power of Self-Belief

There is no such thing as bad publicity except your own obituary.
— Brendan Behan (Irish author & dramatist)

Publicity and promotion are similar but unique activities. Publicity can be construed as primarily the act of gaining exposure in magazines, newspapers, websites and other media. Promotion would be personal appearances, giveaways, contests, et cetera.

When you combine the free publicity opportunities available from trade magazines and other traditional media, blend in direct mail with your advertising and tradeshow exhibits, and commit to some promotional activities, you are hitting on all cylinders.

The way to round out the efforts is to have a regular online presence in the form of social media, including a blog, a website, and regular email marketing to the names you have carefully opted into your list. We'll discuss these topics in the next two chapters.

Traditional publicity results from your effort to get something about you, your artwork or your company mentioned in an editorial feature in some form of media, such as magazines, newspapers, websites, television, radio and these days blogs and online sites devoted to art and artists. While success in this area is critically important for you in creating awareness and synergizing with your other marketing efforts, personal branding is an equally important aspect to profiting from publicity.

If you are an introvert, the suggestion of personal branding might not be your fondest desire, because it means you must become "the brand." That is, your name becomes branded to a look and style that is unmistakably yours. To a degree, it is building on the cult of personality that is pervasive in our culture. The quote below from Steve Hanks, a decades-long successful limited edition artist sums it up:

I used to think if the art was good it would sell itself. Then I worked and starved for 15 years, and I realized that today's art business is about selling your name.

What Does "Selling Out" Mean?

Selling your name is not selling out. And, by the way, what is selling out anyway? Does it mean you do ignoble acts in order to earn crass dollars to feed your family, enjoy your life and possibly do good works with your renown and excess cash?

I think not. To those who would make such statements, I advise them to listen to this refrain from Bob Dylan's "Positively 4th Street." It was written in response to the former friends who turned on him when he plugged for an electric guitar set at the Newport Folk Festival. It was considered a downright revolutionary doublecross in the eyes of the hidebound traditionalists who had come to embrace him as one who would take their movement forward and intact:

> I wish that for just one time,
> You could stand inside my shoes,
> And just for that one moment I could be you.
> Yes, I wish that for just one time,
> You could stand inside my shoes,
> You'd know what a drag it is,
> To see you

I'm never sure how much is plain jealousy or misplaced good intentions when I hear remarks about someone having "sold out." I would love to see the contract they signed when they did. And, even more, I would love to know what Faustian devil they were with when they wrote it.

Did Elvis sell out when he became a lounge act in Vegas? Or was it much sooner, when he traded being a rock n' roll pioneer for being a movie star matinee idol? Was it his job to defend some high ground for rock n' roll's elite? Who makes up these rules?

More on Dylan, he rejected the notion that he was the "Chosen One" or the "Voice of His Generation" or many other unwanted labels people and even old friends and lovers, including Joan Baez, desperately tried to foist upon him. In his 2005 television interview, the first in 19 years, he told Ed Bradley of "60 Minutes" that, as a new young artist, he did not aspire to be anybody's Messiah — except perhaps to be Elvis, but that was the extent of his longing for fame.

When Ed Bradley mentioned that Dylan's song "Like a Rolling Stone" was named the best song of a list of 500 compiled by Rolling Stone magazine and asked if he was honored, Dylan nonchalantly replied, "Yeah," and agreed it was okay to get the notoriety. Bradley pressed him to admit it was an honor, and Dylan agreed with a wry smile and said, "This week." Clearly, he was indicating he knows current tastes are fickle and history is long, and that he isn't concerned with what today's pundits make of his body of work this week.

Likewise, you shouldn't be worried about critics either. In the end, you can only be true to yourself, and if you are genuine in that, it will be abundantly clear to those who want to own a piece of your art. If it happens that thousands of people respond to your creative vision and willingly pay money to make it part of their lives, then you can be proud of your achievements, despite what any critic might have to say about it. Perhaps Frank Sinatra had the best take on critics with this famous quote, "Living well is the best revenge." Henry Ford II, the grandson of automobile magnate Henry Ford, put it this way, "Don't explain; don't complain."

I had more to say about this in my Art Print Issues blog where I penned this post: "The Double Entendre of the Artist Selling Out." It was a tongue-in-cheek look at how we celebrate an artist with "sold out" editions on one hand and think it is crass for an artist to have commercial success on the other. Go figure.

Regarding publicity, I suggest you incorporate branding your name into your marketing and particularly into your promotional efforts. It will give you vastly increased success in selling your art.

For Picasso, the bigger the better

A story that sheds light on how thinking big and promotionally was in the mind of the most famous painter of the 20th century, Pablo Picasso, was related to me by Vince Fazio, Director of Education at the Sedona Arts Center [www.sedonaartscenter.com] where I gave my first live workshop. Coincidentally, my speaker notes from that six-hour presentation formed the basis for the first edition of this book.

As Vince related, a young painter had become acquainted with Picasso and made repeated requests for the great master to come and view and comment on his work. Eventually, Picasso granted him the wish. After taking considerable time in studying the young painter's work without saying a word, he finally spoke. His simple and succinct advice was this: "Sign your name larger."

You will note you never have to look to find a signature on a piece by Picasso. Why? He understood the power of his name. He might never have had a conversation with anyone about branding, but he knew – perhaps through instinctive genius or maybe through crafty wiliness – that to take pride in promoting his name would always work in his favor.

There is an interesting book on publicity and promotion called, Get Slightly Famous: Become a Celebrity in Your Field and Attract More Business with Less Effort by Steven Van Yoder. Although it is not written for artists, it contains many great examples of how people with certain knowledge and skills can use them to promote themselves.

Know Your Industry and the Media It Supports

Although I have mentioned this earlier, it bears repeating: you need to be a student of your competition and of your industry. You also should become a student of the various trade and consumer publications serving the art market. Become a subscriber of all the industry trade publications immediately! Do it now! A list of their websites can be found in the "Resources" section of this book.

You need to learn and understand what trade magazines offer their readers and advertisers, and how they differ from each other. Find out everything about the free publicity opportunities magazines provide artists and publishers. Keep in mind that you don't have to be doing business with these magazines to be mentioned in their publicity columns, but it doesn't hurt either.

Traditional media also produces publicity in the form of free promotional editorials for advertisers. Make sure you are aware of any offerings and what their deadlines are. You can't count on your rep to always look out for your best interest with regard to you submitting your PR in a timely manner. Ultimately, you need to learn to take advantage of all they offer – make it your responsibility.

You can magnify your marketing by mixing in an effective publicity campaign. For example, if you start with a schedule of six ads to run over a 12-month period, and you diligently apply yourself to use every publicity opportunity every publication offers, you can easily double or even triple the number of exposures you will have to the market in that same time period.

Say It, Say It Again; Rinse and Repeat

Steady frequent exposure is a key ingredient to success in this game. As you should already know by now, you are in the business of building a dealer network and a fan base one at a time, and your combined online presence, consumer and trade advertising, publicity, and tradeshow activity are the primary ways you will use to begin to make inroads with the established buying habits of dealers and collectors.

According to an article in the Los Angeles Times Magazine, Howard Fox, the curator of the Los Angeles County Art Museum, annually attends hundreds of exhibitions and visits 50 to 60 galleries regularly. He also gets letters, emails, slides and invitations to shows and to view websites.

Fox says he finds the incredible velocity and volume of the offerings makes it very difficult for the unknown artist to stand out with him. He believes what it takes, besides talent, is the slow steady drip of frequent exposure to make a lasting impression. Working to master the art of publicity will be a huge help to you in keeping frequent mention of your name in appropriate media.

While we are admittedly comparing getting the attention of one curator to thousands of art dealers, the process still is the same. The steady, methodical, patient application of every means possible to put one's message in front of a buying influence – drip, drip, drip away – will lead you to success. Water will carve stone if it drips enough in the same place.

In magazines, the names of the columns change, as do those of the editors responsible for writing them, so often that it can drive you crazy keeping up. By comparison, imagine how hard you will work to build an ad or get ready for a trade show to working on PR. You need to stay focused on being abreast of changes and publicity opportunities.

Actively seeking publicity is not just one more thing to put on your plate; it is an important component of your whole marketing strategy and – unlike everything else you do in that strategy – it's free, aside from the time and effort required. Working hard at publicity is a prime example of how an organized, driven marketing person can use the tools available to gain a competitive advantage over those who don't get it, or who get it and just don't do it.

It is a smart idea to cultivate relationships with the editors of the trade publications. You'd be surprised at how few of your competitors make the effort. To this, I say ... duh! You should be thanking them; their lack of foresight or their laziness helps you garner more attention from an activity that requires a small effort for a potentially large return. Having editorial personnel become aware of your company will invariably lead to more publicity for you; why wouldn't you do it?

Considerately approach your editors. Find out what shows they are attending. Ask for a meeting if you are going to be there too. Let them know you respect their time, and inquire of them how they prefer to receive materials, what their timeline and deadlines are, and ask for suggestions to help you maximize your publicity opportunities.

Do this, and you will have far more success than the average company that drops something in the mail or sends in unsolicited email. Ask your editors if there are story ideas you might be considered for; do your digging, and keep it professional and courteous to get the best results. Find out how you can help them. Offer to provide artwork to fulfill a publication's need for images and graphics. If it is appropriate, ask if there are opportunities to contribute articles to the publication.

If you are seeing a repeat pattern of suggestions to befriend reps, show staff, management and editorial people here, you are right. This advice comes from years of observation about what worked best for those companies and individuals who wrung every possible positive offering from shows, editors and magazines. Because they worked as hard at building good relationships with people who could help them, they received far more in return.

Effective Publicity Starts With Setting Goals

Before beginning a PR campaign, you must determine your goal. Getting publicity is a good thing alone, but getting publicity in the right media, for the right reasons, is a wonderful thing. Wasting time chasing the wrong media with the wrong goals is disheartening.

Your goal could be to become better known within the industry or in some segment of it. Or it could be to become better known locally, regionally or nationally. It might be any combination of these segments. Still, it could be something completely different. Regardless, it must suit you and your needs. The more ambitious the goal, the more planning and brainstorming it will take to pull it off.

Naturally, you have other goals for your art business. We discussed a mission statement in the first chapter. Having a goal for your PR campaign is an offshoot from it. Whenever you have a goal, it gives you a means of incrementally breaking down the steps so you can understand how to attack it methodically.

Do You Need to Target Consumer Media, Specialty Media or Trade Media?

There are consumer general media and specialty or vertical consumer media, and also trade media. One can target all three if you are ambitious, organized and energetic enough to manage it. I reiterate: becoming a student of the business you want to conquer is imperative. Studying the media that serves our industry is different from simply reading it; it means paying attention to the advertising, features and publicity opportunities in them.

Study an ad and ask what the advertiser is trying to do and how effective you think it is towards that goal. You will want to make mental, if not physical, notes of the subject matter, medium, size, color, prices and other invaluable data you can glean from the advertisements and from the feature articles and editorial or publicity columns. This is a great use of creating a SWIPE file, i.e., keeping copies of items you will refer to when creating your own campaign.

Study current and back issues thoroughly, making a concerted effort to understand what is going on with them – especially with their PR columns and features. Take the time to note the names of the editorial staff, the columns they write or the beats they cover. You will find that being conversant about a person's work open doors for you. Editors are always busy, but the right approach is the best way for you to win time with them. When you can talk to someone about their previous work, you will get their attention quicker and with more authority.

There is a host of specialty consumer magazines targeting the art market; you need to spend some time at the library or at a good magazine store or Borders to study which of these might be appropriate for you. The bulk of them focus on original work as opposed to reproductions, which makes them less viable targets for you. While top-shelf, glossy consumer-art magazines may be out of the range of most artists, there will always be some who ignore the obvious, forge ahead, and get noticed as a result.

Part of the art of shameless self-promotion is to never be shy or afraid to tackle what others consider impossible. It is always free to ask; and if done politely and professionally, there virtually is no downside to taking action. As hockey-great Wayne Gretzky says, "You miss one hundred percent of the shots you don't take."

Sometimes the neophyte blindly charging in where others fear to dare is the one who gains access to things considered out of reach by those who study and think too hard before acting. Carrying the hockey analogy further, the highest percentage shots are the ones with the best angle to the goal.

The trade magazines no longer have the pull they once did, and the audience they serve is much smaller and more finicky; nonetheless, they are still important and worth studying to learn what publicity opportunities they offer to artists. You will be surprised at what is possible with a diligent and respectful campaign to get your items published in these publications.

If you can afford advertising in them, do it. It's good for the magazines that serve the industry, and the added visibility will give your publicity more credibility and punch – and vice versa. Despite all that has gone on and changed within the industry, I still see new advertisers committing serious financing to building awareness using trade media.

If you want to target consumer media, whether print, radio or television, you have to stand out from the crowd. There are so many media outlets today that it is a constant chore for them to find suitable content, which makes them open to consideration of your ideas. Competition for content aside, practically all media seeks the unique – and often something that has an angle with a human interest perspective. A charitable component is always a booster. Having an interesting story with a do good angle included is sure to give you a leg up.

Getting Back to Goal Setting

How about making a goal to get x-number of national trade media placements, x-number of local media placements and x-number of regional media placements in for the next 12 months? Success starts with planning and persistence. Make a reasonable, achievable plan and break down the steps necessary to turn the plan into action. Be realistic. Taking on more than you can reasonably handle is a prescription for losing patience before you succeed.

Some media, such as trade publications, are easier to deal with and have shorter deadlines than consumer print magazines. Others, such as national consumer magazines, work many months in advance on publicity. Newspapers work on shorter deadlines. Local broadcast media often works only a couple of weeks in advance for many stories. The proliferating decorating shows on cable also are worthy targets. Although I do not know their typical deadlines, I assume they also need months of advance in planning their content.

Any and all of these are great targets, especially if you weave a cohesive plan to work in as many as make sense to create synergy and momentum together. I reiterate, to find ideas, you have to train yourself to read and review the newspaper and magazines and other media – not for entertainment or information, but as sources. When you see an item of interest, even those things not art related, ask yourself what you would need to do to emulate it, do it better, or put yourself in a position to be involved.

As a Visual Artist, Are You Press-Release Worthy?

Stop now! Think back to what your immediate reaction to the above question was. Examining your self-perception and reaction should be quite insightful to you.

There is no wrong answer.

There are just three basic ways to respond:

1.   You immediately agreed you were press release worthy.
2.   You stopped to assess if you were worthy.
3.   You instinctively felt you were not doing anything to make you press release worthy.

How you perceive yourself is one aspect of this challenge. In addition, your concept of the value of a press release and what they do could easily color your decision. There is little training for visual artists on how to use a press release or what value they might derive from them. This lack of understanding could easily cause the activity to be filed away as intimidating, mysterious, or bothersome.

While you are a product of many things, your self-perception is your choice. If you believe you are press release worthy, good for you. It shows a confidence and self-awareness that helps you in other aspects of your career. Having a healthy ego is a good thing for artists. It's much easier to convince others about the value of your work if your persona portrays confidence and self-esteem. Our society might root for the underdogs, but we buy the winners.

In social settings, we all have radar for how someone feels about themselves. The manner of how self-perception is expressed doesn't matter. We read the person and evaluate them on the subtle clues we observe. Does the person come off as elitist, competent, confident, shy, meek or brash? Your experience, tools and own biases are always in use when you meet someone new, and you never fail to evaluate.

There is practically no reason for any artist not to be press release worthy. If you thought you were not, or were not sure, I hope to help you change that perception. It will come in learning more about how press releases work, what their real value is, and how to get a good one written and submitted. I believe it will be a confidence booster for you when you come to realize you are press release worthy.

After all, what would be the point of going through the motions to prepare for publicity if one lacked conviction or confidence in creating and distributing a press release? I trust you realize you need not be a famous artist to be press release worthy. You just have to have something interesting and viable to publicize.

Analyze who you are, what you do or what you might be interested in doing? Here are some angles to consider. Ask yourself, have you:

- created a thematic body of work that would grab the interest of local or regional media?
- published new work?
- been picked up by a gallery?
- been commissioned to work on an important piece?
- moved your studio or hired an assistant?
- started a blog or revamped your website?
- been asked to demonstrate or speak at a meeting?
- had a piece selected for a prestigious juried show?
- have won an award at a juried show?
- had a well-known person purchase your art?
- had a piece go into a collection or museum?
- decided to exhibit at a tradeshow or consumer show?
- been interviewed on TV, radio, magazine or newspaper?
- been picked up by a licensing company?

- donated a piece for a charitable organization?
- painted a piece for a wine label?
- joined a prestigious art group?
- taken an artist retreat in an interesting place?

These are just examples; you'll need to plumb your own situation to find what works for you. Some of them could be joined, and nearly all could be expanded upon.

Start a SWIPE File: Build a Media Contacts Database

I have already mentioned the idea of a SWIPE file. I should tell you I swiped the idea from a graphic designer who sells Photoshop tricks and who is not shy about grabbing inspiration where he can. As he promotes the idea to is customers, so do I proliferate the notion here.

There is nothing wrong with creative borrowing. When you read anything, keep your mind open to possible PR opportunities. Make a note, put it on your brain, tear out the article and put it in your "Ideas" or "SWIPE" file. The important thing is to tune into what and where the possibilities are and then be organized to make sure you can retrieve the information when needed. The more ways you find to use publicity, the more effective your efforts will be.

Begin building a database of potential prospects to send press releases. This information resource, if carefully constructed, can turn into one of your most valuable marketing tools. If you see an article with a byline, drop a note to the author with a quick sincere compliment. If it is a blog article or online article and you can comment, jump in with something short and sweet. Resist the temptation to use these contacts as an opportunity to promote yourself. Save that for when you have something important to tell the world about.

However you do it, getting all those prospective names in some form of a contact manager will be crucial in your long-term publicity efforts. Make sure you keep good files on everything you submit as well. Maintain a copy of the best pieces to provide to galleries and dealers to help them in their marketing efforts, while keeping separate everything you have submitted or have gotten press on, either in a paper file or electronic file. From websites, save paper and print the pages as PDF files to save in an appropriate folder.

If you have a website, you can setup a private area and use "no follow" robot.txt instructions to keep it from being indexed by search engines. That way you can provide a link to those pages without having to password protect them. In the private area, you can provide images, logos, bios, links and other useful tools for journalists to use in writing about you.

New rules for press releases keep them in style

The press release has been the mainstay of the public relations professionals. Today, smart marketers are finding new ways to use it and to make sure it is as useful as ever. Typically, highly formatted press releases are distributed to promote a company's story to the media. The idea is that the release will catch a journalist's eye and create interest to become mentioned in an article or interview.

While press releases are still cranked out by PR firms, they are not the lifeblood for journalists seeking story ideas. As such, their impact has been lessened. What you find now is that press releases are used in a new way for companies to communicate with their customers, prospects and the media.

If you ask journalists how they get story ideas, you will find they use the Internet for as their primary resource. They information they gather online forms the basis for articles, interviews and quotes. Understanding this new use, smart marketers now write using search-engine-optimization (SEO) techniques to help them craft their press releases. You can use this approach to entice the media to tell your story with the important side benefit of enhanced Web presence.

Formerly, press releases were edited just for journalists. Now, press releases are used by savvy publicity professionals to attract both buyers and journalists. The object is just as much for buyers to find your press release online and click through to your website as it is for the media to pick up your story. The beauty of this purpose is that a buyer can find your art and buy it, or contact you, without your press release being published.

In the past, press releases were only used to disseminate newsworthy stories for the sole purpose of gaining media interest. As with so many other things, the Internet has disrupted the old way of doing things. The rules for press releases have changed, and these days seeing one get to press purely is a bonus. Today's press releases can work wonders for you without media coverage.

As a result of the new rules, you are no longer limited to:

- writing formulaic press releases with the "who, what, when, where and why" information up front.
- keeping to a 300-word length when 500 words works better.
- just measuring media response when finding buyers is equally as – or more – important.

Search Engine Optimization (SEO) Techniques Increases Results

One thing that has never changed when it comes to press releases is that quality content is critical. You always will need to focus on creating quality content and also employ solid SEO techniques to ensure search engines will pick up on the release.

When you properly optimize your press release, you seek to get higher page ranking results in search engines, with page one as your ultimate goal. By including the keywords and keyword phrases focused on your art, yourself as an artist and your art publishing business, you often get page one search results for very little cost.

For more effective use of your resources, and quicker results, your efforts to achieve page-one ranking should focus on long-tail keyword phrases. These phrases use three or more words in a search term. While they do not return the most results, by being specific they are more likely to convert to sales.

The reason long-tail keywords are more effective is because when a searcher is being specific, they know exactly what they want. For example, searching for "art prints" will generate millions of responses, while querying "pet art prints Collies Houston" will generate a few thousand results. Another press release SEO benefit is you are more likely to attain natural back-links from organizations within your own industry, Such links are the sort search engines highly value, especially when the link comes from a website with a higher page rank than yours.

SEO tips to get the best results:

- Gather your list of important keywords, phrases and long-tail keywords in advance. Google's keyword tool will also work [www.google.com/sktool].

- If possible, include your most important phrase into your title and subtitle and throughout the release using natural unforced language.
- Repost the press release content to a page on your site.
- Include links to social bookmarking sites to make it easy to bookmark your release.
- Always use a keyword phrase instead of "click here" or other generic terms when you link to your site.
- If you have a blog and website, make sure you include links to both – or better, to specific pages on them – using keyword phrases.

Common sense, courtesy and conformity are required

You still need to abide by common sense and established patterns of press release usage. These include:

- Covering the most important details in the first paragraph.
- Keep it short: aim for somewhere around 500 words tops.
- Use strong keywords in titles and subtitles.
- Offer quotes from customers or executives in third-person.
- Conclude with a brief paragraph about your company with contact information.

There are numerous sources on the Internet for help on how to write a press release. You just need to search for "press release examples" or "press release tips" to find links to sites designed to help you. Once you have completed and submitted your site, keep in mind that while a call from a major news source would be thrilling, it is not necessary to the success of your press release.

Many press release services will write your press release for you, for a fee. Alternatively, you can use a proofreading and editing service such as Gramlee [www.gramlee.com]. I have personally used this service with great satisfaction. Go to the site and buy a designated amount of words, submit your copy, and usually within 24 hours you get back a professionally edited version for your use. If your English writing skills are poor, or if English is your second language, then this service or another like it will be invaluable affordable tool for you.

Search and you will find numerous press release distribution services available, such as PRNewswire, MarketWire, and BusinessWire. Personally, I have always used PRWeb.com and believe it to be the best for small businesses. For the basic $80 fee, PRWeb distributes your press release to thousands of journalists. Its Online Visibility Engine tool does many of the SEO tasks for you and includes social media publicity as well. Buying in at the $80 level assures that your release makes it to Google and Yahoo News.

There are other paid services available; E-releases [www.ereleases.com] is just one example. For $399, it will submit your press release to its extensive database of newspapers and magazines, plus you can pick two categories from its list of industry specific outlets, which consists of trade publications. Its art category currently lists 71 organizations on the submission list. For $599, it will write your press release (up to 500 words) and do the submissions as well.

As a site dedicated to artists, Art Deadline [www.artdeadline.com] has an extensive media database and also offers members PR services. You can sign up for its free newsletter and get some of the current deadlines available emailed to you monthly, or you can a take subscription and enjoy access to all its resources. For the print-on-demand community, Fine Art America, also offers press release services for artist members on its site: http://fineartamerica.com/aboutpressreleases.html

Some other things to consider regarding publicity are as follows:

- Effectively and properly applied, publicity will pay greater dollar-for-dollar dividends than any other marketing activity in terms of recognition, because of the power of third party influence.
- Don't overlook it even if you are busy; it's too important.
- From the onset, budget for someone to do it for you as part of his or her job function while you work on your business plan.
- Hire a good public relations (PR) firm or publicist with art experience, if you can afford one.
- As an artist, get to personally know editors and publishers, even if your PR person already has a relationship with them – that PR person might leave, but you will still be there.
- Publicity is more important at higher price points, but should never be left off any marketing plan

The Power of Self-Belief

When it comes to being successful, having the power of self-belief cannot be overstated. I am talking about neither egomaniacs nor the self-delusional here, both of which are plainly obvious to the average person. What I am talking about is a grounded belief in one's own talent.

I wrote this Art Print Issues blog post, "The Power of Believing in Yourself," and its message remains current.

> You are an artist. You chose to be an artist. You desire to achieve success as an artist. I've said it many times before: if the fire in your belly is real, then it is as likely art chose you as much as you chose it. Meaning, you are not going to be satisfied doing anything else or settling for less than the best you can do.
>
> The arts are full of hungry, ambitious, talented people. It is not easy to get your share of success. Certainly, no one is going to hand anything to you. You have to go out there and get it, and you have to keep after it when you hit the hard spots and obstacles that end many careers. It can be especially tough when others who ought to know fail to recognize the depth of your talent.
>
> Musician Chris Daughtry is a perfect example of the power of believing in one's self and persevering against the odds. His eponymous debut album, DAUGHTRY, stormed the charts to become the quickest selling rock debut in Soundscan history. DAUGHTRY became the #1 top selling album in the country – not once, but twice – after debuting at #2 in November, 2006 and moving upwards of 300,000 copies in the first week alone. After more than a year on the charts, it remained highly ranked on the Billboard 100 chart. In a further testament from his peers, he received four Grammy nominations for the 2008 awards show.
>
> So how does his success as a musician relate to visual artists? Glad you asked. The short answer is, a lot. And you don't have to be rock music fan to appreciate how it applies.
>
> Daughtry caught his break by being a consistent loser. The thing is, he never gave up on his dream to be a successful recording artist. True enough, he managed to make it on the roster of American Idol, the

juggernaut reality-show singing contest that catapulted him to fame. But he was sent packing in fourth place.

American Idol was not the first time Daughtry had attempted to break his career through a reality show. In a testament to his belief in himself, he also auditioned for a summer fill-in CBS reality show titled Rock Star INXS.

In that effort, he failed to make the cut to be one of the singers on the televised version of the show. In other words, the professionals whose job it is to evaluate talent completely missed the call on him. In the end, it was the judges who failed, not Daughtry. But, can you imagine how much belief in himself he must have had to pick himself up after that experience and soldier through the grueling rounds of auditions that those who make it to the American Idol stage are put through.

At any time, no one would have blamed him for going back home to his family and his mundane job as a service writer at an auto dealer. Undeterred, he kept after his dream and pursued it when it would have easy enough to tell himself he had his shot and didn't make it. That Chris Daughtry has talent to go with his drive and determination is also a key factor. American Idol makes comical fodder of the self-delusional wannabes who are clueless to the fact they have no talent; some repeat year after year in a vicious cycle of crushing failure. Often they are supported by equally delusional family and friends.

It is quite important to get independent assessment and take consistent reality checks to assess your ability and progress; and well-meaning family and friends are often not able to objectively help. But, as Daughtry has proved, in the end you have to trust your own instincts to keep going when lesser people would have long ago folded their tent and gone home, and when those around you are trying to ease you off or demand you give up your dreams. If you have that burning hell-or-high-water desire, I don't need to tell you to not let them steer you away. As I said earlier, art chose you, and part of that choice is pushing for success – often against the odds.

Any of us who are seeking more from our careers can take a clue from Daughtry. He obviously had the talent to make a crack album with a bunch of solid hits on it, but, those gatekeepers weren't giving him the chance. He was measured and marginalized by those who should have known better.

If you are having trouble getting juried shows, galleries or publishers to see the talent and uniqueness of your art, don't give in to despair. Don't let the naysayers deter you. If you know in your heart and head that you have talent that needs recognition, fight for it and don't let up. Perhaps putting on DAUGHTRY for a listen to remind you of what is possible when you put the power of believing in yourself in full motion.

Daughtry's story is outsized in that his success is well documented and easily accessible. You do not have to find outsized success as a byproduct of believing in yourself, but I know whatever success you achieve will be greatly enhanced by it.

Using the Power of Word-of-Mouth Marketing

In the past few years, more and more marketers have come to realize how potent word-of-mouth marketing can be towards creating awareness and influencing sales of their products. As an example, many large corporations and well-known brands have joined WOMMA, the Word of Mouth Marketing Association, in an effort to help them understand how to capitalize on what is sometimes called "water cooler" conversations. It also helps them with measuring their returns on their social media schemes.

A better fit for readers of this book would be the Society for Word of Mouth [theswom.org]. Its stated mission is to help people build word of mouth into the DNA of their organizations using social media. The organization offers lots of advice and support for its members. I think it would be perfect for local artists groups or co-ops to help them market using word-of-mouth techniques.

Another blog post I wrote fits into the concept of word of mouth in slightly different way. It is titled "Six Degrees of You." If you have heard of "Six Degrees of Kevin Bacon," you need no introduction to the concept. Here is an edited version of the post:

The parlor game, Six Degrees of Kevin Bacon, spawned all manner of conversational tidbits and even a humorous television commercial for the Visa check card. I recommend you put its power to work for you!

Those who can best help you are closer to you than you think

A slide from my "live" workshops is "Six Degrees of You." Essentially, I have been conjecturing that you are only six contacts away from anyone in the world. I was using a form of "blink" intuition to make that assumption. It is the gist of bestselling author, Malcolm Gladwell's book, Blink: The Power of Thinking without Thinking. That I was right has been proven by Microsoft researchers when they announced they had found the average to be 6.6 degrees of separation of anyone one person from another.

My point was that there are people close by who can help you greatly, some available just for the asking. Others may require some schmoozing to get what you want, and some will snub you and you will never know why. As an art marketer, one of your top priorities ought to be compiling a list of those people who are in the best position to help you advance your career. The second part of that task is to use Six Degrees of You to seek them out.

The final part is to know exactly what you want from them, how to succinctly ask them for it, and how to eloquently provide the features, advantages and benefits of why they should help you. It's no different than making a pitch to a private investor. Just know what you want and why, and know what's in it for the other guy. In the case of those higher ups you ask, it might be noblesse oblige, or it could be to return a favor, or it might be a way to demonstrate and exercise their personal power. Their motivation only matters insofar as it might help you on how to best present your suggestion for help.

If this sounds like a lot of work and bother, you are right. But when it comes to return on investment, only well-done publicity comes close to offering you as similarly rich a payoff as does using the personal power of influential people.

If you are focused, ambitious and believe in yourself, nothing can stop you. If I am anything, I am a realist. I know suggestions like this are much more complicated to put to use than they are to talk about or think about. Still, when you think about how just one, two or three powerful people can make an enormous difference in your career, what reason do you have to not professionally pursue them?

Compared to how much effort and expense you put into preparing for a consumer- or trade-show, or into an advertising campaign, it is really not that daunting. The hardest part for some readers may be convincing themselves they are worthy of the desired attention. If that rings true for you, then reread my post included in this chapter on "The Power of Believing in Yourself" and look for ways to improve your self-esteem.

To help you with the elevator speech you should have memorized (so you can easily and glibly respond to, "What do you do?" and "What do you want?") try the 15 Second Pitch site [www.15secondpitch.com]. It's free, and it works!

There is real value in being able to quickly and pointedly tell others about yourself. Of course, you will need to be able to elaborate, but having a great opening statement or answer to a question about what you do will help you grow your confidence and lay the groundwork for the more meaningful discussion that will lead to selling your art.

One last suggestion for spreading your influence and awareness is public speaking. If you are the sort who freezes or breaks into a cold sweat at the thought of getting in front of others to speak, then either pass on the suggestion or join a group such as Toastmasters to help you overcome your fears.

Naturally, if you can talk about your work in front of groups in a thoughtful, enlightening and entertaining manner, that would be great for you. The problem is that when you and your art are your only subject you will have limited opportunities to speak. I suggest you become an expert on something of interest to you that you can talk about in speeches to others.

Get to know the art history of your city, state or region. If you have a famous artist from your area, study him or her until you can talk for an hour about them. It could even be about some famous generous benefactor to the arts, or someone who is not local or regional to you. If you decided to talk about the influence of the Saatchi brothers or Eli Broad on modern art, I bet you could find regular venues to offer your speech.

The promotional material released from your speeches will also have to mention you are a local fine artist with your blog and website addresses. You get to be an expert, a local celebrity of sorts, drive traffic to your site and build important back links to it, all in one cause. As with so many other items we talk about in this book, this is another way to help lay a foundation and add those collectors and dealers one at a time in the process.

Chapter Twelve
Websites for Artists

The debate is over. Artists and other small business people should no longer be debating whether having a website is necessary. Today, when 75% of the U.S. population has Internet access, it is not an option. You need to be onboard and represented online.

Like it or not, the Internet has caused all manner of artists to reconsider how they get the product of their creation to market. In this book's first edition, I mentioned how the artist formerly known as Prince signaled a change. To some, it seemed a defiant act of career suicide when he abandoned traditional distribution channels – i.e., recording labels and music retailers– in favor of selling direct to his faithful fans through his website. It turned out to be such a great move for him that he eventually became "Prince" again.

Fast forward a few years and you find him giving away millions of copies of his CD in advance of a series of concerts in London. He knew he would gain enough fans and sell enough tickets to more than cover the cost. The publicity alone was worth incalculable millions.

Giving It Away and Getting It Back

The marketing tactics used by Prince and other artists who used the Internet to reach their fans are worth noting. The Grateful Dead are the most downloaded and traded musical act in history. They proved a multi-million dollar enterprise could be grown on the strength of giving away their product by freely allowing copying and distribution of live performances. There was typically a special section at Grateful Dead concerts where tapers could hook up their equipment.

In the process, the Grateful Dead created legions of dedicated fans, many of whom spend money on tickets, authorized recordings and other ancillary and licensed products to more than make up for the loss in income from the free distribution of recorded music. The actions by these artists have helped to create an ongoing tectonic change in the distribution of information and entertainment, as well as literary and visual art.

The British band Radiohead put a new spin on these ideas when it released a downloadable CD and allowed its fans to pay whatever they thought it was worth, including nothing at all if they wished. After a few million downloads and a steady slew of publicity, the band finally set minimum prices for the CD.

Both the Australian artist Hazel Dooney and British graffiti artist Banksy offer their fans high-quality digital downloads of their work. In Dooney's case, if you send your printed copy to her with a self-addressed and stamped return envelope, she will sign it and return it to you. Both artists have generated great newsworthy mentions for their generosity and created new levels of fans and loyalty from them in the process.

The powerful combination of the Internet and print-on-demand (POD) technology is allowing visual artists, writers and musicians to create works they can sell directly to the public. The dynamics of these developments has affected how all parties involved, including consumers, retailers, distributors, and publishers, receive and are compensated for goods delivered.

These days, consumers are doing their best to avoid traditional distribution. They are listening to music on the Internet and over satellite broadcasts. They are buying music downloads at Starbucks or over the Internet to play on their iPods. To avoid annoying each other with phone calls and emails, they laboriously type in short text messages on their cell phones to be read at the convenience of the receiver. They are avoiding commercials and time-shifting television programs using digital video recorders.

The number of self-published books coming onto the market is exploding. Just a few years ago, the idea for me to write and successfully self-publish a book was out of the question. Now, frustrated artists are using these tools to take control over how their products reach their collectors, readers and listeners. It is not a time to be complacent with how you get your work to market.

You need to be aware of how distribution channels are evolving so you can judge the opportunities and pitfalls. The inestimable American humorist, Will Rogers, could not have said it better.

Even if you are on the right track, you can still be run over if you are not moving.
— Will Rogers

The Internet Changed the Gallery Business Forever

While getting a sale on a first visit was always a huge challenge for a brick and mortar gallery, the Internet has made it more difficult. It allows collectors to price shop and perform due diligence on the gallery's claim about the artist's reputation and the art's provenance and so on. As a result, many galleries are carrying fewer prints, because it is perceived that originals do not have the same competition as prints.

As the economy continued to spin in its downward cycle, it put more pressure on galleries and intensified price wars between those carrying the same prints by an artist. While this has always gone on, the Internet has rapidly pushed this shift in buying tactics. Smart collectors are realizing they can shop fine art prints, as with everything else, thanks to the convenience of the Internet. This is a problem for artists and galleries and, at the same time, it is an opportunity. It's pure Darwinism.

The survivors were those who learned how to adapt to shifting consumer-buying trends. The same will be true for artists.

Formerly, I believed it was bad business for an artist to create channel conflict by competing with his or her galleries unless they were an established name in the industry. It is easy to realize why galleries would not give up valuable retail space to compete with an unknown artist who is selling the same work on his or her website.

In an ideal world, artists and galleries should not have to be in competition. Unfortunately, such is not the case today. Although there is no clear-cut formula for how artists or galleries should co-operate when competition between them is happening, taking the high road on both sides is the best approach.

What I mean by taking the high road for artists is that they need to establish guidelines on what is in their best interest and what is in the galleries best interest. If you are fortunate enough to have a relationship with a gallery that is moving your work, I do not believe you should be in direct competition by selling the same images from your website.

One option is that perhaps the gallery does the originals, and you do the prints, but there are too many options here to explore them all. Each case is going to be unique, and I think it will take creativity and persuasive negotiation to allow you to work deals with galleries when you are also selling work on your site or through other distribution channels.

Selling direct to collectors can be a viable marketing decision when you are a known entity. For example, the premier primitive artist Jane Wooster Scott appears to do well selling from her website, [www.woosterscott.com], while supporting a dealer network. While you can aspire to be able to do this, building your reputation and demand for your work first may be a better way to go.

In Wooster Scott's case, galleries with Americana collectors will want to carry her work despite the channel conflict, because they know she will sell in the gallery due to her reputation and demand for her work. It's a business decision for them, just as it is for her company. Still, galleries will steadfastly reject artists without a following that want to compete directly with them, and who can blame them?

Whatever the case, I do think publishers, artists and galleries need to rethink how they are collaborating in creating a collector base for the artist. What worked in the past may not work best now or in the future, and the changes seen in the shifting buying patterns caused by the Internet are at the heart of that rationale.

There has always been some naturally occurring antagonism between some galleries and some artists. It's a marriage of sorts, and some are rocky relationships while others are solid. Artists feel galleries don't do enough for them, and galleries think artists have no loyalty and are withholding better pieces, ready to jump to the next gallery, and so it goes.

Of course, there also are wonderful stories of galleries and artists sharing blissful success in long-term relationships. However, I've also heard artists ask, with a sneer, in what other business can a retailer get their product for free and then keystone (100% price increase) it when it is sold. And I've heard gallerists lament that it costs them $100 or more per month, per piece on display in rent, not including other expenses such as commissions, benefits, taxes, utilities, advertising, et cetera, all with no appreciation of their overhead from artists.

Galleries often rightly find many artists are clueless when it comes to understanding the difficulty of creating a collector. Artists often find galleries fail in properly representing them and living up to the spirit of their agreement. This is neither a condemnation of either artists or galleries, nor of their actions. Everybody puts self-interest first, which is natural.

Having said that, I think this is not a good time for either side to be working against the other. The best thing that could happen would be for all parties to realize that if they don't find a way to cooperate better and work with the changes that the Internet is causing, they will all suffer in the end.

My advice is as follows: If you are an artist, you need a website. You will have to figure out how to use it to serve your own needs and that of the galleries or publishers who carry your work, depending on circumstances. If you are gallery owner and are not setup to sell online – and don't plan to be – then start thinking about what your next career will be because you will quickly be watching the erosion of your business as it goes to your online competitors.

Domain Names

O be some other name!
What's in a name? That which we call a rose
By any other name would smell as sweet.
— Shakespeare

A domain name is an alphanumeric unique name that identifies individual websites on the Internet. It is the human-readable alternative to the octet series of numbers that make up an IP (Internet Protocol) address.

A domain can be of any length up to 67 characters and is made of the 26 letters of the English alphabet, numbers 0 to 9, and hyphens (-). You cannot begin or end a domain with a hyphen, but you can include multiple hyphens. Domain names have a TLD (Top Level Domain) suffix or extension. While more are added regularly, the most common suffixes include .com, .net, .org, .biz, .info, .us.

Do not let any company hold your domain name for you. Insist on having your domain in an account you control. There is no reason a Web developer or anyone else needs to have your domain in their account. It would be tragic to lose your website because your developer skipped out on you, went broke, or took down your site in a disagreement.

You cannot overestimate the value of your domain name; you can, however, rebuild a website. In the worst case scenario, if you lose access to your website or if it comes down without your consent; you can still rebuild it if you own your domain name. It is not nearly as easy to rebrand yourself and your website if you lose the domain name, or if you never have control of it.

My advice regarding hosting is if you are having a custom website built for you that requires shared hosting or a server that you should have the hosing account in your name and under your control. You can always setup the web developer with a hosting account executive status, ftp access, or some other arrangement that does not take ultimate control from you. Naturally, if you are using a full-service provider that specializes in artist websites, you won't be able to exercise such control of the hosting. But, to reemphasize, there is never a reason to not have a domain name in your own account – never.

When it comes to your domain name, keep it simple. Choosing the best, most suitable name is very important. You will use it on all your communication. It will be an integral part of your effort to brand your name as an artist.

It may seem obvious, but is nevertheless worth emphasizing that you should use your name. The most likely thing for someone to remember about you is your name. Check for yourname.com and register it immediately if it is available. A good source for purchasing domain names is Go Daddy [www.godaddy.com]. You will get a free email address with your registration. I encourage you to use it as your primary business email address.

Do not modify your domain name unless necessary. That is, if you have yourname.com, then stick with it. If you have a common name, it is likely not available; in which case you can consider adding a modifier such as: yournameartist.com; yournamefineart.com; yournamestudio.com, et cetera.

Avoid being cute, clever or generic. Using descriptive phrases instead of your name is not a good idea. Terms such as KittyCatArtist.com or GrandCanyonartist.com will not serve you well. Stick with your name and a brief modifier, if necessary.

Domain names are not case sensitive; they will resolve to lower case in the address bar of a Web browser. However, you can use upper-case letters to make longer names more readable. For instance, I present my blog as: www.ArtPrintIssues.com to make it easier for the eye to follow and to pronounce. As a side note, if I were starting my blog today, I would have used my name and published using the subdomain: blog. BarneyDavey.com.

This leads to the question of what to do if you have years of branding under some domain name that goes against my advice above. My blog is a good example. After working to establish it as a high ranking, authoritative business resource for visual artists, I did not want to lose the momentum and search engine visibility it had gained under ArtPrintIssues.com, so I chose to stick with it. You may make the same decision for similar reasons. You will note, my title is Art Print Issues by Barney Davey, which is the second best thing to do if you don't have your name in the domain name.

For some, who may not have had good advice and thus chose a name poorly, I would not rule out buying a better domain name to replace it. You could begin by redirecting it to your established domain with the long-range goal of re-branding your website with the new, improved domain name.

The .com domain is king! The number of .com TLDs swamps all others. There are about three times more .com domains registered than the total of .net, .org, .biz, .info and .us combined. We are conditioned to think .com, even though we read or heard some other TLD. Why would you intentionally put yourself at a disadvantage by buying something other than a .com name?

While the chances of obtaining a short descriptive .com name becomes more challenging each day, I would resist the temptation to use one of the other TLDs such as .net or .org for your artist website. If you choose a .net and there is another domain registered, such as .com, you can be sure you will send traffic to it.

If you live outside the U.S., you may want to consider getting a country code domain name to go with your .com TLD. For instance, if you live in Great Britain, you may want to promote yourself within your country as yournameartist.co.uk. Should you choose this route, you create more challenges and decisions over which to use in different situations. You could point the country code domain to your .com as any easy fix.

There is a school of thought to protect your domain name's intellectual property value that you should purchase the name with the other popular TLDs, such as .net, .org., .biz, .us and .info. Since this tactic can add considerably to your marketing budget, I tend to believe you would do better to buy more years of the .com and marketing for it. Should your name be easily misspelled, it would be a good idea to purchase the obvious misspellings and forward those domains to your primary domain name.

Using hyphens allows you to claim the same generic name as someone else who has previously registered the name. I recommend against using something such as yourname-artist.com. It will be confusing, and you will send traffic to the non-hyphenated site. In addition, you will have to spend time, energy and money to educate your collectors to use the hyphen.

Make sure you are not violating copyrights. You can check to see if a name is trademarked at the U.S. Copyright office [www.copyright.gov/records]. It can be costly to have to start over again, or to have to defend yourself should legal action be taken against you.

Domain names can be of any length up to 67 characters. That does not mean you should use as many characters as possible. Shorter is better with four or five syllables being optimal. If you do opt for a longer name, make sure it is keyword rich. Do not use slang or incorporate anything trendy that will be dated in a couple of years. If you are using more than your name, set expectations with your choice so that when your domain name is heard, it instantly and accurately conveys the type of content to be found on your site to the listener.

Use a whois lookup service, such as Ajax Whois [www.ajaxwhois.com], to make it easy to find available domains. If you find a name that is taken, you can attempt to purchase it from the current owner. Be prepared to pay a premium for an existing domain, especially if it has a website attached to it. There are domain appraisal services and domain buying services that can assist you.

Website Options for Artists

When you start your investigating, you will find numerous options for getting a website for your art business. Here are the most common options:

- Generic Do-It-Yourself (DIY) site builder programs that use built-in templates and color schemes provided by the hosting company.
- Template and semi-custom websites created specifically for artists.
- Websites built by you, or by someone you know, using Dreamweaver or some other Web building software.
- Custom websites built by a Web developer or Web development company.
- Content Management Systems (CMS), including popular freeware programs such as WordPress, Joomla and Drupal.

There are many "free" options available for newbies to get started. In my opinion, most look amateurish and send the wrong message about how serious you take your career. You can find free sites from your ISP and other sources, but you get what you pay for.

When something is free, you usually have to put up with ads and banners on your site that are not related to your product, or from which you derive no income. It is a tacky way to display your artwork and yourself as a professional. Do not fall to the temptation to cut corners on investing in your career; avoid them.

I find the generic site-builder programs are too limiting for most artists, and I do not recommend using them. It is difficult to make them work, especially for creating galleries in which to properly showcase your work. Moreover, the idea is to do the work yourself, which can lead to uneven or unpolished results.

Just as I advised in an earlier chapter to hire a graphic designer to help create advertising and print materials (because most likely you do not have the talent or experience to get the best outcome), the same is true with Web design. Your website will be one of your most important marketing tools. Do not shortchange yourself by getting in over your head on when doing your own design and implementation.

There are a number of Web developer companies that focus on visual artists. Use your favorite search engine to query for the search term "websites for artists" to find a good representation. You should look at as many as necessary for you to understand what options are available and what you must have.

While you may find other providers, I recommend you include in your search Fine Art Studios Online [www.faso.com] and Folio Twist [www.foliotwist.com]. The former is helmed by Clint Watson, a longtime gallery owner and artist advocate. The latter comes from Dan Durhkoop, a painter and creator of the painter's friend Empty Easel Website [www.emptyeasel.com]. I commend both the Empty Easel site and Clint's Fine Art Views blog [www.fineartviews.com/blog], to you with high praise. See the Resources directory for more links from this category.

You should take the time to compare the sites for services and pricing. It is easy to see examples of their actual work. However, you may not want to contact artists directly; it may be burdensome for some artists to get unsolicited requests to vouch for their website provider. It is easy enough to learn how long a site has been hosted by a particular provider. Together with the information you glean from inspecting your potential provider's websites, this should be sufficient in helping you decide which provider to choose. Of course, word-of-mouth is still one of the most reliable sources for suggestions on any services you seek to use.

Your other options are to build a site yourself using Dreamweaver or some similar site building software, or to have a site built for you by a developer. The drawback to the first option is you have to take the time to learn how to build a site, and you may not have any training on website design or graphic design. You may also need to learn html or php languages to be able to accomplish all your goals.

The upside to building your own website from scratch is that you have full control over the entire process. You make all the decisions, from layout, navigation, color schemes, to fonts and more. You will know how your site works, and you can make changes without having to rely on a third party to help you.

Rather than building from scratch, you may choose to use a CMS type of software. The most common are WordPress, Joomla and Drupal, although more are available. These open source programs allow you to build a website using various components and plug-ins, which means you do not have to know how to code everything to pull your site together. These programs have free and commercially available themes you can use to hang your site on. The themes typically allow for a high degree of customization.

In 2009, Google announced that page loading speed would become a more important factor in its page ranking algorithms. Internet professionals took notice, as they always do when the search behemoth speaks. Besides simplifying page design, one of the top methods of speeding up a site is to use a CDN (Content Delivery Network.)

A CDN uses a group of web servers distributed across multiple locations to deliver content more efficiently to users. In this system, the server with the fewest network hops or the server with the quickest response time is chosen. The cost of a CDN to a small business is prohibitive, but as your business and online traffic grows, you may find using a CDN helps your user experience, as well as helping your Google Page Ranking and keyword rankings to enjoy better search engine results.

Content

Your website is a personal reflection of you and your work. Keeping it updated with interesting content is a key to gaining repeat visits to your site.

By proactively addressing questions and concerns, you can help ease any buyer anxiety about doing business with a new online marketer. Here are some key items you should incorporate into your website:

- Include both the company and owner's name with complete address.
- Include testimonials from actual collectors to generate a human touch and interest potential clients.
- Include a FAQ. If you get repeat questions, then providing clear answer to them to make it easier on you and your visitors.
- List the products used in creating your work.
- Explain shipping policies. Who takes the risk of transportation damage or loss? Is transportation insurance included?
- Post a return policy. A reasonable suggestion is seven days

from the receipt of the painting with a 100% refund.

- Be straightforward about what you offer and your terms.
- Include a privacy policy, especially if you intend to ask for any kind of information.
- An SSL certificate is required with a merchant account and shopping cart. You should have one if you collect any kind of personal data in a form on your site, including just asking for name and email address.

One of the most important pages on your site will be your "About" page. I know from experience that writing about one's self can be difficult. Although I believe artists should be able to toot their own horn, I am realistic to know it does not always happen easily.

Alyson Stanfield, the Art Biz Coach, provides insight into this project. She says you need to inject personality into your About page, and I agree. This is a chance to let your personality shine through. It should not be a dry recitation of facts about where you were born and went to school, or the accolades you have collected along the way.

In addition to using this page for bragging rights, give your readers a glimpse at your life beyond being an artist. What other passions do you have? Do you love to cook? Are you addicted to the Project Runway television show? Are you a closet or unabashed fan of American Idol? Do you belong to non-art related groups? Do you play an instrument, sing, dance or act? Do you have a partner in your business that makes it go for you? Are you an avid poker player, NASCAR fan or college- or pro-sports fanatic?

Do not be shy about including amusing or interesting items from your life history. It can make your prospects and collectors feel more attached to you. So if you have been a firefighter, fallen in a tub of holy water, or met your wife on American Airlines – wait, that's me – you can connect on levels beyond an appreciation for your creativity. I like writing in the first person – Hi there; it's Barney – but I find it stiff to write in the third person. Whatever you choose, just be sure to be consistent. Otherwise, it will be confusing to your visitors.

When it comes to writing Web content, it is a good idea to get professional help. Good copywriters can make a huge difference in your presentation. They will use your words and style and help you polish your copy and, equally important, they can make sure you are using good keyword rich phrases to help with your SEO.

Contact information should not be a just submittal form. They are not totally reliable. When I find a site with no physical address, phone number and regular email, it turns me off. I always wonder what someone is hiding, or are they arrogant or incompetent. Whatever it is offering has to be very compelling, or I will leave the site and not return.

Under construction pages are okay if that is all you have on the home page while in site development. Otherwise, do not use them and avoid having links to pages with "Coming Soon" on them. It is annoying to take the time to go to a link only to find nothing there. It makes you look amateurish. Be respectful; take the link for any pages with no content off the site.

Include your prices. People shopping on the Internet expect convenience. If you make me go somewhere else, or if I have to contact you to get prices, I will go elsewhere. If your pricing policies are fair and consistent, why would you leave them off? You cannot control what others will think.

When they cannot find prices, you leave it to their imagination as to why you have done so. Is the artist a snob and too important to put prices on the work? Does the artist not provide pricing so I have to contact him or her to get a sales pitch? Are the prices left off so the artist can play "Let's make a deal?" If you think it harms the presentation, then include a pricing grid and a special page where a visitor can learn what things cost without having to either leave the site or call or email you.

Gathering Email Addresses and Privacy

In this book's first edition, I emphasized the importance of building a dealer network, and while it is still crucial, your horizons should now include building a direct following with your collectors and fans. Working on both target audiences should be a daily ritual. One of your most vital tasks is to be constantly focused on harvesting email addresses from those interested in your work.

Despite justified clamor about spam, you will be pleased at how many people will still trust you with their email address when you promise not to use it for any other purpose but to contact them about your work. To accomplish that end, you should have a privacy statement with a link to it on your website. Further, you should clearly state that you promise never to share or sell the email addresses you collect. You can find help to create a privacy statement here: http://www.freeprivacypolicy.com

Having a link to a privacy statement on your website will make you standout as professional and courteous. It is also something you can refer to when you are attempting to collect email addresses. If a person knows you have a posted privacy policy, it is just one more reason to trust you with his or her email address.

Using Flash-based sites can create a pleasant, even exciting visual experience. However, they do not do typically rank as well with search engines because the information on them cannot be crawled and indexed. The same is true for sites using lots of java-based script. While this is changing and search engines are finding ways to rank flash pages, I advise against a flash site at this point. A compromise is to have a section of a page using Flash while the rest loads in HTML.

Flash intro pages are not recommended. You may entertain me – and I emphasize, MAY – for one time on a first visit, but after that, you are wasting my time on something trivial. The same is true for music openings. They are annoying. I expect it on a musician's MySpace site and no other place. These concepts are passé and are likely to turn off many visitors.

Navigation and Design

Your site can have a stunning visual design, but if it does not convert sales, or generate leads, it is dysfunctional. Your visitors need to be able to easily navigate your website to the information they want. They also need to clearly understand what other goods and services are available.

Make it easy to find things, and keep items in relevant categories. If you paint and sculpt, do not bury your sculpture on some deep link within the site. Put it in a category on the home page, along with whatever else you have to offer.

One piece of feedback I hear from clients who are selling online again and again is that they are astonished at how quickly their products sell once I update their sitemap and add some simple searches which break down categories. They also tell me products are now moving from categories they had struggled to sell things from for ages.

Have you heard of the 8-second test? Research indicates that this is the length of time your website has to make a first impression on visitors. Graphics are important, but even more so is your bold headline. Use it to give your visitors an exciting and compelling reason to stay on the site. This is contrary to advice you may hear from a Web designer, but don't listen to it. Pictures, graphics and logos each have their place, but not to replace a strong opening headline.

Coming up with a bold headline that contains a strong promise or benefit is how you arrest the attention of casual Web surfers and begin to convert them to customers. Spend the time to succinctly tell me the dominant reason why I should choose to do business with you. There is a fine line between puffery and effective promotion. Dial it in and win.

This information is not be construed a primer on creating compelling website copy. As mentioned above, if writing compelling copy is not your strong suit, you may be well served in finding a professional copywriter to help you. Yes, it costs money to hire good help; but when you think about how important it is to create an effective website, it is worth the investment. Your website will tirelessly sell for you, day and night. It can open doors like no other media. When well done, it will be your single most valuable marketing tool.

Each page on your website should exist for a reason. Starting with a powerful, benefit-oriented headline, your pages should follow with a strong paragraph that supports the headline and draws the reader's interest. The goal is to arrest attention first, and then involve the reader further and finally come to a call to action. That is a lot to try and do, but it is worth doing. It is how you will make your site as successful as possible. You have to make it so interesting you keep your visitors past the initial 8-second test.

Your site is more than a virtual mall or electronic brochure. It is a means of lead generation unlike any other. There is an unspoken quid pro quo on the Internet. If you expect your visitors to respond to call to action and give you their name, or buy something, you will get the best response when you give something of value to them.

What is a qualified name worth? I previously mentioned how Hazel Dooney and Banksy offer free high-quality digital downloads of their work. There would be nothing wrong with copying that successful idea. As with a headline, the more time you spend crafting a good offer, the better your results will be. The same is true for buyers. How about giving any buyer a free mini-print, a pack of gift cards, or free shipping on the first order?

E-commerce

An important decision for you is to determine whether you will sell direct from your site. If you go this route, you will need to take payments. The simplest method is to setup a PayPal account. With it, you can collect payments and even arrange shipping. It does not require you to have a merchant account. If you are just starting, this is your least expensive option to take payments for online sales.

The drawback is that the transaction takes place on PayPal and some potential buyers may not realize they do not have to have or create a PayPal account to make a payment. It appears more professional to some buyers to see that you have a merchant account, because they know your bank would have approved your credit before letting you use this.

To use a merchant account, you will also need shopping cart software to make the transaction. Also, you must have an SSL certificate before you can be approved for your merchant account. There are usually application fees, monthly fees and a percentage per transaction and a transaction fee. This means you need to be doing volume to afford a merchant account.

Self-Representing Websites and Print and Fulfill Websites

This chapter is about you getting your own website, in your own name, established. There are many other types of websites where you can show your work. However, they are not about you; they are about a collection of artists. While I believe that participating in some of them can be worthwhile, I suggest looking into them after you have your own website up and running.

Search Engine Optimization (SEO) for Artists

Your website must be attractive not only to your visitors, but also to search engines. To be successful at SEO, you or your Web master will spend considerable time and energy to create:

- human-readable URLs;
- XML sitemaps. Keyword-rich alt and title tags;
- deep-linking architecture, internal links within your site;
- W3-compliant code;
- on-page search engine optimization;
- in-bound links.

There is more to SEO than the above items, but if you manage each of them, you are well on your way to gaining high page rankings from Google and other search engines. I suggest you use your favorite search engine to learn more about the bullet points above. Search for each one individually and study the results. Then search for "SEO for artists" to find specific for your art-based website.

Learn to think in "keyword phrases" when it comes to creating copy for your site. You do not want it to be a bunch of copy-pasted, unintelligible gobbledygook or overused phrases. It should read in natural unforced language that contains keywords and phrases. For instance, never use a generic "click here" text link when you could be linking with a keyword phrase such as "still life paintings" or "photorealism prints."

Search engines are about one thing: relevancy. It is the goal of a search engine to return the most relevant results to every query. Keep this in mind as you work on making your site as SEO friendly as possible. Dead links are unfriendly and a search engine no-no. You will be dinged for having broken or dead links on your site. Search, and you will find there are numerous broken-link checkers available.

Meta data, including the title, description, meta tags and keywords, are very important to SEO success. Matt Cutts is a senior software engineer for Google, and is also the face of Google on YouTube. If you are interested, I suggest subscribing to its Google Webmaster Central Channel. You will find a growing list of more than 200 informative and useful videos aimed at demystifying Google's vaunted search algorithms and SEO in general.

One thing you will learn from Cutts is Google does not index keywords in meta data, that is the information viewed by search engines rather than Web visitors. While Google ranking is the primary target for all SEO activity, there are other search engines that matter and some do still index keywords in meta data, so it is still a worthwhile task.

Pay-Per-Click (PPC) Advertising

Employing SEO tactics will help your site rank higher in organic or natural searches. These listings on search-engine result pages appear purely due to how relevant they are to appropriate search terms. They are the coin of the realm, or the Holy Grail of the search. The non-organic search results you see on a page primarily consist of pay-per-click advertising.

Since Google owns a dominant portion of online search, its Adwords program is the most popular source of paid advertising. You can use its Search-Based Keyword Tool [www.google.com/sktool/#] to help you identify the best keywords and keyword phrases that are most appropriate for optimizing your site, and to find the best keywords to bid on in Adwords and other paid-advertising programs. My advice is to work at getting your site optimized as much as possible before considering the PPC alternative.

Should you decide to pursue it, spend the time to study how PPC – especially Adwords – works before you start because you can waste a lot of money learning what not to do with an unfocused and amateur Adwords campaign. You will find Microsoft and Yahoo return fewer results, but also that you will spend less money on the learning curve. Facebook and MySpace also offer versions of PPC advertising. You may want to look into their programs if you plan to pursue this form of advertising.

Local Search

Statistics show that somewhere in the neighborhood of 79% of households do some kinds of search for a local product or service on a daily basis. Many of your best prospects are searching for local artists using the Internet. Major search engines are competing to replace your local phone book. It is important for you to get your business listed and take advantage of the growing number of people using local search.

As a visual artist, you are likely seeking a broader audience than your local market, although by no means should you be ignoring it. I have a blog post titled, "Local Search for the Local Artist – Grow Where You Are Planted," which you can find on Art Print Issues. It extols the virtues of building a homegrown following.

Getting listed in local search engines also helps create more quality back links to your site. You want to make sure you stake your claim on the "Google 10-pack." When you search for a term such as "fine artist Phoenix, AZ" you want to be included in the 10 listings beside the map on Google's first page of results. Don Campbell on his www.Expand2Web.com site offers tutorials on how to use local search.

You will want to start with the top three local search engines:

- Google Local Business Center – *www.google.com/lbc*
- Yahoo Local – *http://listings.local.yahoo.com/csubmit/index.php*
- Microsoft (Bing) – *https://ssl.bing.com/listings/ListingCenter.aspx*

Do not stop with the big three local search engines. Get yourself listed in every local, regional and national directory you can find. All of them are eager for listings; it is how they become and stay relevant. You should not have to pay as most are happy to have your listing and for an opportunity to pitch paid services to you.

Your list should include the Yellow Pages, White Pages, cable company listings, and local search engines, such as Scottsdale.com. If you search for "directory listings your town" you will find dozens of places to add to your free listings.

If you have not concentrated on your local market, you should. It is easier to develop contacts that can help you in the media and small businesses. You can eliminate shipping charges and include free hanging services to further stimulate sales.

Here are some common sense ideas you can use to promote your business:

- Include your URL on everything you print or email, including letterhead, business cards and in e-mail signatures.
- Create or purchase promotional items. Mini-prints, greeting

cards, coffee mugs and T-shirts are good items and provide a regular reminder to visit your site.

- Include your website address in every directory listing you make.
- Get a magnetic sign or a back window graphic with your website address.
- Launch a sweepstakes that offers anyone who registers on your site – or anyone who subscribes to e-newsletters within a certain time frame – the chance to win or receive a free gift.
- Add a resources page to your website and use it to create your own link exchange by asking sites complementary to yours to swap links. Keep the links relevant and check to make sure your link is being posted on the cooperating site.
- Become active by commenting in online discussion groups, chats and blogs, and always include your URL in your signature. Be polite, do not spam with unwanted messages. Make sure your comments add value.
- Put an "e-mail this link" on every page of your site.
- Create a survey to help you determine what your customers want and what they like.
- Use online classified advertising and online auction sites such as Craigslist.org and eBay.com to increase exposure to your site and products.

Site Submission and Statistics

Search engine crawlers will likely eventually find your site without help. However, that is taking much for granted and it increases the time before your site is crawled. You should submit your site yourself, or pay a service to do it for you. There are numerous sites that offer to help you with search-engine submission for free.

Many of these sites also offer other tools to help you with keyword density, meta tag generation, checking broken links and link popularity. The tradeoff for free service is that you agree to receive their marketing messages. Using all of the named services will help you make sure your site is toned up as much as possible.

You need to know the "who, what, when and why" of your website visitors. Once again, Google has an excellent free resource to help you with this called the Google Analytics tool [www.google.com/analytics]. Ensure you have a good traffic statistics program installed. If you don't have them as standard with your webhost, ask them what packages they have available and get them to install one for you; these are generally free.

In addition to Google Analytics, there are other free site-statistics services. A couple of the most popular are Stats Counter [www.statcounter.com] and Sitemeter [www.sitemeter.com]. You will find using them gives you slightly different results. Consider adding at least one to your site in addition to Google Analytics with the caveat that any such app will affect your page loading time.

As you begin to use your statistics to understand how traffic is arriving at your site, you can then apply it to making smart choices when it comes to online advertising. You also can start to write blog posts based on keywords that generate the most traffic to your site. As the saying goes, "Knowledge is Power."

If you blog frequently and authoritatively, search engines will take note. Having an effective blog is arguably the best SEO tool in your online marketing arsenal. Blogging will be given an in-depth view in the next chapter

Chapter Thirteen
Online Marketing and Social Media

A wise man will make more opportunities than he finds.
— Irish painter, Francis Bacon

One of the chief purposes to having a website is to help you sell and promote your art using the tremendous efficiencies of email marketing. Email is the most cost-effective method of getting your message out to a targeted list of buyers and collectors.

While the irritations with spam and social media have both reduced its effectiveness, email marketing should be an essential part of your marketing mix. This makes collecting email addresses a top priority task for your business. One you should strive to include in all your marketing efforts.

Building your List

When it comes to marketing, it is easy to say that everything is important, and to a degree this is true. However, besides crafting a consistent and impressive tone and style to your marketing, there is arguably no more urgent task than list building. How you go about it is ... every way you can imagine.

Start by systematically and automatically asking any potential collector if you can add someone to your list. If in person, you can ask for their card and then send a single follow-up to remind them you met and acknowledge you have added them to your list. It is illegal and bad netiquette to add names to your email, not snail mail, list without permission, so just don't do it.

Your contact manager database should have a field to indicate whether you have permission to use email an address. If you don't, use direct mail to communicate with those whose permission you lack. Make sure you have a call to action when you send snail mail to get people to come to your site or blog and subscribe.

Just because someone has their email address on their site, this is not an invitation to send them unsolicited email. This is particularly true with broadcast email. A single thoughtful email to someone regarding something other than a blatant solicitation to buy your art is acceptable as normal business correspondence; however, it is not a license to build a form letter and insert names in fields to give the impression of personal correspondence.

Here are some ways to help you build your list:

- Ensure your email offer is prominent on your home page and on other relevant pages of your website and your blog.
- Offer something for free. You might recall how Hazel Dooney and Banksy both give free high-quality digital downloads. It could be a three-pack of note cards, a mini print or a report you have done on some art topic, which will get you snail-mail or email address.
- Start a blog with content that will build traffic over time. Have your email newsletter sign up visible and easy to use.
- Create a publicity campaign about your newsletter, your most recent work or your charitable activity.
- Comment on other artist's blogs and sites.
- Write and submit e-zine articles for article directories, such as ehow.com and ezinearticles.com.
- Join and participate in art-related or culture-related forums. (This is not to be confused with art business forums where you will find other artists who your best prospects for encouragement, but not for sales.)
- Write about artists you admire, or about art history, or about some other aspect of art that will drive traffic to your blog or website.
- Ask your subscribers to share your newsletter, and give them link to tweet or add to their Facebook page.

Use Proper Email Etiquette on Initial Follow-ups

Start with reminding your recipient where they met you. Was it at an event, a show or social gathering? Did they inquire about something specific? Do you have common acquaintances? Have they commented on your blog? Include something in the subject line that jogs the memory, e.g., "Met You at the Scottsdale Art Walk."

Do not delay your follow up. The sooner you send your email, the more likely they are to remember you and open it. Most people set their email up to put mail they open on their accepted list. Using an inviting subject line helps get your mail open. Avoid words or phrases that trigger anti-spam filters. You can search for "spam filter words" to find them. This will keep your email from going in the spam or junk mail folder.

Choose a Reliable Email-Services Provider

You will not be able to manage a subscriber list using Outlook or some other email desktop client. It is likely your Internet Service Provider (ISP), or email provider will have limits on the number of emails you can send in a day. I suggest you use your favorite search engine to query for "email service provider reviews" to find a suitable reliable service to use.

Your provider should have customized email creation tools you can use to build any kind of templates, including newsletters and surveys. I recommend you get a list and then spend time on at least three or four of the ones that look the best to you. Most have free tutorials and tours of their sites and features.

Some email programs have an auto-responder feature. This allows you to send a series of emails on timeline. Using a feature like this is great way to add value and encourage subscribers to join.

Your topic will be the key to your success. Whether it is art history, local lore, seasonal offerings, recipes, poems, short stories does not matter as much as the passion you put into it and the relevancy to your readers' interest.

Here again is a place where you might hire a copywriter to help you create a knockout series of drip emails. Look for one who also has SEO experience and consider having him or her work on your website content as well.

Tips on Newsletter Mailings

- As mentioned with individual emails, your subject line is critical. It should be keyword- and benefit-driven.
- Add value. Give your readers a reason to open and read your email; for example, tips for hanging or displaying art,

- discounts on purchases or shipping, partner discounts, et cetera.
- Ask questions. Include polls or surveys to help you learn what is important to your readers.
- Consider adding video; many email provider services offer this option.
- Educate and entertain. Reciting dry facts about you or your art won't get it, but offering insights and anecdotes will.
- Do not keep mailing to those who never open you emails. Consider a special direct mail campaign to re-engage them or, ultimately, weed them off your list.
- Think about segmenting your list demographically or geographically.

Anything you can do to make your mailing more specific to your audience will make it more effective.

Publishing an electronic newsletter is a great use for email marketing; it can incorporate announcements about everything you are doing. Include any new pieces in the works or those that have just been made available, as well as any appearances or openings you have scheduled or upcoming show where you will be exhibiting.

You can make your newsletter a source of information that goes beyond what is happening with you. Use it to reprint, with permission, articles of interest to your readers. For example, if you paint in an abstract style, educate your readers about the history of the style. If your market is local or regional, talk about museums, fairs, gatherings and other culture related topics.

If you are a gourmand, a great chef, or a wine connoisseur, then use your knowledge to write entertaining articles about these topics. The point is to make your newsletter something your subscribers will want to open and read. If you provide details that are not all self-serving and aimed directly at making art sales, you will make yourself and your art that much more appealing.

Ask your readers to forward your newsletter to their family and friends. Have an email sign up prominent on the first page and other appropriate spots throughout. You can use a mix of text links and html sign-up box scripts to vary the offer.

Blogging

Blogs (short for weblog) began as web-based journals or diaries. As a blog author, you are known as a "blogger": someone who regularly publishes content on a certain topic or range of topics. As a blogger, you want to be known for something. You should be able to describe the mission of your blog in one or two sentences.

By adding frequent and regular postings, you will begin to create a virtual community around them. The community is comprised of likeminded folks who are interested in the topics you write about. When you allow your blog visitors to post feedback to your journal entries, they become even more committed to the community. This interaction tends to intensify your relationships with your collectors and potential buyers, which you can leverage into greater sales.

With regards to art marketing and developing an online presence, I consider having a personal blog to be a primary tool in the hierarchy of what is most important. From my perspective, a blog ranks in importance only behind a good domain name and a personal website.

If it seems that having an online newsletter and a blog is redundant, you would be partially correct. However, by overlapping the two, you create a synergy with the effect that both become more successful. When you understand how each serves a unique purpose, you begin to realize the significance and use of each. A newsletter is based on the push concept of marketing, while a blog is on the pull.

You push out your newsletter to subscribers who have opted-in to it. A blog, on the other hand, is pulled by a reader who has interest in you or your subject matter. You gather newsletter readers by using email capture techniques, while blogs use those and also offer RSS feeds where the content is delivered to your followers in a blog reader, such as Google Reader [www.google.com/reader]. There are dozens of other reader applications that capture blog posts for those who subscribe to a blog's feed.

Wikipedia describes RSS as:

> RSS (most commonly expanded as Really Simple Syndication) is a family of web feed formats used to publish frequently updated works—such as blog entries, news headlines, audio, and video—in a standardized format. An RSS document (which is called a "feed", "web feed",[3] or "channel") includes full or summarized text, plus metadata such as publishing dates and authorship. Web feeds benefit publishers by letting them syndicate content automatically. They benefit readers who want to subscribe to timely updates from favored websites or to aggregate feeds from many sites into one place. RSS feeds can be read using software called an "RSS reader", "feed reader", or "aggregator", which can be web-based, desktop-based, or mobile-device-based.

Now that you know about feeds, you will want to list your blog with a free service that syndicates your blog feed to the Internet and to your readers. A good choice is Google's Feedburner [www.feedburner.com] service. It has many additional features to help you publicize your blog and track your subscribers.

A blog is more interactive, more like a conversation. Your readers can interact with your topic in the form of comments. Some blogs – either by design or because of the content – are more suitable for reader comments and interaction; you will gain a feel for how you want to work this as you develop your own blogging style.

Search engines love blogs because they are dynamic. Your website and newsletter, on the other hand, are static. You publish the information, and it stays as is – indefinitely. Blogs are a continual source of new, fresh information. If you establish a blog and begin to write consistently and authoritatively on topics of interest to you and your readers, you will begin to find your blog gaining high page-rank value on Google. You will also find it ranking high for keywords and keyword phrases important to your art business.

Search engines are about one thing: relevancy. The goal of a search engine is to provide the most relevant results to any single query it receives. In a perfect world, if you enter a query, you should find the source or answer you seek in the top five results. In most cases, search engines consider newer information to be more relevant than older information. In addition to the many other positive marketing aspects you derive from using a blog, the SEO results alone should encourage you to begin one right away.

Although I emphasize the value of email marketing, it is not as effective as it once was due to spam and junk mail filters, general inbox-overload and fears of viruses. Blogs help fill the void left by the downturn in email marketing. They offer a means to communicate with your reader base of collectors, prospects, artist friends and industry-related contacts.

Blogging helps support your email marketing efforts by enabling subscription options that allow your visitors to be notified each time you update your blog. Since your blog is archived on your blogging software site, they can be retrieved and searched by your visitors at any time. This is in contrast to your newsletters, which typically are deleted soon after being read.

Blog Essentials

To begin, you need to decide on these four things:

1. Blogging software/platform
2. Blog title
3. Blog theme
4. Content

A blog is a website that is specially configured to allow you to easily maintain all the functions of effectively managing your blogging activities. While there are both free and paid services you can choose from to use as your blog platform, I recommend avoiding the free sites. Here is why:

- The site is on a subdomain of the provider, e.g., worldfamousartist.blogspot.com
- You have less control of your settings.
- You must abide by terms of services for the provider.
- Blogs may be deleted without notice if considered as spam.
- Blog may be deleted if your site is hacked.
- Custom design and range of templates available is limited.

But the main reason to pay for your own blog hosting is you own the domain. When you use a free service, it owns the domain. It is not portable. You cannot go into the control panel and forward your blog and all its content to another provider. Each post you write will have a unique URL for it. Should you want to move your content, you cannot do a 301 redirect from the old URL to a new one. You potentially lose years of archived posts, in terms of both search engines and with your readers' links to your blog. That is a nightmare. Besides, your own domain looks more professional.

When it comes to a blog title, I believe you should make it a subdomain of your website, such as blog.yourdomainname.com. It might be tempting to purchase a cool domain name to use, but I believe you are watering down your primary website domain in the process. You will also be required to market two unique domain names, which is too much extra effort for no gain, in my opinion.

If you have already started down the path of a unique domain for your website and your blog, you have to weigh whether to stick with your decision or not. That will depend on how long your blog has been published, how many posts it contains, what your blog Google Page Rank is and how difficult it will be to make the change. In many cases, you will be better served to stick with the two domain names than go through the trouble to change.

I built my www.ArtPrintIssues.com blog using Typepad. It is a paid service that overall offers many valuable options for its users. While it does allow me to do domain mapping so that my real blog URL – barnedavey.blogs. com – is masked, from an SEO perspective, it is still far from ideal. What's more, I am stuck using the themes it provides, which – while numerous – are more limited than I would like. If I were beginning a blog today or making a recommendation for a new blogger, my suggestion would be to use WordPress on a paid hosting site.

A theme is what gives your blog its unique look. No matter how you choose to publish your blog, you will have options for selecting a theme to go with it. The theme will include color, type and graphic options. Additionally, you can choose from one, two or three columns within a theme. I suggest you keep your sidebar columns on the right so your main content will load first. Using a single sidebar column minimizes clutter and distraction making the choice better for most blogs than using a three-column format.

If you take my suggestion and go with WordPress, then you will need a theme. There are both free- and paid-theme options available. You will find more customization with the paid options and likely more features as well. One of the most popular paid options is the Thesis theme from DIYThemes.com.

Thesis is not a framework for beginners, so unless you have a modicum of ability to follow instructions to modify CSS and HTML, you may require help getting a skin for it. With this theme, you can build websites as well as blogs, or a combination of both. My www.barneydavey.com is built with the Thesis theme. A common fear among bloggers is if they change their page design, it will hurt their rankings. Since Thesis is a framework, not a real theme, you can change your design without changing your code or worrying about losing your ranking as a result.

If you like WordPress and want to use it for an e-commerce solution, there is a theme called Market Theme [www.markettheme.com]. It will help you turn WordPress into an online store. It is not a full-fledged inventory management system, but for visual artists, that is not a serious drawback. To get online store software for $55 is a bargain.

Content is King

When it comes to what to write, you will find that no rules apply. However, while you are free to discuss any topic you choose, that does not mean you should. I suggest avoiding controversial subjects. Your mission is to find readers who will buy your art and help you promote your art career. Getting entangled in politics, religion or even about "rights" content is going to distract you and your readers.

I wrote an Art Print Issues post titled "A Year of Blog Topics for Artists – No Reason to Hold Back Now." It offers useful ideas on blog topics you can use to help you get started. If you are committed, you will find a side benefit from having the discipline to write regularly will be the blossoming of your blog voice. Just as you paint with a certain flair or style, so shall you write your blog posts in a unique style. As you develop your style, you will find topics are everywhere.

Here are some things to keep in mind as you write your posts:

- Make them creative and interesting. You want to touch your readers with your sincerity and passion about your creative process.
- Include keywords and keyword phrases in your blog post title and in your content. Being consistent with both will help you get top rankings with search engines.
- Post frequently; twice a week or more is great, or once a week at a minimum. Doing so will bring you more return visitors, increase your blog subscriptions and garner more comments from site visitors.
- Do not rely strictly on a spell checker. You need to proofread your entries or have someone else do it for you. If your writing skills are weak or your English is poor, consider using a service such as www.gramlee.com to get professional help. There is no shame in getting help; but there is shame in publishing shoddy and poorly written blog posts.
- If you have the budget, there are companies that specialize in creating social media content for you. They will ghost write blog posts and items for your Twitter and Facebook accounts for you as well. That said, I have a difficult time seeing how this would work for artists because the content is more personal than say for some corporate account.

Now that you have published your blog, you need to promote it. I suggest you get about 6 -10 posts under your belt before you put too much effort into your promotion. It is so easy to start a blog, and even easier to quit one. As a result, there are many abandoned blogs out there. As a longtime blogger, I am not inclined to promote new bloggers until I see they have established some continuity.

When ready, you should publicize everywhere you can, including sending out free and paid press releases. You can use your Facebook, Twitter, LinkedIn, Friendfeed and other social media platforms to help you build your following. Rather than regurgitate the hundreds upon hundreds of suggestions on how to promote your blog, I suggest you search the phrase, "how to promote my blog." You will find more great ideas than I have room to display here.

Finally, there may be no better resource for learning about blogging for artists than the Wet Canvas forums. Search for "wetcanvas.com internet sales strategies," and you will find a couple sticky threads at the top of the page with hundreds of posts on blogging for artists, including some from me.

Social Media

I could write a book on social media. Certainly, dozens of really good ones are already published. One of my favorites is Crush It: Why Now is the Time to Cash In on Your Passion, a bestseller by Gary Vaynerchuk. He gives great examples of how to use social media, including suggestions on the best products and services to tap them.

As with blogging, the amount of available information on social media – from what it is to how to use it – is overwhelming, and it is all available from a few keyboard clicks. Therefore, I will not try to cover in this book this huge topic with the tremendous number of variables. I believe you will learn most of these things by trying them out and by doing your own research to help you discover the best ways to make them work for you.

Setting aside the idea of getting specific instructions here on how to use Twitter, it is overwhelming just to try and figure out where to spend your time and what social media tool will give you the best bang for your buck. This is where I can help you, because I do have strong preferences on which social media options are best for you.

I believe you can concentrate on four options and forget about the rest, or give them only an occasional indulgence of your time. The four top choices in order of importance are:

1. Facebook
2. Twitter
3. LinkedIn
4. YouTube

The size of Facebook and its importance cannot be underestimated. I suggest you have an account in your name, preferably the same name as in your website domain name. For instance, my Facebook address is: www.facebook.com/barney.davey. Facebook's terms of service do not allow for business use on their personal accounts; however, you can set up a Facebook "Fan Page" or a "Group" for your business. Your Facebook personal account cannot have more than 5,000 friends.

Here is the difference between a Facebook Fan Page and a Group, according to Mashable.com:

Facebook Groups are set up for more personal interaction. Groups are also directly connected to the people who administer them, meaning that activities that go on there could reflect on you personally. Pages, on the other hand, don't list the names of administrators, and are thought of as a person, almost like a corporate entity is considered a 'person' under the law.

For visual artists, I believe a Fan Page is the better solution.

I recommend the same naming strategy for Twitter. Here again, my Twitter account name is: www.twitter.com/barneydavey. I am seeking to brand my name with Facebook and Twitter; but where that is not possible, I look for other ways to include my name. For instance, my blog title is: Art Print Issues by Barney Davey. I want it to be easily understood that I am the author of 300 posts written to help visual artists succeed at the business of art.

A primary difference between Facebook and Twitter is closed versus open. On Facebook, I have to approve anyone who wants to be my friend so they can access my information. On Twitter, anyone can choose to follow me, whether I choose to follow them back or not. For this reason, I feel like Facebook is more homey or clubby than Twitter.

I use software called Hoot Suite [www.hootsuite.com] to help me manage my tweets. There are competitors, primarily Seesmic [www.seesmic.com] and Tweet Deck {www.tweetdeck.com] that both do the same thing, which is to integrate social media and allow you to publish on one and have the same information appear on the other automatically. A very nice feature is one that allows you to create posts and set them up for a time you choose. By the time you are reading these words, I expect other competitors to have arrived. Eventually, as with social media platforms, these applications for utilizing them will find some to be the de facto choice while others fade away or remain relegated to small market share.

While my posts to social media go everywhere now, as is the case for many others, you can find arguments that this is a strategy that cannot last. Because the real-time effects of social media are now causing search engines to figure ways to include posts from social media, it is thought having duplicate content might hinder your SEO for your tweets or Facebook posts causing them to fall in search rankings. There are other reasons as well, but so far I am not inclined to create unique content for different social media outlets. Who has the time? But, give me enough motivation and I will find the time.

There are plenty of books, blogs and other sources to help you fine tune your Twitter strategy. My suggestion is to create a following of your choice. I do not automatically follow everyone who follows me; I have no interest or time for the "get rich" "multi-level marketing" crowd. I use Topify [www. topify.com] to decide whether to follow or not. It shows me how long an account is open, how many friends/follows/tweets are in the account and a list of recent tweets. I can choose to follow or delete the email.

Yes, it can flood your email, especially when you are building a following; but it is so worth it to control who you follow. The ones you are not interested in will fall away eventually when you do not follow back. I work at creating a community of followers on Facebook that are either family or friends, but mostly artists. I have the same mission on Twitter, but I include a mix of social media, business and tech gurus to help me stay informed on interesting developments in those fields.

YouTube is included because video content is growing in importance. Google has a beta program called Gaudi that allows it to capture the spoken word to index and archive. So for those who think they should avoid vlogging (video logging), think again. It can be a wonderful way to gain page rankings and stand out from your competitors who have not caught on.

Gary Vaynerchuk grew his father's discount liquor store from $4 million to $60 million in annual sales by using the Internet and vlogging. He has created more than 650 videos where he answers questions from viewers about wine or discusses some new or vintage wines from the store. The production is decidedly low tech, but highly effective. It has made him a bona fide Internet marketing star, sought after speaker and subject of numerous traditional media interviews and stories.

Do not worry if you think you will not come across as chic, hot stuff or telegenic; Gary Vee has proven you need to be none of these to use video successfully. Besides, you have your art to talk about and display, which should be the real star anyway. I have blogged about Valentina at Val's Art Diary [www.valsartdiary.com] and Natasha Wescoat [www.artcandy.tv], and how both have used video to promote themselves and their art.

It is not lost on me that Val and Natasha are both what one of my readers called "adorable" in a comment about my post on them. While looks and personality may help drive some traffic, we are interested in real buyers – not wooing admirers. That means if you work on delivering solid content, you do not have to be on the camera the whole time. You can find a way to let your personality and art shine through, and you will get results.

There are other options to YouTube, include Daily Motion [www.dailymotion], Vimeo [www.vimeo.com] and Viddler [www.viddler.com]. Gary Vee likes Viddler and says he was able to climb higher with it than he would have with YouTube. I kind of like the millions of visitors and the name brand that YouTube offers; but done right, any of these options will work for you.

Ustream [www.ustream.com] is another video option. With it, you can broadcast live to your audience, as opposed to creating and uploading your video. Some in the tech community think it may be able to rival YouTube to contend for large video audiences. I think it may be too much for the average reader of this book to ponder, but I include it as a resource because of its potential importance. It is worth having on your radar for now and the future.

LinkedIn is different from other social networks. It is more closed and attracts more professional types than either Facebook or Twitter. For instance, many Fortune 500 CEOs have profiles on it. Here is information about it directly from the site:

LinkedIn is an interconnected network of experienced professionals from around the world, representing 150 industries and 200 countries. You can find, be introduced to, and collaborate with qualified professionals that you need to work with to accomplish your goals.

When you join, you create a profile that summarizes your professional expertise and accomplishments. You can use your connections to help you professionally. Your network consists of your connections, your connections' connections, and the people they know, linking you to a vast number of qualified professionals and experts. Through your network you can:

- manage the information that's publicly available about you as professional,
- find and be introduced to potential clients, service providers, and subject experts who come recommended,
- create and collaborate on projects, gather data, share files and solve problems,
- be found for business opportunities and find potential partners,
- gain new insights from discussions with likeminded professionals in private group settings,
- discover inside connections that can help you land jobs and close deals,
- post and distribute job listings to find the best talent for your company.

LinkedIn is setup and positioned as the professional's choice of social networking. There are some very good groups you can join in which you can meet interesting and helpful people. You can also use these groups to find answers to questions or get help for professional issues you might have.

So far, what I see on LinkedIn are communities of artists seeking help and offering help. There are some art appreciation types of groups there, but there are many more with artists primarily as members. I have nothing against participating in these groups and know artists can find help and support in them. However, your goal should be to extend your reach to potential buyers as opposed to making more contacts among fellow artists.

My advice on all these social networks is to limit how much time you spend building relationships with other artists. While you can use your connections with them in the networks to get help and answers, that is not the best use of your time. Many of those questions can be, or already have been, addressed on discussion boards, such as on the copious threads on the General Business forum of WetCanvas.com.

As stated above, your mission in using social media is not to make friends with thousands of artists. It is to make friends, followers and associates of potential art buyers. You have a finite amount of time to work on social networking. It can be instrumental in your career growth, but only if you keep your focus on why you are doing it in the first place. Just remember, it is not for fun, but for business. Fun may be a natural by-product, but should not be the reason to allocate time to social networking.

There are so many books, blogs, articles and other valuable sources of great ideas on how to use social media that it can be overwhelming. Here is a link to a series of articles published by Kate Harper on her blog. She is a greeting card designer who has published her own line of cards and now works with licensing companies. I also provided an article for the series [http://kateharperblog.blogspot.com/2010/03/social-media-month.html]. You will find a wealth of practical information and insights among the many 22 contributors to the series.

The number of other social media and social bookmarking products and services is seemingly endless. If you use some – such as Flickr, Stumbleupon, Delicious and so forth – I trust you will use them well and to your advantage. If you work on the four options I have given here and have the time and energy to do more, go for it. The ones I have given you are those I believe will give you the best return on your time and effort. Nevertheless, I would not argue the efficacy and return on investment in any of the others.

Article marketing is one last idea for you. It involves writing and publishing knowledgeable articles for online services, such as for ehow.com and ezinearticles.com. Done right, article marketing can help establish your credibility and drive traffic to your blog or website. There are art-specific sites that take article submissions on a regular basis. A couple of notable examples are www.fineartstudiosonline.com and www.emptyeasel.com. Both publish frequently and are always seeking new voices to add to their mix. Here again, you can employ the services of a copywriter to ghost articles on topics you choose.

Online Galleries and Online Art Venues

If you feel confused by the sheer number of sites offering to sell your art, you are normal. Literally, there are thousands of sites attempting to sell art online. They range from the pure ecommerce poster and print market (represented by industry leader art.com and its sister-site allposters.com) to local or regional sites that represent a few artists from any defined geographical area.

Since we are concerned with the print market, you will find fewer sites selling reproductions as opposed to original art. Still, the numbers are daunting and the choices many. There are various types of sites that sell art prints:

- Traditional online ecommerce vendors such as art.com and allposters.com
- Print and fulfill such as fineartamerica.com, artistrising.com, imagekind.com, and deviantart.com
- Auction sites such as eBay.com and overstock.com
- Artist community sites, such as ebsqart.com and artflock. com
- Artist promotional sites where you upload images to a gallery and fulfill upon sale. Examples are artspan.com, yessy.com, artbyus.com and picassomio.com
- Juried sites including artfulhome.com, artthatfits.com and 20x200.com
- Brick-and-mortar galleries that sell prints through their Websites

The above represent the broad categories of places where you can sell your art online. If you do enough searching, you will find other varieties of sites among the numerous that sell art prints.

From my observation and research, there are few artists, if any, making a living by selling through online sites. While some artists are known to have done well marketing their art on eBay, it seems that in around 2006, the site lost many top sellers, including Natasha Wescoat and Michel Keck [therawartist.com], who reportedly earned $20,000 a month there on average with a high gross of $42,000 one month at the peak of her experience there.

Most of the sites mentioned here have membership fees; some have basic membership at no charge and fees for premium services. You will need to perform your own due diligence to determine which, if any, of these sites offers a viable way for you to expand your art sales. Some sites are juried, such as The Artful Home and 20x200, where you need to apply in order for your art to be accepted and sold through the venue.

In early 2010, Boundless Gallery abruptly closed its doors. It simply said that although the business was not bankrupt, it was not generating enough profit to make the venture worthwhile. This news came as quite a shock to the artists who had invested their time in promoting their work through the site. I am guessing none of them were making a full-time living from the site, but that some were financially hurt by its closing.

The point of mentioning the sad tale of Boundless Gallery leads to one of my deepest convictions about long-term success for artists in the print market. It is my strongly held opinion artists should do everything they can to control as many different distribution channels as possible. To varying degrees, this is true for all artists these days, on nearly every level – but especially those in the print market. That means becoming self-reliant and selling direct.

I do not advocate abandoning sites that sell art. Many of them offer very good programs that can help an artist make more sales and grow awareness for them and their art. In fact, I believe it is worthwhile to investigate and get involved with as many as possible after doing proper research on them. At the least, the site's results are searchable and it is likely your name will rank higher on some of them than on your own site. Steady blogging and proper SEO on your own website can change this result.

In the long run, it is your career; and it is your responsibility to manage it. The more you rely on others to bring you along, the more vulnerable you are to decisions beyond your control that shut down sales of your art. When you sell direct and build meaningful personal relationships with your collectors, you give yourself the best odds of sustaining your career through the ups and downs of the overall economy and of surviving the changes in the market place.

Chapter Fourteen
Galleries, Dealers and Alternative Spaces

I love the gallery, the arena of representation. It's a commercial world, and morality is based generally around economics, and that's taking place in the art gallery.
— Jeff Koons

While I can understand how, by reading parts of this book, one might come to the conclusion that I have lost faith in the ability of brick-and-mortar galleries to deliver for artists; it would be an incorrect assumption. Having worked in two thriving galleries, I have nothing but respect for anyone who can own and manage one successfully. It is my belief that owning a gallery is a labor of love, because it is a business fraught with peril, drama and – without question – it is not the easiest choice to make for entrepreneurs.

Once, when I was being introduced in a joint teleseminar workshop with the Art Biz Coach Alyson Stanfield, I said that her followers should be thrilled she chose to work in the art field, because with her talent it would have been easy for her to make more money doing other work. The same is true for successful gallerists. It goes beyond a way to make a living; for most it is a lifestyle choice based as much on the love of art as anything.

I have often encountered artists who are bitter about the commissions that galleries take. It just seems unfair to them to give up half of the proceeds, and that is after waiting months or even years for a piece to sell. Who wouldn't be a bit grumpy after investing in making the work, then printing, framing and shipping it, only to have to be patient until it sells? It is a natural human reaction.

However, there is another side to the coin. Here is an example of how a gallery owner looks at the finances of selling art. If the gallery overhead is $5,000 a month, which would be very low, and the gallery is able to exhibit 100 pieces, then the monthly cost of exhibiting each piece is about $50.

Undeniably, it is more complex than that scenario, but it helps illustrate how much a gallery owner puts into bringing work to market. If it takes six months to sell, about $300 of the galleries takings has gone to pay overhead. For sure, few artists would be willing to help with gallery expenses in order to get a larger commission.

The question artists need to ask is, "In the current environment, can I build a gallery network as the exclusive distribution channel for my work?" The short answer is "yes." However, it is more difficult now than it was in the past to achieve success or to make a living solely on gallery sales. It seems to me that for most artists, especially emerging artists, this may not the best choice.

If you are going to use galleries in your distribution scheme, then the likelihood is that you will have to include other means of finding buyers for your work to generate the income you need to make your living. Coopetition, which means cooperative competition, is a word to describe this situation. That is, there will be times when you are competing for sales with the galleries, and other times when you are cooperating for sales with them.

I had the pleasure to speak with artist Charles Pabst in his Scottsdale gallery. He has been successful in the print market for many years and sells both originals and giclées in his gallery. His giclées are very limited, between 50 and 200 in an edition. I asked him how he is able to compete with galleries that carry his work and also keep them happy. His reply was that they service the daylights out of their galleries, and also that he gives them the best images to sell.

His giclée pieces are reworked and embellished by him to the point they look nearly like an original. His galleries know they get the best work and can assure buyers they will not get a better price or better work by shopping elsewhere. At the heart of his success is that he paints the kind of work that begs to be bought. Knowing what to paint and how to make it the most alluring takes as much a skill as knowing how to draw, or how best to put paint to canvas, in the first place.

What you can learn from Charles Pabst is to do your best, treat your galleries with respect and do not take advantage of them by undercutting your prices when you sell direct. I believe that for most new artists, the best thing to do is to create work exclusively for your galleries. Whether it be a series of works or just individual prints not available except in certain galleries, you give yourself a chance by creating work galleries know cannot be picked up on the Internet or through other galleries. Many galleries have quit the print business to concentrate on originals just to avoid the heartbreak of losing sales to cheap buyers who shop them and then look for better prices on the Internet.

As mentioned throughout this book, things are not the same as before, and they are not going back. If you are going to include traditional galleries in your marketing mix, you are going to need to be creative in how you deal with them. When Hazel Dooney works with a gallery, it is on a temporary basis until whatever project at hand is complete. What she brings to the gallery is a full marketing program. She will do mailings and email blasts, blog posts, publicity and other chores traditionally done by a gallery. She comes fully equipped with a large loyal collector base.

This model may be too much for a relatively new artist, but it is worth striving to be able to offer such things. It emphasizes the importance of using the Internet, email and social media to develop your own large loyal following. These are things you should be working on no matter what stage of career development you are at.

There are art dealers in the market place, but they are not obvious or easy to find. Many are retired or former gallery owners or employees who have developed a great contact database of potential buyers along with artists and gallery sources. They use their knowledge, influence and contacts to purchase art for their clients. The financial arrangement is much the same as working with a gallery.

There is a far greater probability they will find you, as opposed to you finding them. Again, steadily working to build your presence in the art community will help you gain exposure to these potentially valuable sources of sales that mostly fly under the radar. It is worth knowing such dealers exist so you can keep your own radar tuned to help you identify them. Do not make the mistake of thinking that because someone does not have a retail location or fancy website, they are not a good prospect for you. Take the time to get to know who they are and then treat them with the same respect you would a gallery owner.

Art fairs and shows will continue to be an important way for many artists to make sales and find buyers. When you are working shows, it makes sense for you to expect to make as many sales as possible during the show. However, what you do with the folks who do not buy can be as important – or even more important – to you in the long run.

Ask any gallery owner who has stayed in business for a few years. They will all testify that it is the buyers who come back months or years later who keep them in business. You cannot expect to get a large percentage of buyers on first blush; it is unrealistic in a gallery or a show. What you can expect is to have effective ways to get those buyers' permission to put them on your email and snail-mail lists.

Not every tire kicker is a deadbeat. One way to flush out who is and who is not is to get them on your list. Most nonchalant, noncommittal buyers are going to pass on your offer, even if you sweeten it with a gift card, postcard, mini-print or piece of chocolate. The ones who will take you up on such an offer are telling you they may be a prospect at some future date.

If you have followed the other advice in this book, you will have an email capture and a broadcast email program in place. Get their details on the list, and then use it wisely to communicate regularly (without becoming perceived as a pest or spammer). Those names may be the kicker that makes you a star-artist in a gallery.

When it comes to working with galleries while also competing with them, strive to be fair, creative and ethical. Keep the drama out of the equation. Not every gallery owner is going to be easy to work with, just as not every artist is either. You decide what works best for you. If the deal or the relationship is not what you expect, move on, leaving on the most cordial and professional terms as possible. Your reputation and your self-esteem go hand-in-hand and are priceless assets.

Specialty Marketing

If there are ways we have not yet touched on to get to market, then they probably can be classified as specialty marketing. Here are some good examples:

- home and hospitality design
- health care marketing
- spas and salons

- restaurants
- temporary spaces
- shows with other artists
- home parties
- antique malls

Home design would be working with interior designers and their suppliers. In my experience, residential designers are not the best prospects. Typically, they need work for a specific project. If you have what they need, it is great; but they are not steady repeat buyers, and they may not be the easiest clients to manage either.

Contract design and hospitality design are different. These designers are working on commercial buildings, including hotels, resorts, et cetera. While their needs can also come and go, often when they need something, they make very large orders. With contract designers, who are specifying paint, flooring, windows and furniture, art is usually the last to be ordered.

Keep an eye on building projects in your area and try to learn about the design firms handling the jobs. That is your key to making a pitch. If you are small fry without a huge portfolio, you may need to put together group of artists with complementary looks to make a pitch. It can make for good publicity if a project does agree to bring in all local artists, which could be a great angle for you. I recall a few years ago reading a story about a new hotel in Florida. All the art was commissioned from local artists in the area. It could have been an art association that managed the deal, but there is nothing from you going after a prize like that. You could round up your own group to make a presentation.

If you are interested in the hospitality-design field, which can be lucrative, you need to check out HDExpo.com [www.hdexpo.com]. It is held in Las Vegas in May and is the premier show for those who are interested in getting the attention of designers and others who specify and buy for hospitality construction jobs. One hotel job can require a huge amount of art.

If you do not have a huge portfolio, your purpose in attending or perusing the show directory would be to find the art print publishers who are active in the market. There are many worse ways to take a working vacation to Vegas than to walk a show like this.

Another specialty field that requires large amounts of art is health care. Medical office buildings, hospitals and other ancillary construction jobs related to the health care market are a huge market. As with the hospitality market, a single artist is at somewhat of a disadvantage; but if you have the right looks for the field, it would be worth investigating.

There are no shows in this field that I know of, but you can find resources by using your favorite search engine to look for relevant companies. Also, there is an aptly titled Healthcare Fine Art blog [www.healthcarefineart. com], which you will find informative and useful in researching this potentially lucrative field.

Alternative Space Marketing

Alternative spaces include any location not primarily operating to sell art. Some examples are:

- coffee shops
- gift shops
- spas and salons
- restaurants
- retailers
- antique malls

The trick to working with retailers, restauranteurs and shop keepers is being able to discern what their real level of interest is in working with you. Granted, each of these has their own business to attend to and you are always going to be an afterthought, but there is potential in each of these ideas.

I would not get excited just because you have someone who offers to help you. You need to believe your work is appropriate for the space and, equally important, have some assurances your art will be displayed and promoted in a way that makes your effort worthwhile. This is where the power of "six degrees of you" can come into play. If you know in your bones that a location is right or the owner is a good fit for setting you up, then work your network to get an introduction.

I know of artists who worked a deal with the local Nordstrom's department store and who have done quite well setting up a small display a couple of times a year. Likewise, I know a local skincare salon owner in high-priced, residential and commercial real-estate zip code who uses the salon walls as a gallery. The same goes for a local hair salon in a hip area of Centrai Phoenix who represents local artists and helps put on events in the evening when the salon is closed for business.

Some other creative ways to get your art displayed and promoted are temporary spaces, shows with other artists and home parties. With the number of empty commercial real-estate places, there are some opportunities for artists. Offer to use your art to dress up the windows in street-level spaces of empty shops and offices. Perhaps in return you can negotiate to use the space on a temporary basis, or to put on a weekend art show.

The idea above is perfect for working with other artists; for example, performing artists, poetry readers and so on. Take an empty space and make it into a temporary venue for art events. A situation like that also lends itself to garnering publicity on local TV, radio and print media.

I mentioned networking above. You do not have to have a specific goal when you start networking. You just need to get your name out there. Start attending local business gatherings. For many, meeting an artist will be a breath of fresh air compared to insurance agents, real-estate agents, chiropractors, network marketing people and others who are as thick as fleas at these types of meetings.

If you can do public speaking, put together a couple of speeches on something related to art in your community. Maybe it is on architecture, or it could be on the history of abstract art or impressionism. All you need is the courage to get up in front of people and talk. The amount of images and information available on the Internet to help you put together a PowerPoint presentation is huge.

Now when you meet someone, you can tell them you are local artist and you do public speaking. You would be surprised how many groups seek entertaining speakers who can give their group 15 to 30 minutes on a topic. If you have studied the ideas on publicity earlier in this book, you can use some of them to develop you ideas for this purpose. Instead of you submitting a press release of your own, you get the group to do it for you. Offer to help them with a pre-written release, or by providing the name, address and email of the best media prospects to contact.

If you have a marketing person, spouse or someone else more suited to do this, they could work the networking and give the speech. If they are introduced as your partner or representative, you could be invited to be in the room and shake a few hands afterwards.

These suggestions are just creative ways to think about raising awareness for you and your art on a local or regional level. Do some serious brainstorming around concepts like these, and you will amaze yourself at the number of creative, unique ways you can come up with to promote your art business.

Finding and Working with Art Reps

In the first edition of this book, I offered the opinion that planning to use art reps to build a dealer network was not a good idea. This opinion came from the understanding that they were too difficult to recruit. That has not changed. Art reps are still a rare breed, and it can be a chore to find ones suitable for you.

The problem is not that those who represent artists do not add value, but more that the typical road warrior who has the moxie and skills to make a living calling on art galleries, art dealers and interior designers can make more money doing the same work, but focusing on repping picture-frame moulding, furniture, decorative accessories or gifts.

From the rep's perspective, there is nothing wrong with art, except that either the volume or commission is not as substantial for wall art as it is for any of those categories. If one can get 25 to 50% more turns on a product, and at higher price points with better commissions, then why not get into that line of work? Thus, many would-be qualified art reps never enter the field, or they quickly migrate away to more lucrative opportunities. This adds to the difficulty in finding a good art rep.

That is not to say there are none or that it is pointless to seek help in this area; however, I will say it is not a good idea to base a marketing plan on being able to recruit enough art reps to adequately build your business. While I do not have any statistics to back up this opinion, I believe there are more art reps working to get originals into galleries than there are art print reps. Here again, the price points can be dramatically higher for originals. In addition, an elitist mentality may be at play. If a rep is working to get his artist into Art Basel Miami, he or she probably does not have the interest or the contacts to work for artists in the print market.

One thing that has changed my outlook on what a rep can do since the first edition of this book was meeting the inimitable Richard Harrison. He was an artist and full-time art rep traveling a territory in Florida for 20 years. He supported his family for those decades from the 1980s to the 2000s, working the trade in galleries and interior design shops.

I ran into him by participating on the WetCanvas.com "General Business" forum, where he was working to gain some interest in a series of podcasts he had put together. He had generously recorded hours of sage advice on how to work as a rep, how to work with a rep, and other important information about art marketing – and he was giving all of it away for the benefit of any interested listener.

When I listened myself, I immediately contacted him and took to helping him promote his podcasts. We have been friends ever since, and my admiration for him has grown steadily the longer I have known him. As of this writing, he was near celebrating, as he likes to put it, "the 40th anniversary of his 39th birthday."

It was refreshing, invigorating and inspiring to watch him master the techniques of creating podcasts and building a website [www.salestipsforartists.com], while also learning to blog and generally having a great time staying involved with the many artists who sought his freely offered advice. I encourage you to visit the site above to listen to his free podcasts. You will come away learning a great deal of valuable information about art marketing and how an art rep works the business.

Dick retired at a good time. The forces gathering to change the business had not yet gained full strength so he was spared from watching his gallery base dwindle and feeling the effects of cheap Chinese oil paints flooding the market or the rise of big-box retailing. Likewise, he escaped the relentless pressure of dealing with the changes brought on by the increased reliance on the Internet for buyers of all kinds, including art print collectors.

How do you find a rep?

The best way to find a good rep is to go to the galleries and companies they call on. Who better to tell you what reps do a good job than a gallery owner or a picture framer? You will find many picture-frame molding reps also pick up pocket change by repping artists. Many galleries that sell prints also offer framing. The facts are that most print galleries could not survive strictly on art print sales alone. The margins on picture framing are greater, and often the framing component is greater than the cost of the print.

You can look at gift shops and furniture or decorative-accessory retailers to inquire whether there are any good reps you should meet. Should you decide to exhibit at a tradeshow, you may find reps coming into your booth. Do not be shy about asking your fellow exhibitors for recommendations as well.

If you spend enough time using a search engine, you can uncover art reps that way as well. Because the results of doing this are spotty and hard to achieve, I would not recommend spending too much time on this approach. The other suggestions here are likely to get you better and more satisfying results. Should you persist in building a base of art reps to help distribute your work, I wish for you to find ones with the quality, wit, personal charm and dignified approach to handling their careers as Dick Harrison did for his artists.

Chapter Fifteen
Licensing

Business art is the step that comes after Art. I started as a commercial artist, and I want to finish as a business artist.
— Andy Warhol

The subtitle of this book is "Creating Cash Flow from Original Art." It is meant to convey the concept that reproducing your art as prints creates a multiplication process whereby you repeatedly make money more from your original art. Doing so develops a steady secondary stream of passive income for you.

Now imagine having your same images used to create a third stream of income. Art licensing is such a source, one that can create a steady third-revenue stream for your creative output. While for many artists and publishers licensing is nearly "found money," for others it is a primary source of income.

In the strict sense of the term, when you enter into a royalty agreement with a publisher who will reproduce your work as posters, giclées or prints, it is a form of licensing. However, in the art world, licensing has come to mean everything but licensing your work to publishers.

Licensing is the business of offering royalties or commissions for the use of art, logos, likenesses and entertainment characters, et cetera. Licensing comes into play when an image or graphic element is printed or placed on any number of a huge variety of products, including greeting cards, note cards, wallpaper, linens, puzzles, playing cards, stationery, apparel and much more.

Since there are books and blogs devoted to helping you understand and capitalize on art licensing, this will be a fairly short chapter. The point here is to introduce you to the concept of licensing, make you aware of how licensing works in general and encourage you to learn more about it.

Until the last decades of the 20th century, most of the licensing of fine art was limited to publishers licensing original art from artists in order to make prints. You might not have even thought that having a publisher make your work into a poster was considered licensing, but it is. To this day, having publishers create prints and posters of their art represents the majority of licensing deals for artists. And the royalties for licensing fine art images to become prints remain the largest in the industry.

What happened in the 1990s was an explosion of licensing for all manner of things, including fine art, which became a consumable commodity of sorts when it was pulled into the mix. Do you recall the "Dancing Raisins"? If you do, that was around the time licensing took off. Once it started, you began to see the cross-promotional marketing between retailers, fast-food companies and other companies everywhere. For example, movie, television or comic book characters began appearing on lunch boxes, pajamas, interior decor, and linens, or became available as action figures in McDonald's Happy Meals, and so forth.

In addition to books on the subject of licensing, there also are tradeshows and magazines exclusively devoted to the field. License! is one of two publications serving the field. It is published by Advanstar Communications, which also produces the annual Licensing Show [www.licensingshow.com], formerly in New York and now in Las Vegas. Total Licensing [www.totallicensing.com] is a British publication that covers licensing events worldwide.

The License Show is considered the premier show by some because it draws the biggest names in the field, with all the comic book, motion picture and other top brands exhibiting and attending. However, many art publishers find the Surtex show [www.surtex.com] to be the better venue for fine art. They have found it to be more lucrative in generating licensing deals for their work. The description below of the Surtex show, lifted directly from its website, helps you understand why this is so.

Markets Represented:

Art and Design for Bath Fashions, Bed Linens, Cookware, Decorative Fabrics, Floor Coverings, Home Accessories, Home Apparel, Housewares, Infant/Juvenile Merchandise, Kitchen Textiles, Specialty Appliances, Tabletop, Upholstery Fabrics, Wallcoverings, Window Treatments

Profile of Attendees:

Manufacturers of Bath Fashions, Bed Linens, Decorative Accessories, Floor Coverings, Home Furnishings/Textiles, Home Apparel, Home Furnishings/Textiles, Home Storage, Juvenile Merchandise, Kitchen Textiles, Packaging, Personal Care, Private Label, Tabletop, Upholstery Fabrics, Wallcoverings, Window Treatments. Retailers: Bed, Bath & Linen, Department Store, Design/Lifestyle, E-commerce, General Gift, Gourmet, Home Furnishings/Decorative Accessories, Home/Garden, Mail Order/Catalog, Specialty Stores. PLUS: Buying Offices, Interior Designers, Licensing Executives and Wholesalers/Distributors.

Perhaps the strength of the Surtex show for publishers is that it is more concentrated on art and design than the Licensing International show is, which instead covers the entire gamut of opportunities. Undoubtedly, its most important strength is that publishers typically come away from exhibiting at the Surtex show with more contracts for their artists.

If you are an artist working with a publisher, most likely that publisher already has representation at shows such as Surtex and perhaps at the Licensing International Expo. If you are working with a publisher, you will want to know what its plans and marketing efforts are for securing licensing deals for its artists. Most publishers worth their salt realized long ago the great opportunity that licensing presented to them and their artists, and therefore they have full-time staffs concentrating on that aspect of the business. There are a few who leave it to their artists to find and make their own licensing arrangements. However, in some ways – especially if you are industrious and have the time and ability to manage this component on your own – this could be a more rewarding contract for you.

Licensing Information Resources

There are a couple of books on licensing for you to read. They are Licensing Art & Design, by Caryn Leland; and Art Licensing 101, Third Edition, by Michael Woodward. Having the information they present in your library will be invaluable, particularly if you plan to self-publish. As with other publications listed in this book, if you find purchasing them would hurt the budget, consider borrowing them from the local library.

In addition to the books, shows and magazines available for art licensing, there are very good blogs devoted to the subject. These include the following:

- "The Art Licensing Blog" [www.artlicensingblog.com], by Tara Reed
- "All Art Licensing" [www.allartlicensing.com], by Jeanette Smith
- "Joan Beiriger's Blog on Art Licensing" [http://joanbeiriger. blogspot.com], by Joan Beiriger
- "Something to Cherish" [www.somethingtocherish.com], by Cherish Flieder
- "Greeting Card Designer" [http://kateharperblog.blogspot. com], by Kate Harper

Licensing is an area where having a rep can make a big difference. While I said earlier that reps for selling fine art prints are hard to find and are probably not the best way to build a print business for self-published, it is the opposite case with licensing. Often, having a good rep will make all the difference between getting lucrative contracts with companies that want your images and being on the sidelines.

Susan January, the vice-president of Leanin' Tree, a greeting card company with 750 artists, shared her views on Kate Harper's blog. She says she sees both artists and agents, and finds both work well, depending on the relationship. From her perspective, you can go it alone or have a rep handle your work for you.

The art-licensing mogul Mary Engelbreit has a great article on her website, www.maryengelbreit.com. It is titled "Art Licensing 101." Here is an excerpt:

I'll be honest – starting out in the licensing business is difficult. Producing and marketing designs is an enormous, expensive undertaking that I didn't try until I was well known in the industry and had a partner with a lot of business experience and good contacts at the bank. Allow me to explain:

I borrowed $60,000 (and this was a long time ago!) to print 5,000 greeting cards of each of my 20 designs (that money was spent on printing alone) and focused on drawing because I was told I needed 100 to 120 designs to establish a legitimate line. My partner found sales representatives throughout the country to show my cards to every shop owner in their territory. We also ran booths in national gift and stationery trade shows, took orders and subsequently attracted new reps.

We were successful, I think, because more and more people became familiar with my work and my name. My drawings were very different from anything else already on the market – giving me an edge. It's something for you to keep in mind with your designs. Whatever you do, don't copy another artist, because originality can lead to success.

We paid our staff (a warehouse person and two secretaries), the local printer, and our reps, but we didn't pay ourselves for a year and a half. In short, getting started from scratch is more than a MONUMENTAL, full-time task, and I needed income from another source all the while.

You do not have to start as big as Mary Engelbreit. You can work on your scale. I have mentioned this before, and it is worth repeating: you will enjoy your success and achieve your goals if you set them on realistic expectations. That means you need to have an honest assessment of your resources and capabilities in the equation. When you have that, you can set your sights on achieving goals within your reach. By being honest with yourself, you avoid feeling overwhelmed or defeated.

Kate Harper mentions on her blog that she started out building 2,000 outlets for her cards. Then she went into licensing and now has 200 deals with some large manufacturers. No matter what you decide, you are going to have a learning curve to get to where you want to go. That means learning about the business and building your contacts within it.

The licensing business is largely about the Rolodex — who you know and how well you know them. Those artists and agents who have the right contacts will quickly get their images in front of the best prospects, because they have the established relationships and a reputation that they are reliable and have good taste and instincts.

Because there is so much work to do to when getting a publishing business off the ground, I recommend that all but the most determined and organized self-published artists seek an agent or rep to handle this aspect of the business, at least in the first few years. The usual licensing agent-commission runs at around 35%, but nothing is set in stone. It can be lower or higher, depending on circumstances. Nevertheless, those agent commissions can be considered cheap if they bring you multiple deals.

Whether working with a publisher or an agent or dealing directly with licensing contacts, when it comes to deals you'll find you have little time to make up your mind. Often they are looking for a specific image, and usually they have more than one source for it. Those that dither will find the window of opportunity closes on them while they are still trying to decide.

An aspect of the licensing business that you need to be aware of is, unlike with a poster or print where the artist maintains some artistic control in the printing process, you give up all control when your image goes to licensing. That means your images can be reversed, truncated, colored differently, made in different sizes and more. If it troubles you to think your art is going to be treated this way, you need to think about whether or not licensing is really your cup of tea.

A company that specializes in art licensing is Porterfield's Fine Art Licensing. You can learn much from visiting its website [www. porterfieldsfineart.com]. Go there and you will find the site offers many articles about the licensing business, as well as imagery from the artists represented. If you feel you have a fit for its look and are so inclined, you can also submit an application for representation.

While most artists aren't getting rich on a few licensing deals, the good ones with good representation find that over time their imagery creates a nice steady stream of cash flow. What happens is the same companies come back to license the images for new products. Each generates its own royalty stream, and when these deals begin to overlap is when the process becomes lucrative for artists. It gets better when multiple licensing deals with multiple companies kick in.

If you want to study some of the top licensing artists, besides the previously mentioned Mary Engelbreit, look into the careers of Thomas Kinkade [www.thomaskinkade.com] and Paul Brent [www.paulbrent.com]. Unlike Engelbreit, who went straight into the licensing field, Kinkade and Brent spent years building their print businesses and the licensing ultimately became a huge financial offshoot for both. It just proves there are more ways than one to become a successful artist in the licensing field.

It is said Mary Engelbreit has more than 6,000 license agreements for her images, all which help propel her company to its annual $100 million in sales. While she and Thomas Kinkade have to be near the top of the heap in terms of licensing deals, just imagine getting a fraction of that pie. For most artists, the idea of making $50,000 or $100,000 for licensing royalties on their images is just a dream. But it doesn't have to be if you work hard and smart at including licensing in your creative and business prospects.

One must still have chaos in oneself to be able to give birth to a dancing star.
— Friedrich Nietzsche

Chapter Sixteen
Giclées and Digital Prints

What is a Giclée?

This digital print format has become the most broadly used form of limited edition prints sold today, and it is making big gains in open edition prints as most poster publishers now use it to expand their offerings.

Print-on-demand (POD) technology has forever changed how fine art print reproductions are created and marketed. It has also changed the music recording and book distribution industries. Musical artists can now affordably make their own CDs and distribute directly to their fans. Authors, me included, can self-publish a book and distribute either directly or through online bookstores such as Amazon.com without having to pre-print thousands of copies to keep printing prices low.

By avoiding the costs associated with inventory, you only pay to print when you have orders. You can endlessly make exquisite replicas of your original work. You can print on a wide variety of substrates, including paper, canvas, metal, Mylar, wood and more. And, the color gamut range is higher than with traditional offset printing. Multiple sizes are easily made within equipment and aspect ratio capabilities.

Custom projects for collectors are easily and affordably fulfilled.

It took years for the giclée print format to gain full acceptance in the industry because of the controversy surrounding colorfastness reliability. It also suffered from the then-stigma of being computer-generated. New inks, solvents, printing processes, substrates and finishes have eliminated the criticism. Also, the resistance to technological advances, which contributed to the hesitancy of many in the art community to embrace the giclée as a legitimate medium, has faded with time.

Since these prints are digitally produced, they can be printed in small (even one-off) runs, which are the major attraction for artists and publishers. It means you don't have to eat your mistakes, as you do with other forms of printmaking.

The term "giclée" was coined in 1991 by Jack Duganne. He was then and is now a printmaker who uses inkjet-based digital-printing technology to create digital fine art prints. The intent was to distinguish what were commonly known at the time as "Iris proofs," which were used by the commercial printing, graphic arts and advertising communities for proofing purposes. These proofs were much different from the fine art prints that he and others were producing using the same printers. While the name was originally applied to fine art prints created on Iris printers, it ultimately came to describe any high-quality ink-jet prints.

The Internet is full of websites selling art reproductions made with a digital printer, including home desktop versions, using the term "giclée" to describe them. It can be a humorous adventure to read the vain attempts to explain:

- what the word means;
- its genesis;
- how to pronounce it;
- the process of creating digital reproductions.

The reality for the art industry is these misguided, sloppy efforts are not a laughing matter. There are thousands of poorly informed, poorly worded and futile attempts to describe giclées floating around cyberspace. While the intent may be to help inform collectors and Web surfers about what a giclée is, the misinformation distracts from the original purpose of coining the phrase.

The result of this onslaught of misguided amateur attempts to define the term is that it has become as nondescript and amorphous as the word "print." The more the word and its description gets mucked up, the more confusing the term becomes to the public, and the less ability it has to be the powerful, valuable descriptor as originally intended.

I believe if you use "giclée" to describe your art, then it is incumbent on you to use the term correctly in your description of it. It is inevitable that so long as are using the term that you also will be explaining it. Do yourself and the industry a favor and take the time to be accurate. The more you are correct, the more confident you will be in your answer, which can only help your sales.

The attempt here is not to provide a full history of the word's meaning and origin. Rather, I recommend to those of you truly interested in understanding what a digital print or giclée is to spend time with the following links:

- What's in a Name: The True Story of "Giclée" [http://www. dpandi.com/giclee/giclee.html].
- Digital, Fine Art Printing Comes of Age [http://www.dpandi. com/history/]

These articles provide the best and most accurately detailed history I have seen. They are penned by Harald Johnson, the author of Mastering Digital Printing. Many consider his book to be the Bible of digital printing. Johnson is a digital printing pioneer and a long-time colleague of Jack Duganne.

If there is a soapbox here, it comes from the frustration some artists and printers have with the loose use of "giclée" to represent digital fine art reproductions. Unfortunately, the term is now used to describe both the highest quality digital prints and homemade prints coming off a desktop printer from a low-resolution digital photograph.

Loose usage of the term is regrettable because the original meaning was to describe a meticulously produced digital print. One where hours would be spent to perfectly capture an image, manipulate the RIP software, and fine-tune the color and printer calibrations to produce a masterful, faithful reproduction, such as a fine art digital reproduction. The broad uncontrolled use of the word giclée is a problem for all in the digital art print market.

Now one can even find advertising from lamp companies promoting "giclée lampshades." This proves at once that the word had become widely accepted and the unique, exotic implications it once had are being lost as it passes into the lexicon of everyday language. I do not expect artists, publishers or printers who are heavily invested in the use of this word to abandon it. Nevertheless, I believe there is a case for moving forward with another way to describe the process. It is easy to see why some artists and printers are turning away from using "giclée" to describe their prints.

Essentially, a giclée is a digital print with a fancy name. What it comes down to is education. You cannot control how others are going to use the term. You have to decide for yourself if it is a term that adds value to what you are doing. There is certainly nothing wrong with using "giclée" as a way to describe your art prints. You will find yourself in good company if you do, as many well-known artists and print publishers continue to market using it.

Personally, I think using digital fine art reproduction is a perfectly serviceable and satisfactory marketing term. The question is, do you run with the crowd and get lumped in with not only the top-selling print artists but also lampshades, or do you rely on your work, your reputation and your marketing skills to use the arguably more mundane – but inarguably more precise and less-confusing – term? It is a question only you can answer. It is not just about your own perceptions and prejudices; it is about what makes the best business decision for you.

The Case for Convergent Media

For artists who work using a combination of digital tools, I came up with the term "convergent media." I have written about it as a guest blogger on www.AbsoluteArts.com and on my Art Print Issues blog.

The question came up on the excellent www.DigitalPaintingForum.com about what to call one's work when the outcome is a print derived from digital painting techniques. I do not lay claim to being the first to have uttered the term "convergent media" – not when there are thousands of Google query results for it on a variety of issues and concerns. However, I do believe I am the first to apply it to digital fine art prints or giclées, where the original files to create the print come from multiple sources.

The following commentary is excerpted from a guest blogger post I made on Absolute Arts [www.blog.absolutearts.com].

Where I am going with this is to say I think we need a term to define what is going on with digital art. I am not talking about something like how the French word giclée was, as some think, misappropriated into usage as marketing jargon. The term did successfully allow printers, publishers and artists get away from using the terms "computer-generated print," "digital art" and "digital printing" at a time when using such terms were certain to cool the ardor of potential buyers of this new media, especially at their price points. It is inarguable that the use of "giclée" as a descriptive term helped ramp up the acceptance of digital fine art printing.

To keep things in context, in 1990 there was no Internet to speak of; the desktop computer revolution spawned by Windows 95 was still five long years into the future. Cell phones and digital cameras were not the norm as with today. Fax machines exemplified the cutting edge of instant communication technology. (For those of us who worked in an office then, standing around waiting to send or receive a fax was the modern day equivalent of the proverbial water cooler.) So, at the time, using "digital" to describe anything related to art was not going to warm the hearts of any buyer, and as such the adaption of giclée was brilliantly, if not luckily, conceived, received and passed into the vernacular.

Today, we have a much different environment. People are awash in digital gadgets everywhere. I recently watched part of a football game on an iPhone. The iPad is poised to become a ubiquitous household item. Photo manipulation software is commonly a free add-on with digital cameras and printers. As a result, we are no longer afraid of using the word "digital" to describe exquisite things.

The process of creating art using digital means is involved and multi-stepped. There is image capture, whether through digital photography, image creation using a Wacom Tablet or other hardware/software combinations. There is a manipulation of the imagery through any number of software programs, such as Painter, Photoshop and Illustrator and so on. What follows is the work's output onto a myriad of substrates, including paper, canvas, vinyl, metal, wood and more. To produce a final desired result, the artist must print or collaborate with a printer on calibrating the equipment to get the output desired. Often pieces are further enhanced post-printing to make them unique, one-of-a-kind and nearly original.

To my mind, the term "convergent media" makes sense. It reflects the usage of "mixed media," which is an ages-old, widely accepted art term. Mixed media describes a multi-stage process of using different techniques and media to render an original piece of art. Convergent media does the same thing but implies the use of technology not available to previous generations of artists.

"Giclée" is a marketing term. I see "convergent media" as a descriptive term. As with use of its cousin "mixed media," the artist is required to give only a simple explanation of the blending of techniques and media. In describing how a piece was rendered, typically an artist using mixed media will give details up to a point, and then let it go at that; and collectors who like the piece are fine with receiving only this brief information. That is, there could be torn paper, cloth, paint, wax, items from nature and so forth that went into the piece; but exactly how it was rendered is rarely a talking point or subject of conversation.

Just as a mixed-media artist doesn't give minute trite detail such as, "I used a No. 2 lead pencil to outline on a gessoed canvas," I don't believe a convergent artist needs to give all the details and a step-by-step of how an image was created in order to satisfy a buyer. They are subjectively and emotionally buying the finished vision of the artist's imagination and creativity, not her or his computer skills. The buyer is still buying on emotion, not on the technical merits. That said, sophisticated buyers always appreciate technical talent along with creative ability.

"Convergent media artist" is an accurate, honest description of a person using any number of current technologies and techniques to create art. Convergent media distinguishes from using giclée and expands on the limited term "digital art." Agreed, it requires a brief explanation, as does "mixed media," but it does not obfuscate as "giclée" does. I think it enhances without detracting, and it embodies what is available now and in the future for innovative artists to incorporate into their oeuvre.

Having made the above argument in my Absolute Arts guest blog, I will move on from terminology by saying I believe any term you use will probably be okay. So if you are happy with giclée, digital print, digital fine-art reproduction, digital painting, fine-art digital photograph or convergent media, then stick with it. My only admonishment would be to remain consistent in your usage.

How Digital Fine-Art Prints (Giclées) Are Made

This section will be brief as this is a business book, not a technical manual. There are many excellent books on digital printing. If you are inclined to delve deeply into learning about the process, get a copy of the previously mentioned Harald Johnson's Mastering Digital Printing (Second Edition). There also is Fine Art Printing for Photographers: Exhibition Quality

Prints with Inkjet Printers (Second Edition), by Uwe Steinmueller and Juergen Gulbins. If you do your own printing, you will find 301 Inkjet Tips and Techniques: An Essential Printing Resource for Photographers by Andrew Darlow to be an invaluable asset in your library.

For more details and information than you probably will ever care to know, there is an industry research group known as FLAAR [www.fineartgicleeprinters.org]. Here is a description of the organization from its website:

FLAAR Digital Imaging Technology Center concentrates its experience on the evaluation and testing of high quality scanners (35mm slide scanners, flatbed scanners, drum scanners); 1200 dpi laser printers for graphics design and printing photographs; and large format printers of all kinds for limited editions of fine art and photo prints. We also do evaluations of printers for signs, posters, banners and are gradually moving into evaluations of printers for textiles.

The technology for giclée printing continues to evolve. For instance, UV-cured flatbed printers can now handle ceramic wall tiles, wood, aluminum and other metals, as well as glass and a diverse range of thick materials. There are printers capable of printing on curved surfaces, and metallic inks are also becoming available. The equipment and processes used just a few years ago are already out-of-date.

There is no reason to believe the march toward improvements will not continue. Artists, being the creative sorts they are, will eagerly pursue these developments in developing new never-seen-before methods of rendering art.

Giclée Printing Workflow

As with preparing and printing any fine art reproduction, there is a workflow procedure to follow. This includes having the proper equipment and the tools and skill to calibrate them. Starting with the very best image capture is absolutely essential.

Topnotch ateliers will have a Better Light [www.betterlight.com] scanning back, a Cruse flatbed scanner [www.crusedigital.com] or the equivalent to begin the process of getting the most accurate in-depth digitization of your original work. They will have professional lighting equipment to perfectly illuminate your original, and the monitor, image capture equipment and output device all need to have exact calibration.

After the original is precisely digitized, the digitally captured image is processed using appropriate software, such as Adobe Photoshop or other tools of the trade. Once your preferred media is selected, the printer, ink, and media are profiled for color balance and management.

A proof is printed and is used for color-matching to the original. The artist and/or technician oversees and adjusts the color balance using state-of-the-art computer-image enhancement, until the most faithful representation of the original painting is achieved. Or, should the artist or publisher choose, changes to the print from the original can be applied. More than once an artist seeing that more red, for instance, could be pumped in a section of the print and enhance it, specifies such a change to be made at this step. After all adjustments are made, final prints are now ready to be printed.

When final prints come off the press, hand embellishing can be applied. Some artists prefer to do this part themselves, while others use services offered by their printers, or hire their own "highlighters" as with Thomas Kinkade to do the work for them. Others pass on this step because it adds time and expense to the process.

A protective top coating finishes the print. If it is printed on paper, it may have the edges deckled; if it is on canvas, it may be mounted on stretcher bars. The finished print is then packed and made ready to ship. Some full-service giclée ateliers offer framing and fulfillment. Others offer a combination of serigraphy and digital printing to expand how prints are created.

Advice on Working with Giclées and Giclée Printers

The following information is excerpted from an Art Print Issues blog post with the above title.

Now that you have decided to create giclées of your work, here are some important things to know. These items are by no means all you need to consider, but should help inform your decision on how to best proceed and succeed with adding giclées to your portfolio. The savvy suggestions provided here come courtesy of Barry Glustoff, master giclée printer and owner of Digital Arts Studio [www.digitalartsstudio.net] in Atlanta, GA. with added notations from me.

Tips for Great Results with Giclée Printing

Image Capture

Quality is essential to effectively compete in today's print marketplace

- The best result for your final output starts with your initial step, which is your image capture.
- Quite simply, the most critical part of producing the highest quality finished work begins with a obtaining the highest caliber digitized file of your work available.
- The adage "garbage in equals garbage out" is an inarguable proven fact here.
- Creating the best possible digital file of your work requires a professional's skills, equipment and expertise.
- Some artists may possess such skills, most will not.
- Along with skills, you need proper tools, equipment and software.
- Although technological advances have brought costs down, professional-grade digital scanners and cameras used for fine art reproduction still cost tens of thousands of dollars.
- Equally important is the specialized filtered lighting needed to properly illuminate artwork, capture its subtle textures and details, and to eliminate glare from canvas varnishes and glossy paints.
- The best latest 10 to 15 megapixels digital cameras using flash or outdoor lighting are still incapable of creating highest quality image capture.

Selecting a Giclée Printmaker

Finding the right printer is more important than finding the closest printer

- When shopping for a giclée printmaker, look for those that do their own digital capture and printing.
- Prices for this service range from $75 to $300 per image for color corrected and proofed files ready for print.
- Some printers companies waive this fee with a minimum

print purchase causing you to weigh the pros and cons of paying a set-up cost versus ordering more inventory than you need.

- A first-hand recommendation or warning from someone else's experience might be the best criteria for finding your ideal giclée printmaker.
- Make every attempt to contact other artists who have used or currently use a printmaker you are considering.
- Some printers, especially those only that operate exclusively online, might appear to be full service or less expensive than others, but they may not be able to provide the attention needed to "get it right." Or they may be shipping work offshore without your knowledge.

Tips for Working with Your Giclée Printer

They may be the experts, but you need to maintain control

- Your printer should strive to establish a cooperative, working collaboration with you, understanding your needs and goals, and be able to easily communicate with you in "non-technical" language.

- It is highly recommended you maintain an actual print in your portfolio of each substrate you print on as a reference sample.
- Don't let any printer hold your artistic property "hostage" in case you're not satisfied with their print quality.
- It is critical you archive your own backup copies of your digital files for safekeeping.
- Whenever possible, get actual printed proof copies of your work, printed on the canvas and/or paper type you intend to use. Don't be "fooled" by companies who refuse to provide this option.
- Every giclée printer attempts to accurately match your work, but depending on equipment, types of inks, papers and skill, it is not always possible to get 100% accuracy. This is often the case when attempting to reproduce one media with another, such as printing a copy of an oil painting with water-based, pigmented inks.
- The color range of the pigmented inks used in giclée printmaking is not always equal to the colors achievable

with solid, pigmented oil or acrylic paint.

- Seldom, if ever, will the original and the reproduction be displayed side by side. That said, a competent giclée printmaker will have a great understanding of color control and correction techniques and should attempt to make any corrections as directed by the artist, until satisfied.

Protect Your Copyright

If your work is good enough and important enough to send to a giclée printer, it should be copyrighted [www.copyright.gov] to give you full legal protection. Yes, you have automatic copyright when you make your work. However, it is advisable to protect your artwork by registering it before it is infringed. While original artwork and giclée prints are protected prior to registration, the damages available to an artist for infringement are limited to actual damages. Actual damages may be hard to prove, and therefore often this is not practical to pursue. Infringement of registered works will allow you to receive actual damages, plus legal fees, plus statuary fines of up to $150,000 per infringement.

I am not suggesting any professional giclée printer would steal your copyright. Nevertheless, if they do make enough changes to your original work, the new work may fall under the "Derivative Works" section of copyright law.

Here is a description of "Derivative Works" from the U.S. Copyright office [http://www.copyright.gov/circs/circ14.pdf].

Derivative Works

A "derivative work," that is, a work that is based on (or derived from) one or more already existing works, is copyrightable if it includes what the copyright law calls an "original work of authorship." Derivative works, also known as "new versions," include such works as translations, musical arrangements, dramatizations, fictionalizations, art reproductions, and condensations. Any work in which the editorial revisions, annotations, elaborations, or other modifications represent, as a whole, an original work of authorship is a derivative work or new version.

A typical example of a derivative work received for registration in the Copyright Office is one that is primarily a new work but incorporates some previously published material. This previously published material makes the work a derivative work under the copyright law.

To be copyrightable, a derivative work must be different enough from the

original to be regarded as a new work or must contain a substantial amount of

new material. Making minor changes or additions of little substance to a preexisting work will not qualify the work as a new version for copyright purposes. The new material must be original and copyrightable in itself. Titles, short phrases, and format, for example, are not copyrightable.

To understand how this could potentially affect you, read the article "Who's Copyright Is It – Anyway?" [www.artslaw.org/owncopy.htm] from Ocean States Art Law.

Your best course of preventative action is to ask your printer to reassign any and all reproduction rights incurred under U.S. Copyright Law by the printer back to you as a condition for doing business with them. I cannot imagine any printer who desires your business to object to complying with your request. If one should, there are plenty more who will do so without question.

As with all questions of the law, accessing qualified legal help is the wise thing to do. Anytime you are not sure of what to do or how to proceed to protect yourself, hire a competent attorney to help you.

DIY versus Service Bureau Printing

Do-it-yourself (DIY) giclée printing

From my observation, I believe most artists have more than enough to do painting their originals and getting their work to market. It seems to me that taking on the additional task of printing their work is not a wise decision. There is the time in investigating what equipment, software and tools are needed. Then there is the substantial financial investment in obtaining all that is needed and the substantial time investment in learning to become proficient using the equipment.

It is interesting to me that while I have repeatedly made this argument I have rarely succeeded in discouraging those who already had their mind made up to print their own work. For argument's sake, let's say a printer can make a giclée for you at $.12 per square inch. The question is this: for how much less can you make one yourself?

When you factor in the cost of owning and insuring the equipment as well as the space to house it, and take into account the time to run it and the inventory required to manage it, can you truly save enough money to justify printing yourself? If something happens to your work at the printer, the printer eats the cost. If it happens to you, you eat it. How many mistakes can you afford before you are losing money?

If you are going to go into full production mode, here are categories of items you will need to consider, purchase and learn to use: printers; inks, papers, and other media; RIP software; color-management equipment; scanners; LCD Monitors; laminators and films; giclée finishing; frames; canvas mounting equipment; trimmers and cutters; computers; software; accessories; digital cameras; studio equipment; and photo accessories.

Besides the time and money you will put into printing your work, you have to contend with the obsolescence of your equipment. Like it or not, it will suffer wear and tear, and you will be faced with repairs and replacement costs. You should consider this into your decision making when contemplating whether to print your own work.

I hope I have sufficiently dissuaded most one-artist shops from jumping into printing their own work. I do realize there are valid reasons for not taking my advice, whether it is your desire to just let the geek inside you rule or because you have run the numbers and decided it makes financial sense to take the plunge. Should that be the case for you, just make sure you take the time to investigate thoroughly to make the best decisions possible.

For those who do have the resources to make giclées for your art business, you can look at a one-stop service such as DTG Web [www. dtgweb.com]. While far from the only source, it consistently markets to the art print market and offers a wide range of equipment and services specifically for capturing fine art images and printing them, including training. Although the site offers a huge variety, there are some printer brands not represented; I am sure a representative from the company would tell you why.

Service bureau considerations

Much of what could be said here was covered earlier in the excerpt from my blog on "Advice on Working with Giclées and Giclée Printers." Some obvious factors are proximity, reputation, staff, experience, cost, equipment, other assets and marketing assistance. Each of these factors can vary and are worth considering.

For some artists, being able to drive to their professional printer is a prime concern; while for others, it is far enough down the list that it does not affect their decision. Although I fully understand why proximity is important to some, I personally believe finding the right printer is more important than easy access.

The changes in the market place have battered professional giclée printers as much as any other segment of our industry. There has been a shakeout of weaker players, which had to be a concern for the artists whose work they printed. While reputation alone will not protect artists from the fallout should their printer fail, it is nevertheless a good measure of both the quality of the work and the potential longevity of the printer.

Some professional printers also provide marketing services. It could be in the form of a gallery for artists on their site or live events to showcase their artists. These kinds of extras can be the deal maker in situations where you find all else to be equal.

Limited Editions versus Open Editions

When it comes to the decision of whether to make a digital print a limited or open edition, I strongly favor open. I have covered this topic numerous times on my blog and as a guest blogger on Absolute Arts. To me, going with a limited edition is going backwards and makes no sense.

Limited editions came about because making more was neither technically nor financially possible. Etching plates or silk screens would wear out in the printing process and could not be used indefinitely. There is a huge upfront cost in preparing a press for four-color offset printing, which makes going back on press for additional small runs unfeasible.

Given the situation, it made sense to limit the number of prints, and then numbering them became a common practice. Limiting the editions of fine art prints is a centuries old technique for tracking and – more importantly – marketing the work. Since we are now in a digital age with the capability of making endless perfect reproductions of an original, it raises the question, Why are we still limiting editions of digital prints? The only answer is that it is both a nod to tradition and is still valued by many as a valid marketing ploy. In my mind, it is nothing more than a gimmick.

The average giclée buyer realizes the print came from a digital printer. As such, they also realize that the allotment arbitrarily assigned by the artist or publisher has no real basis other than marketing purposes.

Look at it as a consumer rather than an art marketer. Do you believe there is some great intrinsic value in a limited edition that would make you want to pay more for it? Do you believe digitally printed art is investment-quality piece work that you may sell for more than the original price in the future? How many limited edition prints make it to the secondary market?

The reality for a large percentage of artists is that they do not sell out their editions. So why go to the trouble and additional administrative work to create limited editions if this is likely to be the case? I understand the motive behind limited editions: it makes the art seem more special, which in turn gives it the potential to be more valuable and easier to sell, especially when there are only a low number of editions left. However, I also know smart marketers can sell art based on its visual appeal and on the reputation of the artist – without having to make the edition limited.

I am certain that art buyers will pay a fair price for a work they want to own, regardless of whether it is open or limited. I further believe most would prefer to buy the art in the size that best suits their needs, as opposed to being forced to buy the size specified by the limited edition. Yes, I know there are ways to sell multi-size editions, but that seems really hokey to me.

If you feel the need to number the pieces, that is fine. Just do not limit them. You can use any numbering convention that works for you; for example, you could use 1/oe, 2/oe (for open editions) or 1/unl, 2unl (for unlimited). Because of the way collectors are, I believe that if your work becomes collectible, special numbers – such as the lower numbers, or the artist's birthday, or something about the print or subject matter – will become collectible, despite the edition being open.

Ask any open edition or poster publisher who has been around for a while. They will all tell you there have been certain prints that got legs and sold thousands upon thousands. Often times, it is a print from a series where no one could understand what the special appeal was. It just happens sometimes.

When you limit your art, you cheat yourself out of future sales. You cannot count on being able to knock yourself off and reproduce a winner that is similar to the original. It doesn't work that way. If you feel the need to limit your art, then create a special edition of 200 or less that is hand-embellished, remarqued or otherwise worked in hand by the artist after the print is made. Be upfront with your limited edition buyers to let them know you are offering the lower quality work as open edition.

Another factor with limited editions is the laws in 14 states that require you to comply with their guidelines when you sell limited editions, including sales made to state residents over the Internet. This means you need a Certificate of Authority that is legally compliant in those states. One rarely hears anything about enforcement of these laws, but that is not a license to ignore them. Do your own research to learn what you need to do to be in compliance, or go open and be free of this extra encumbrance.

Signing, Numbering and Dating Art Prints

You should not sign your work on the printed area. Some ateliers will digitally remove your signature from your original for you. The common method for signing works on paper is to sign and number in pencil in the margin below the work. With canvas and now other substrates coming into use, you have to find a place to sign that will not detract from the art. On canvas, signing on the back is typically how it is done.

Many artists are not diligent in dating their work. I am not a fan of dating an original with the signature if it is going to be sold in a gallery, because a piece that is several years old may still be fresh and relevant to a prospective buyer; but when they see it has been in the gallery for a long time, they may wonder why it has not sold.

Here is what Alan Bamberger has to say about dating art on his highly regarded website, www.artbusiness.com.

Many artists don't pay enough attention to dating their work, digital or otherwise, but the more art you make and the longer you make it for, the more important dates become – especially on your early work, especially if you have a long and productive career. Dates come in mighty handy when retrospective time rolls around too. And once again, given the choice between two identical works of art, one that's dated and one that's not, knowledgeable buyers will choose the dated one over the undated one approximately 100% of the time. Keep in mind that you don't necessarily have to date the art on the front if you don't want to, but date it somewhere.

When it comes to making giclées, convergent media, or digital fine art reproductions, you have many choices to make. Do yourself a favor and try to think through as far as you can with those that matter. Ask yourself, how will this decision be working for me in five or ten years?

To be at the peak of your profession, you need to be consistent and fair. The more you mull over your decisions before acting, the more likely you are to come up with a plan that you can live with for years to come. There is elegance in simplicity. If your buyers know they can always find your signature in the same place and that your policies towards limited editions or open editions are available, consistent and fair, it will help you build a layer of trust around all that you do. Other than asking someone to buy your work, the most important thing you can ask of them is to trust you.

You have noticed advertisements for companies throughout this chapter. I realize that it is unusual to find advertising in a book. Perhaps it is my three decades of magazine advertising sales that stirred me to think about this idea, but I more wanted to be able to offer readers easy access to the best companies to help them print and get their work to market.

There is a Resources section beyond this chapter. It has been greatly expanded to about 300 listings to assist you locating companies and sources to help your art print career. Since I knew believe there was enough room to list every business that serves artists in the digital printing field, it is limited it to those who wanted to support distribution of this book and advertise to connect with you. Also, because there are constant developments with companies coming and going in this part of the market, I was concerned about the effectiveness of a directory with too many dated listings.

The solution was to limit giclée business companies to advertisers in the book, and to create an online directory to post a more robust directory with as many current listings as I could find. The result is a new website called the Giclée Business Guide. Its Web address is: www.gicleebizguide.com.

While I lament above the term giclée is overused and misappropriated by lamp manufacturers and others, I also believe it is not going to leave the art lexicon anytime soon. Publishing this important industry as the Giclée Business Guide is one way I show my belief the term remains valid for our industry.

The years ahead will be both challenging and exciting in the art print market and the near continuous development of digital image creation and printing show no signs of slowing. The online giclée business guide will be there to keep you informed of opportunities and changes in the market place.

Resources

This Resources section consists primarily of companies, artists and services mentioned in the book. It does contain other references sure to be helpful to my readers. While I have made every effort to provide accurate details, there may be errors. Because I do not firsthand knowledge of every listing here, caveat emptor applies as is it should for every savvy businessperson.

Use **GicleeBusiness.com** for the Most Up-to-date Information

Since the book is print-on-demand, there will be some opportunities for an occasional update to this section. If you have a listing that needs changing or you feel is important enough for inclusion, contact me. My advice for those looking for the most current information is to go to the directory at **www.GicleeBusiness.com**. It is certain to have the freshest data and contacts as compared to the static listings in this Resources section.

Advertising

I admit the idea for advertising in this book was inspired by ads I've seen in the Artist's & Graphic Designer's Market, now in its 35th annual edition. I believe "creative borrowing" is important to expanding any business. Additionally, just as I encourage my readers to extend their art into new markets such as licensing, or healthcare, for instance, tasteful advertising in this book is an extension of the same philosophy.

There will never be more than a few select companies advertising here. As mentioned above, the book is print-on-demand, and thus can be updated at anytime. If you are a marketer with an appropriate message for the readers of this book, feel free to contact me with your interest.

When it comes to advertising, I owe a debt of gratitude to the fine folks at Digital Arts Studio in Atlanta. Their company is one of the industry's premier digital printmakers. Not only have they been longtime great supporters of my first edition, they are the first charter advertiser in this book. Check them out at: www.DigitalArtsStudio.net.

My thanks also go to Jason Horejs, owner of Xanadu Gallery. It is one of the top galleries on Main Street in Scottsdale. He has been a good friend and a steady source of first edition book sales since we met. Check out his ad to learn about his book, 'Starving to Successful' The Fine Artist's Guide for Getting Into Galleries. Get the details on Xanadu's online gallery and art inventory software. You will be glad you did.

Resources

Art Market Related Tradeshows
Art Print Publishers Mentioned
Artist Business Resources
Artist Forums
Artist Software
Artists Mentioned
Artists Website Providers
Blogging Software
Books
Contact Manager & Bookkeeping

Software
General Business Resources
Giclée Resources
Home Furnishing & Contract Design
Shows & Magazines
Legal Resources
Licensing Shows, Magazines, Blogs
Online Art Auction Sites
Online Art Print Venues
Print-on-demand Communities
Social Media

Art Market Related Tradeshows

ArtExpo New York	www.artexpos.com
West Coast Art & Frame Show	www.wcafshow.com
HD Expo	www.hdexpo.com
Surtex	www.surtex.com
The Licensing Show	www.licensingexpo.com
Toronto Art Expo	www.torontoartexpo.com

Art Print Publishers Mentioned

Haddad's Fine Arts	www.haddadsfineart.com
McGaw Graphics	www.brucemcgaw.com
Applejack Art Partners	www.applejackart.com
Bentley Publishing Group	www.bentleypublishinggroup.com
Mill Pond Press	www.millpond.com
Wild Wings	www.wildwings.com

Hadley House	www.hadleyhouse.com
Greenwich Workshop	www.greenwichworkshop.com
Bentley Publishing Group	www.bentleypublishinggroup.com
Somerset Fine Art	www.somersetfineart.com
Wild Apple Graphics	www.wildapple.com
Royo Art	www.royoart.com
Palatino Editions	www.palatino.net
Aaron Ashley	www.bentleypublishinggroup.com
Fortune Fine Art	www.fortunefa.com

Artist Business Resources

Alan Bamberger's Art Business Website	www.artbusiness.com
Art Business News	www.artbusinessnews.com
Art Business Today	www.fineart.co.uk
Art Calendar	www.artcalendar.com
Art Print Issues	www.artprintissues.com
Art World News	www.artworldnews.com
Color Marketing Group	www.colormarketing.org
Decor Magazine	www.decormagazine.com
Decor Sources	www.artandframingdirectory.com
Empty Easel	www.emptyeasel.com
Fine Art Views Blog	www.fineartviews.com/blog
Healthcare Fine Art Blog	www.healthcarefineart.com
HGTV	www.hgtv.com
International Fine Print Dealers Association	www.ifpda.org
Liebermans Wholesale Prints & Posters	www.liebermans.net/
Picture Framing Magazine	www.pictureframingmagazine.com
Robert Genn Twice-weekly Letter	www.painterskeys.com
Sedona Art Center	www.sedonaartcenter.com
Southwest Art	www.southwestart.com
Wildlife Art News	www.wildlifeartmag.com

Artist Forums

Wet Canvas	www.wetcanvas.com
Online Visual Artists	www.onlinevisualartists.com
Digital Painting Forum	www.digitalpaintingforum.com

Artist Software

Archer Artist	www.archerartist.com
Art & Craft Business Organizer	www.jaminmark.com/acbo
Art Tracker 2.0	www.xanadugallery.com/ArtistSvcs/ArtTracker

ArtAffair Software	www.artaffairsoftware.com
Artist's Butler 3.6	www.lynndavison.com/lynnsoft
Artlook Software for Artists	www.artlooksoftware.com
ArtSystem for Artist Studios and Estates	www.artsystems.com/solutions/studioestate.htm
Artworks Artist Software	www.artworkspro.com
eArtist v4.0.0	www.artscope.net/eArtist
Flick! 4.0.2	www.arawak.com.au/flick.html
Gyst	www.gyst-ink.com
VamP Visual Artist Management Project	www.vam-p.net
Working Artist	www.workingartist.com

Artists Mentioned

Arnold Friberg	www.fribergfineart.com
Banksy	www.banksy.co.uk
Bev Doolittle	www.greenwichworkshop.com
Bob Byerley	www.wildwings.com
Bob Timberlake	www.bobtimberlake.com
Cao Yong	www.caoyong.us
Carl Brenders	www.millpondpress.com
Charles Pabst	www.charlespabst.com
Charles Wysocki	www.hadleyhouse.com
Christian Riese Lassen	www.lassenart.com
Flavia Weedn	www.flavia.com
G. Harvey	www.somersetfineart.com
George Sumner	www.sumner-studios.com
Hazel Dooney	www.hazeldooney.com
Jane Wooster Scott	www.woosterscott.com
Jody Bergsma	www.bergsma.com
Mary Engelbreit	www.maryengelbreit.com
Michael Godard	www.godardart.com
Michel Keck	www.therawartist.com
Natasha Wescoat	www.artcandy.tv
P. Buckley Moss	www.pbuckleymoss.com
Paul Brent	www.paulbrent.com
Robert Bateman	www.millpondpress.com
Robert Lyn Nelson	www.robertlynnelson.com
Royo	www.royoart.com
Stephen Schutz	www.bluemountain.com
Steve Hanks	www.hadleyhouse.com
Thomas Kinkade	www.thomaskinkade.com

Thomas Pradzynski	www.palatino.net
Warren Kimble	www.wildapple.com
Wyland	www.wyland.com
Yuroz	www.yurozart.com

Artists Website Providers

Art Dealers	www.artdealers.com
Art in Canada	www.artincanada.com
Art Studios Online	www.artstudiosonline.com
Artist's Websites	www.artistswebsite.org
ArtSites.ca	www.artsites.ca
Artspan	www.artspan.com
ArtWebsites.net	www.artwebsites.net
Beautiful Artists Websites	www.beautifulartistwebsites.com
Big Black Bag	www.bigblackbag.com
Espresso Artist Websites	www.espressoartistwebsites.com
Fine Art Studio Online	www.faso.com
Folio Link	www.foliolink.com
Folio Twist	www.foliotwist.com
Heavy Bubble	www.heavybubble.com
Impact Folios	www.impactfolios.com
Markettheme for WordPress	www.markettheme.com
Mosaic Globe	www.mosaicglobe.com
Other Peoples Pixels	www.otherpeoplespixels.com
Q Folio	www.qfolio.com
Quanta Web Design	www.quantawebdesign.com
Scot Style	www.scotstyle.com
Sitewelder	www.sitewelder.com
Springboard for the Arts	www.springboardforthearts.com
Website for Artists	www.websiteforartists.net

Blogging Software

Blogger	www.blogger.com
Feedburner	www.feedburner.com
Google Reader	www.google.com/reader
Live Journal	www.livejournal.com
Market Theme	www.markettheme.com
Squarespace	www.squarespace.com
Thesis Theme	www.diythemes.com
Typepad	www.typepad.com
WordPress	www.wordpress.org

Books

Jason Horejs - *"Starving" to Successful: The Fine Artist's Guide to Getting into Galleries*

Andrew Darlow - *301 Inkjet Tips and Techniques: An Essential Printing Resource for Photographers*

Michael Woodward - *Art Licensing 101, Third Edition*

Editor's of Writer's Digest Books   *Artist's & Graphic Designer's Market*

Malcolm Gladwell - *Blink: The Power of Thinking without Thinking*

Tad Crawford *Business and Legal Forms for Fine Artists*

Gary Vaynerchuk - *Crush It: Why Now Is the Time to Cash In on Your Passion*

Mary E. Carter - *Electronic Highway Robbery: An Artist's Guide to Copyrights in the Digital Era*

Uwe Steinmueller and Juergen Gulbins - *Fine Art Printing for Photographers: Exhibition Quality Prints with Inkjet Printers, Second Edition*

Steven Van Yoder - *Get Slightly Famous: Become a Celebrity in Your Field and Attract More Business with Less Effort*

John Mullins, Randy Komisar - *Getting to Plan B: Breaking Through to a Better Business Model*

Mike McKeever - *How To Write A Business Plan*

Tom Peters - *In Search of Excellence: Lessons from Americas Best Run Companies*

Tad Crawford - *Legal Guide for the Visual Artist*

Caryn Leland *Licensing Art & Design*

Harald Johnson - *Mastering Digital Printing: Second Edition*

Dr. Stephen R. Covey - *Seven Habits of Highly Effective People*

Marilyn Sholin - *The Art of Digital Photo Painting*

Guy Kawasaki - *The Art of the Start: The Time-Tested, Battle-Hardened Guide for Anyone Starting Anything*

Susan Fader - *The Artist's Giclée* Handbook*

Daniel Grant - *The Business of Being An Artist*

Michael E. Gerber - *The E-Myth Revisited: Why Most Small Businesses Don't Work and What to Do About It*

Kaleil Isaza Tuzman - *The Entrepreneur's Success Kit: A 5-Step Lesson Plan to Create and Grow Your Own Business*

Malcolm Gladwell - *The Tipping Point*

Roy H. Williams - *The Wizard of Ads: Turning Words into Magic and Dreamers into Millionaires.*

Xanadu Gallery helps you sell more of your work and keep more of the selling price.

When You're Successful, Xanadu Is Successful!

Xanadu offers the following services for professional artists.

In this newly published book, Xanadu Gallery Owner, Jason Horejs, shares a comprehensive overview of how an artist can prepare to approach galleries. The book will help both the emerging and the established with concrete strategies for preparing artwork, researching galleries, and seeking representation. You will learn more about how the book will help you take your art career to the next level on the "For Artists" link on our site.

Upcoming Live Workshops

Visit our website and sign up to learn more about upoming live workshops by Jason Horejs, Owner of Xanadu Gallery and author of "Starving" to Successful.

Xanadu Studios

Reach a whole new world of collectors through Xanadu Gallery's website. When you join Xanadu Studios you will receive your own studio page on our site. You will be able to upload as much art as you like, sell your work through the site and enjoy increased exposure to art collectors from around the world. Disover all the exciting profitable benefits of joining Xanadu Studios today at:

Art Tracker

You will love how easy it is to track inventory, sales, and collectors. You get a simple, affordable way to take control of your inventory tracking. Get the details on the site.

Writing Services for Artists

You will be thrilled to see how our professional writer handles all your communications. Remember: Once you get the art right you still have to market it, and every artist needs a strong written piece, usually an artist statement or bio. Our seasoned pro has extensive experience writing for artists. Visit our writing services page to see how he can help you find the words that will make your art dazzle even more

Xanadu Gallery | 7039 E. Main St. #101 - Scottsdale, AZ 85251 | 480.368.9929 - 866.483.1306

www.XanaduGallery.com

Contact Manager & Bookkeeping Software

ACT!	www.act.com
Batch Book	www.batchbook.com
Bento for Mac	www.filemaker.com/products/bento
Contact Plus	www.contactplus.com
Filemaker Pro	www.filemaker.com
Highrise	www.highrisehq.com
MS Outlook	www.microsoft.com
Prophet	www.avidian.com
Quickbooks	www.quickbooks.com

General Business Resources

15 Second Pitch	www.15secondpitch.com
9 Speed Creative Graphic Design	www.9speedcreative.com
Don Campbell Local Search Information	www.expand2web.com
eHow.com	http://www.ehow.com
eReleases.com	www.ereleases.com
Ezine Articles	http://ezinearticles.com
Free Privacy Policy Generator	www.freeprivacypolicy.com
Go Daddy	www.godaddy.com
Google Analytics	www.google.com/analytics
Google Local Business Center	www.google.com/lbc
Google Search-based Keyword Tool	www.google.com/sktool
Google Webmaster Central Channel	www.youtube.com/user/
GoogleWebmasterHelp	
Gramlee Editing Proofreading	www.gramlee.com
Info for US Government grants	www.grants.gov
MagCloud	www.magcloud.com
Microsoft (Bing)	https://ssl.bing.com/listings/ListingCenter.aspx
National Endowment for the Arts	http://arts.endow.gov/
Official Business Link to US Government	www.business.gov
PRWeb.com	www.prweb.com
SelfPromotion.com	http://selfpromotion.com
Service Corps of Retired Executives (Score)	www.score.org
Sitemeter	www.sitemeter.com
Society for the Word of Mouth	www.theswom.org
Stats Counter	www.statcounter.com
United States Small Business Administration	www.sba.gov
Word of Mouth Marketing Association	www.womma.org
Yahoo Local	http://listings.local.yahoo.com/csubmit/index.php
Business Plan Pro - software	

Giclée Printing Resources

There are too many printers and service for fine art digital printing to list here. Go to **www.GicleeBusiness.com** to discover a huge up-to-date list of giclee printers and giclee printing resources, including image capture, substrates, inks, dyes and much more.

Home Furnishing & Contract Design Shows & Magazines

World Market Center Las Vegas	www.lasvegasmarket.com
International Home Furnishings Center	www.ihfc.com/
High Point Market	www.highpointmarket.org
Hospitality Design Expo	www.hdexpo.com
Neocon	www.neocon.com
Spring Fair Birmingham UK	www.springfair.com
Home Furnishing News	www.hfnmag.com
Design Trade	www.designtrade.net
Neet Magazine	www.neetmagazine.com

Legal Resources

Artquest	www.artquest.org.uk
Arts Law	www.artslaw.org
Canadian Artists Representation	www.carfac.ca
Free Legal Advice	www.freeadvice.com
Ivan Hoffman	www.ivanhoffman.com
Joshua Kaufman	www.venable.com
Joy Butler	www.joybutler.com
LawHelp.org	www.lawhelp.org
NOLO	www.nolo.com
Starviing Artists Law	www.starvingartistslaw.com
US Copyright Office	www.copyright.gov
Volunteer Lawyers for the Arts	www.vlany.org

Licensing Shows, Magazines, Blogs

License! Magazine	www.licensemag.com
Licensing Show	www.licensingexpo.com
Surtex	www.surtex.com
Total Licensing	www.totallicensing.com
Kate Harper	http://kateharperblog.blogspot.com
Cherish Flieder	www.somethingtocherish.com
Tara Reed	www.artlicensingblog.com
Jeanette Smith	www.allartlicensing.com
Porterfield's Fine Art	www.porterfieldsfineart.com

Giclée Printer Directory

When it came time to list the giclee printers I had in my database, I realized a static listing for this important category was not going work. It was obvious to be the most helpful resource for my readers to get all the data they would need to locate and contact the printers that an organic updatable electronic database was the best solution. That is how the online Giclee Business directory came into existence. Since I was going to the effort, I decided to add other art business and art marketing resources to the directory as well. The result is there are nearly 500 companies in a growing list of available resources for artists in the directory. Check it out at:

www.GicleeBusiness.com

If you did not find your company listed, go the site, setup an account and create a listing. There are both free and paid listings available. Naturally, the paid listings offer enhanced services, position and promotion. And, there are some select advertising spots available. You can see a splendid example of an effective ad from Digitial Arts Studio on the opposite page. DAS is one of the premier giclee printmaking operations you can find anywhere. It satisfies artists needs from all over the U.S. and beyond.

Artists, please encourage those companies to come to the site and add their information to the directory. The more robust the site, the more effective it will be for all who participate, especially the artists seeking new sources for giclee printing and marketing partners.

Online Art Auction Sites

Bidz	www.bidz.com
eBay	www.ebay.com
Overstock	www.overstock.com
Property Room	www.propertyroom.com
Quality Art Auctions	www.qart.com
Ubid.com	www.ubid.com

Online Art Print Venues

20 x 200	www.20x200.com
Absolute Arts	www.absolutearts.com
Allposters.com	www.allposters.com
Art Flock	www.artflock.com
Art.com	www.art.com
Artspan	www.artspan.com
Deviantart	www.deviantart.com
EBSQ Art	www.ebsqart.com
Etsy	www.etsy.com
Picassomio	www.picassomio.com
The Artful Home	www.artful.com
Yessy	www.yessy.com

Print-on-demand Communities

Art for Conservation	www.artforconversation.org
Artist Rising	www.artistrising.com
Café Press	www.cafepress.com
Fine Art America	www.fineartamerica.com
Finer Works	www.finerworks.com
Image Kind	www.imagekind.com
Red Bubble	www.redbubble.com
Zazzle	www.zazzle.com

Social Media

Facebook	www.facebook.com
Twitter	www.twitter.com
LinkedIn	www.linkedin.com
Seesmic	www.seesmic.com
Tweet Deck	www.tweetdeck.com
Hoot Suite	www.hootsuite.com
Topify	www.topify.com
Vimeo	www.vimeo.com
Daliy Motion	www.dailymotion.com
YouTube	www.youtube.com
Ustream	www.ustream.com

Additional Resources from the Author

Use the terrific resources listed below to learn about new career opportunities and to stay on on top of developments to forward your art marketing plans.

This blog for visual artists is one of the most highly trafficked art business blogs. While it began to help my readers keep current with fast pace of changes within the industry, ultimately it has become a business blog with information suitable to help all indie artists. Check it out at: **www.ArtPrintIssues.com**

If you are looking for a giclée printer, or related services, this is the best place to start. With nearly 300 giclee printers, the job of finding digital fine art printing services is easier now than before. The directory is organic and needs constant input to be most helpful. As you use it, if you have suggestions for companies or the directory, please let us know

BarneyDavey.com

You may have bought the book from my site, or found other helpful information there. Besides that, you can go there to learn about the consulting I offer and the workshops I present. Some of you may want to use my affiliate program to earn money for yourself or for your arts group by helping me promote the book. The details are on the site

Experience shows directories better serve their audience when they work in conjunction with a publication. Go to **www.GicleeBusinessNews.com** to read reports on industry news, technology and product developments. You also will coverage of artists, vendors and events, plus stories about and interviews with the people whose vision and actions shape the industry.

Final Words

I trust you have enjoyed reading this book. It was a pleasure to revisit and create a second edition of it for you. To finish reading a book such as this one shows your commitment. Although it's not a guarantee of success, it's a sure sign you are serious about achieving it, which is no small part of the equation.

If you are ready now to commit to or advance your print career, my wish is for you to find inspiration, as do I, in the following quote from the great German poet, writer and scientist, Johann Wolfgang Goethe. Best known for his epic work of literature Faust, he also influenced abstract painters, including Kandinsky and Mondrian, with his non-Newtonian, unorthodox theory of the character of light and color.

I come back to Goethe's eloquent timeless words over again for the sagacious motivating encouragement they offer:

Until one is committed, there is hesitancy, the chance to draw back. Concerning all acts of initiative (and creation), there is one elementary truth that ignorance of which kills countless ideas and splendid plans: that the moment one definitely commits oneself, then Providence moves too. All sorts of things occur to help one that would never otherwise have occurred. A whole stream of events issues from the decision, raising in one's favor all manner of unforeseen incidents and meetings and material assistance, which no man could have dreamed would have come his way. Whatever you can do, or dream you can do, begin it. Boldness has genius, power, and magic in it. Begin it now.

About the Author

In 1988, Barney Davey joined DECOR and Decor Expo, the business magazine and industry tradeshow producer for art and picture framing retailers, as a sales and marketing executive. For more than 15 years, he made major contributions to the meteoric sales growth of the magazine and the shows.

As the rise in importance of the Internet evolved, in 2000, Barney added the position of Director of Strategic Alliances. He used that platform to help foster growth with dotcoms and other companies seeking to form mutually rewarding relationships with DECOR and Decor Expo. He launched Decor Websites to offer easy-to-use affordable template-based Websites for art and picture framing retailers. He was responsible for starting Decor Expo Online, the industry's first virtual tradeshow.

Along the way, Barney enjoyed a bird's eye view of the print market as he consulted with hundreds of self-published artists and established publishing companies on the most efficient and effective ways to market their art prints to retailers. Barney has developed many friendships and close business relationships with the industry's leading print publishers. His observations with regard to their common traits and best practices are the basis for this book.

In 2005, Barney launched an online newsletter called Art Print Issues [www.artprintissues.com], which he morphed into a blog in 2007. Since its inception, there have been 300 posts published with virtually all the content designed to help visual artists further their careers. Barney has been a frequent guest blogger on Absolute Arts [www.absolutearts.com], one of the industry's most highly trafficked retail sites for fine art.

The first edition of this book was excerpted in The Artist's Magazine. It was also picked up by the North Light Book Club, which is owned by F+W

Publications, the publishing company for many of the top magazines for visual artists, including Watercolor Magic, The Pastel Journal, The Artist's Magazine and others.

Barney is the son an accomplished fine artist and a serious fine woodworker in his own right. He is the former president of the St. Louis Woodworker's Guild. He has spoken to numerous artist groups around the country, and conducted art marketing seminars. He resides in Arizona where he practices art-marketing consulting, writes and does public speaking.

Consulting Services

Barney Davey provides clients with consulting on art marketing, book publishing and media sales. Work with clients primarily is done over the telephone and Internet. No travel means more time for you with out having to leave your studio, office or home for your session. All consulting is done directly with Barney Davey.

A information gathering worksheet that is provided in advance must be completed and returned prior to the first session so that less time is taken getting basics understood, leaving more time for working on your specific needs and questions. You can find more information on benefiting from Barney's consulting services at: www.barneydavey.com/consulting

Speaking Engagements

Barney Davey is available for speaking engagements on the subject of art marketing, art print marketing, book publishing, social media for small businesses, artists and for other topics. Sessions from one hour to a full day can be conducted over the Web, by tele-conference and in-person. Please call or email with your questions regarding how you can reserve time on Barney's speaking schedule.

Barney Davey
Bold Star Communications
PO Box 25386
Scottsdale, AZ 85255
602-499-7500
barney@barneydavey.com